Praise for *Stepparenti*

MW00812707

"If you are the stepparent of any child, one grieving a parent's death or the loss of his or her original family, I urge you to gift yourself with Diane Ingram Fromme's wonderful book, *Stepparenting the Grieving Child*. With wisdom born of experience, insight, and education, the author has written an engaging, encouraging, hopeful, and *helpful* book. It is excellently written and beautifully formatted, easy on both the eyes and heart of the reader. Reading it uplifted me and brought me understanding and solace that, as a stepmom of forty-two years, I was surprised I still needed."

—Sue Patton Thoele,
Author of *The Courage to Be a Stepmom, The Mindful Woman*
and *The Courage to Be Yourself*

"All stepfamilies are preceded by loss, but not all loss is the same. Stepparenting a child whose parent has died has unique challenges and needs a unique roadmap, which *Stepparenting the Grieving Child* provides. Honest, revealing, and compassionately written, this book offers practical insights to support both grieving children and the stepparent who is striving to find their place in the child's life. Diane Ingram Fromme shares intimately from her own experience and others' while integrating research-based insights to create a user-friendly roadmap you can follow."

—Ron L. Deal,
Bestselling Author of *The Smart Stepfamily* and *The Smart Stepmom*,
Director of FamilyLife Blended, familylife.com/blended

"New stepparents of grieving children face a perfect storm—the effects of trauma from a parent's death coupled with new family relationships. The landmines are many, the sources of relevant wisdom few. *Stepparenting the Grieving Child* offers guidance on a topic that's barely touched upon elsewhere, which is why this book is so important, both for the children, who suffer the most, and for the adults, who hope to 'do it right.'"

—Mary Ann Emswiler,
Coauthor of *Guiding your Child through Grief*,
Founder of the Symposium on Children's Grief

"Diane Ingram Fromme enlarges our awareness of the impact of grief and loss in stepfamilies. She does so against the backdrop of the complicated worlds of child rearing, parenting, maintaining the adults' relationships, and building healthy stepfamilies. Through real-life examples, Fromme pulls you into a deeper understanding of the challenges that occur when these worlds collide. Reading this book is like being in a supportive and caring grief group for stepparents, facilitated by someone who understands what you're experiencing, someone who really cares about you and your family. Fromme goes right to the heart of what truly matters about grieving and stepparenting."

—Earl Hipp,
Author of *Help for the Hard Times: Getting Though Loss* and *Fighting Invisible Tigers: Stress Management for Teens*

"Stories of loss and hope lift the weight off stepparents' shoulders while filling their hearts with compassion for a child who longs for a parent forever gone. This is a go-to resource for any person dating, engaged to, or married to someone whose children have experienced the loss of a parent. Diane Ingram Fromme's words jump off the page and land deep in your soul. You are not alone on this journey!"

—Heather Hetchler,
Author of *Quiet Moments for the Stepmom Soul,* Director of Learning2Step.com and Speaker for Sisterhood of Stepmoms Ministry

"If you or someone you know is stepparenting a child or children after the death of their biological parent, read this book! Diane Ingram Fromme's conversational style, combined with practical suggestions and helpful research, provides a resource deeply needed as families navigate a new family structure. I highly recommend it."

—Donna L. Schuurman, Ed.D., FT,
Senior Director of Advocacy & Training, *Executive Director Emeritus,* The Dougy Center for Grieving Children & Families

"In *Stepparenting the Grieving Child*, Diane Ingram Fromme brings a wealth of experience, insight, and a lovely compassionate awareness to an important and under-discussed aspect of stepfamily life. This book will provide a lifeline for stepparents who so desperately want to support their grieving stepchildren but have no idea how to do it or where to begin. This is a resource I am grateful to include on my bookshelf and one I'll be sharing with clients."

—Jean McBride,
Licensed Marriage and Family Therapist,
Author of *Encouraging Words for New Stepmothers* and
Talking to Children About Divorce, and Founder of the Colorado
Center for Life Changes and divorcehelpforparents.com

"Having lived and worked in stepfamily land for over 35 years, I highly value *Stepparenting the Grieving Child*'s personal stories about what works in stepfamilies and what doesn't. This book also shows the similarities and differences between stepfamilies formed by either divorce or death. Either way, the children are the ones impacted the most. Maturity is crucial on the adults' part, and Fromme presents a realistic, researched, and resourceful approach toward growing into this mature understanding. *Stepparenting the Grieving Child* is a good read no matter how a stepfamily is formed."

—Carri Taylor
Opportunities Unlimited, Executive Director, Producer of two DVD
series on stepfamilies and children of divorce www.cgtaylor.com

Stepparenting the
Grieving
Child

Stepparenting the Grieving Child

Cultivating Past and Present Connections with Children Who Have Lost a Parent

DIANE INGRAM FROMME

MERRY DISSONANCE PRESS   CASTLE ROCK, COLORADO

*Stepparenting the Grieving Child: Cultivating Past and Present
Connections with Children Who Have Lost a Parent*

Published by Merry Dissonance Press, LLC
Castle Rock, CO

FIRST EDITION
2017

Library of Congress Control Number: 2016920332

Fromme, Diane Ingram, Author
Stepparenting the Grieving Child: Cultivating Past and Present
Connections with Children Who Have Lost a Parent
Diane Ingram Fromme

ISBN 978-1-939919-47-2
1. **FAMILY & RELATIONSHIPS** / Parenting / Stepparenting
2. **FAMILY & RELATIONSHIPS** / Death, Grief, Bereavement
3. **SELF-HELP** / Death, Grief, Bereavement

Book Design and Cover Design © 2017
Cover Design by Victoria Wolf
Book Design by Andrea Costantine
Editing by Donna Mazzitelli, The Word Heartiste

Printed in the United States of America

To my husband, stepchildren, and their mother:
You helped me realize
what truly matters
about grieving and about stepparenting.

CONTENTS

FOREWORD   **15**

INTRODUCTION: How Did I Get Here?   **21**

My story   23

Why I decided to write this book   27

Who is this book for?   29

How this book can help you   30

Stepparenting the Grieving Child roadmap   31

What's so different about stepparenting after a death?   33

The Stepparent Stories   37

PART I Exploration: Engaging in Self-Reflection and Stepparent Education   **41**

CHAPTER 1: The Dawn of Understanding   **43**

Stepparenting preparation: foresight or hindsight?   46

SIDEBAR: Preparing for a Role   48

CHAPTER 2: Your Marriage and Stepparenting Mindsets   **51**

The mindsets   54

Develop your willing attitude   61

CHAPTER 3: Blood is Thicker Than … Everything   **67**

The power of biology   69

Mother substitutes: relatives come close   70

Father substitutes: similar conclusions   72

The third set of relatives   73

How to cope with rejection   74

Six schemes to depersonalize rejection   76

Ain't nothing like the real thing   82

SIDEBAR: NOT the Mama!   83

CHAPTER 4: Debunking Stepfamily Myths   **85**

Common stepfamily myths   87

The Stepfamily Cycle: what to expect   94

CHAPTER 5: Your Identity in the New Family   **107**

Mission identity   109

Reclaim the authentic you   110

Build your support network   112

SIDEBAR: Support and Step-mountains   114

Invite the natural parent to claim his or her role   114

Reframe yourself in a larger identity picture   121

Manage your ego   122

Connect with your confidence   123

Weave traditions side-by-side   124

Special guidance when children have lost both parents   125

PART II Empathy: Reaching Out to Your Family   **129**

CHAPTER 6: The Lifework of Grief   **131**

Understanding loss   133

Understanding grief and grieving   135

SIDEBAR: Grief and Mourning Differ by Culture   139

Understanding mourning and its four tasks   140

Continuing bonds   144

CHAPTER 7: Is Everyone Really "Fine?"   **149**

Creating memory-keeping opportunities   152

Age-appropriate ways to cope with grief and loss   157

An angel's child faces special struggles   162

Allowing and encouraging re-grief   163

Is grief counseling necessary?   165

What do I do when family members won't seek help?   167

SIDEBAR: Are the Kids Really Fine and What Do I Do?   168

CHAPTER 8: A Heart for Differences   **173**

Developing empathy   176

SIDEBAR: Finding Common Ground Among Differences   180

Find the good   182

CHAPTER 9: Straight Talk and Honest Communication   **187**

The challenge of honest communication   191

Talk about what you see   192

How to talk   195

What to do when it's too difficult to talk   197

What to do when your kids won't talk   198

How to listen   200

SIDEBAR: The Power of Family Meetings   202

Stand together to resolve family conflicts   204

PART III Equilibrium: Finding Balance Day by Day   **207**

CHAPTER 10: Zigzag Evolution   **209**

Stepparent zigzags help you gain perspective   213

SIDEBAR: How Do You Deal with Zigzag?   216

What to do when you feel angry   218

Measuring stepfamily progress   219

CHAPTER 11: Acceptance, Not Attachments   **223**

Choose your attitude, choose your gratitude   227

Inevitable dissonance   230

You're not just a role, you're a person   232

SIDEBAR: There's No E-G-O in A-C-C-E-P-T-A-N-C-E   234

CHAPTER 12: Milestones and Miracles   **237**

Wedding ceremony balances honor and acceptance   240

SIDEBAR: What I've Discovered I Like About Being a Stepparent   242

Celebrate the miracles   244

SUPPLEMENTAL MATERIAL   **247**

Common Stepparent Ponderings   249

How to handle Mother's and Father's Day   249

How to process your feelings about your stepchildren and
    your own children   251

How to manage school breaks and time off   254

How to ride seasonal energy to make your ownchanges   257

How to help people of varying ages with their grief   259

How to recognize when a child isn't coping well   260

How to keep connected with adult stepchildren   261

How Can I Best Help My Stepfamily Overall?   265

Resource Guide   267

Acknowledgments   271

About the Author   273

About the Press   275

Foreword Clarion Reviews   276

BlueInk Review   278

Foreword

Dr. Patricia L. Papernow

DIANE FROMME'S *STEPPARENTING THE GRIEVING CHILD* is a tenderly illuminating and eminently practical book that fills a yawning chasm in the stepfamily literature. The bottom line of Fromme's message: Assume that children who have lost a parent are always grieving. *Is everyone really fine?* No.

Fromme chronicles her own difficult journey of moving toward honoring, rather than fighting, the reality that her stepchildren's deceased mother was, and would continue to be, a permanent part of her family. Along the way she compassionately embraces her own longing to feel effective, loved, and accepted, and she fully acknowledges the strength of her determined optimism (shared by so many in her position) that if she just loved her stepchildren enough she could fill the hole in their hearts left by their mother's death. As Fromme wryly comments, "The stepparent does not get hero or heroine points from the kids for stepping into stepfamily central." Consistent with the research, Fromme states succinctly that stepparents are the *and,* not the *instead of* for their stepchildren. "When I recognized I could not occupy an insider position," Fromme writes, "I stopped being so hard on myself for falling short."

The popular myth is that the death of a parent more easily paves the way for a stepparent to move into the family as a replacement. Fromme eloquently describes the reality—that the truth may actually be opposite. In divorce, children continue to have contact with both of their living parents. When divorce goes well, children can hold on to all of their important relationships. Even in a conflicted divorce, children can often maintain some real connection with both of their parents. Grieving stepchildren do not have any ongoing contact with their missing parent. It has been my own experience that grieving children may not only carry a much larger burden of loss, but may struggle with even tighter loyalty binds, often feeling that "If I let in my new stepparent, I will lose whatever threads I still have of my missing mom/dad." As Fromme also accurately notes, the longing for a deceased parent is often laced with idealization. All of this combines to make it especially challenging for stepparents.

This book stands in stark contrast to an expanding plethora of blogs, twitter posts, and trade books that dispense well-meaning but misleading, and often quite destructive, "advice" to stepparents. Fromme, in contrast, has clearly done her homework. She has immersed herself in some of the few solid sources of research-informed guidance about stepfamilies, and she has fully educated herself about the realities of the grieving process for children who have lost a parent. The result is a book that is at once profoundly personal and firmly grounded in established family scholarship. Readers will find good counsel throughout. For instance, she describes the ways in which stepparents enter as outsiders to "biological connections … a biological family comfort and rhythm of which the stepparent is inherently not a part." The parent in a stepfamily is the center of the family, not the stepparent. Fromme's advice that parents need to retain the disciplinary role is consistent with the research. Only when stepparents have formed a trusting caring relationship with their stepchildren can they begin to, slowly, step into "authoritative"—both loving and moderately firm—limit setting. As I often put it, stepparents need to begin by practicing connection, not correction, often for a very long time. Meanwhile, stepparents need to have input, but parents have final say about their own children.

Fromme honors the need for the new family to build an "us." However, especially when the previous parent has died, she notes the critical importance of maintaining respect for established beloved rituals and practices. New threads need to be woven very slowly "side-by-side" with established family fabric, not replace it.

Perhaps most challenging, Fromme describes vividly her own process of learning that stepparent-stepchild relationships must be built very slowly over time, a lot of time. She describes her chagrin when, five years down the road, her family's therapist, clearly someone with some knowledge of stepfamilies, informs her that she and her stepchildren were still in the relationship-building phase. Again, she offers a way forward consistent with stepfamily scholarship: Stepparents can build relationships with their stepchildren by finding bits of common ground with stepchildren for what I call "shoulder-to-shoulder" one-to-one activities without the parent present. For Fromme, these included inviting her stepdaughter to share in training the family's dog, and, with her stepson, playing indoor beach-ball volleyball during the winter.

The research clearly tells us that the healthiest stepchildren feel positively connected to both of their parents, and with both stepparents. In my own experience, stepchildren of all ages often need the important adults in their lives to proactively release the loyalty binds that can appear when a stepparent enters the family. One aspect of this is what I call "loyalty bind talks." Fromme provides an especially moving example. She suggests telling a grieving stepchild, "I realize that this family is not the family you wished you had. You're missing an important person in your lives, and I'm sorry for that." She adds, "Eventually I want to help you remember that person and get to know me as well." Because parent-child attachment is permanent and forever, it may be important to add here that children with a parent who has abandoned them, or who was inadequate or rejecting, are also grieving and may need very similar support from their parents and stepparents.

Because the parent remains "the hub" and "the stabilizing center," Fromme reminds us that the surviving parent is in a position to support the process of slowly building step relationships, by saying something like, "We've been through a lot and we are all missing [mom/dad]... I want you to know that as we move forward as a family, we will not forget [him/her]. We also have someone new in our family who wants to help us, and who is already helping me so that I can help you."

Throughout, Fromme's honesty and practicality are laced with good humor. One of my favorites is a story of an earnest but failed attempt to force family blending by getting her stepchildren to call her "Snoopy" rather than "Diane" or "Mom." "The lesson?" Fromme says, "Do not try this at home."

Fromme does not stint on the emotional demands, and the losses involved, of stepparenting grieving stepchildren. She warns, "Your stepchildren's need for biological connection" with their missing parent "is not personal or an assault on you. But it will feel like one. Be prepared for rejection." Very moving to me, she is deeply real and honest about the challenges that come with facilitating "good communication." When her normally silent stepdaughter blurts, "You're not a mom in my heart," Fromme describes the muscle required to bear the initial jolt of hurt and then reach for the knowledge that her stepdaughter was taking a risk that could be a huge step forward in sharing her grief. As a result, Fromme was able to respond with, "This is important. Tell me more."

Over time, Fromme comes to understand that her central task is not to replace her stepchildren's mother. It is to actively help them carry their mother in their hearts. "We might take some of our most demanding stepfamily journeys when we encourage our stepchildren to keep their lost loved ones close. Although this process might bring up difficult feelings, honoring our stepchildren's needs ultimately builds the soundest, most trustworthy stepfamily relationships. The sooner you can transition to honoring, not fighting" children's abiding connections to their missing parent, "the more likely your stepchildren will be able to find a place for you in their hearts and in the family."

The book offers a treasure chest of specific concrete guidance for what Fromme poignantly calls, "honoring the gap." Acknowledging that "bereaved children crave blood relatives of their deceased parent," Fromme counsels stepparents to actively support their stepchildren's intense needs for connection with their lost parent's siblings and parents. For the stepparent, the aunts, uncles, and grandparents connected to the deceased parent are a "third" "extra" family. For grieving stepchildren, they are precious connections that help to fill a deep hole in their hearts. Indeed, she suggests, the couple needs to "become the team that helps children to continue their bonds" with their missing parent. She encourages stepparents to gather a repository of stories from aunts, uncles, and friends. She encourages stepparents who knew the children's missing parent to share stories, memories, and what they miss the most. Fromme stresses the importance for children to keep photos of their missing mom or dad prominently displayed. She suggests, as she learned from Jennifer Aberle, to engage in ongoing conversations with stepchildren like: "You can still have a bond with your mom and she will remain important to you. How would you like her to be important to you? Where do you think your mom is? When do you feel her during the day? Let's give her a place." She reminds both stepparents and parents to be especially attuned to anniversary dates, birthdays, holidays, and Mother's Day/Father's Day, and she provides a well-researched list of age-specific guidelines for developmentally appropriate ways to facilitate children's grieving.

This is a profoundly hopeful book, filled with such epiphanies as, "You'll reach a point where your heart will melt because you understand what they need." This book moves the field a huge step forward from what long-time stepfamily researchers Larry Ganong and Marilyn Coleman have called a "deficit comparison" model of stepfamilies as broken first-time families to a picture of healthy, open-hearted stepfamily relationships. *Stepparenting the Grieving Child* provides much needed guidance for stepfamilies with grieving children, for those who love them, and for the mental health, religious, medical, and education professionals involved with grieving stepfamilies.

Dr. Patricia Papernow is a psychologist and an internationally recognized expert on stepfamily relationships. She is the author of one of the leading books in the field, *Surviving and Thriving in Stepfamily Relationships: What Works and What Doesn't,* and Director of the Institute for Stepfamily Education and the National Stepfamily Resource Center.

Introduction

How Did I Get Here?

"We must be willing to let go of the life we planned
so as to have the life that is waiting for us."
–E.M. FORSTER

Brittany: Six years old
Ian: Five years old
Time since their mom died: Six months
My relationship status: Dating Brian
Season: Spring

THE MESMERIZING BLUE OF YOUNG BRITTANY'S EYES matched that of the cloudless sky over the softball field. I had offered to watch Brittany and her younger brother, Ian, at the playground adjoining the field while Brian—my date and their father—played a tournament game.

All the other times I'd hung out with the kids up to this point, Brian had been right by their side too—as we ate, watched TV, or played games together. This was my first time caring for Brittany and Ian on my own. Brian and I were dating exclusively now, and I craved to know more about his kids.

Today's outing presented an opportunity to search Brittany and Ian's eyes for whatever lay within. Until this moment, I think I'd feared what I might find there, considering the children had so recently lost their mother to cancer.

In Brittany's expression I saw an unexpected calm. I was not acquainted with any other young children who had lost a parent, and I thought Brittany might face me with more anxiety or signs of mourning. Only the slight, purplish-grey smudges under her eyes yielded a clue of strain, dark crescents in the soft, ivory skin. When the sunlight flickered across her eyes, I imagined questions—the kinds of hard inquiries that had no satisfying answers—such as "Who are you?" and "Where did my mom go?"

Ian's eyes were a little darker and appeared stormier than Brittany's: "seawater blue," I immediately thought. He was so active that I couldn't get a deeper look, or perhaps he wasn't going to let me connect with him gaze-to-gaze. If Ian showed any signs of mourning, he masked them with constant motion.

The kids dug around in the wood chips near the swings, climbed on the geo structure, and played a fantasy game concocted from the depths of their imaginations. Sometimes I watched the action on the softball field, but most of the time I studied the children. I was taken with the creamy perfection one finds in the faces of the young—unblemished skin and innocence on the outside in marked contrast with the potential scars on their hearts from losing their mom.

Their lives were so unlike mine–I had just spoken to my mother that morning. She and I had even argued a little, as most of us do in the trenches of real life. I expected that Brittany and Ian were hurting, but I couldn't feel any understanding of their pain in my heart, completely oblivious to how naked they actually were to the world ahead of them without their mom in their lives.

When Ian asked me to take him to the bathroom, he still didn't meet my eyes, but he did grab for my hand. I'd never held his before, and it felt strange at first, but then very warm and very much alive. For a moment, I felt connected to him. We could get used to each other, I thought. This could work out just fine.

My journey with my stepchildren started out with brief interactions, simple and peaceful. I appreciated time to observe Brittany and Ian engage in their uninhibited children's play. As the relationship between Brian and me grew and became more serious, the thought of having stepchildren didn't raise red flags for me. "Optimistic" is a word I use to describe myself, and I brought this attitude to the way I approached the upcoming adventure of stepfamily life.

"Prepared" is another word that's an essential fiber in my fabric. However, I didn't think about preparing to be a stepparent. I was looking down the nose of taking on first-time parenting and stepparenting all in one bite, and still I felt ready to move ahead. As I look back, I wonder how that was possible.

To the best of my recollection, I believed I could make anything work, spurred on by my love for a man and my desire to help him. Just past thirty years old, a flood of idealism overtook the practical me, my blissful optimism fueling my high spirits. Later I would discover that love and determination were not enough to fully serve the real needs of my grieving family-to-be. I would need some assistance in order to open my eyes and my heart to stepparenting my grieving children.

My story

When I was growing up, my mother told me about her adventures as a stepmother during her second marriage to my father, whose first wife had passed away, leaving two teenage daughters. My father also adopted my mother's son from her first marriage. My mother shared with me about my father's experiences as well—especially the temporary phase of "you're not my father" from his stepson. I was born into this blended family with a half-brother and two half-sisters. My mom told me many times that the "working out" of step-relationships was agonizing for everyone, including the children. Apparently my mom even threw her wedding ring across the room once or twice. While she sometimes ended the stories by cautioning me not to marry a man with children, I know now that she treasured her marriage despite the difficulties. She was just hoping to prepare me, and possibly spare me, by sharing her cautionary tales.

Life, however, has a way of repeating patterns and lessons we need to learn. At age twenty-eight, in a common workplace, I met Brian. Brian the kindhearted. Brian the brave husband, coping with the mystery of his wife Cathy's cancer, which was in remission at the time. He was also Brian the concerned father. In addition to feeling panicked about the prospective course of his wife's illness, he worried about the ramifications for his children.

I was separating from my first husband when Brian and I were co-workers, following on the heels of the death of my father. I ended up in the same software division as Brian when I was forced to change jobs after the company I worked for merged with another large high-tech company. During that time, I began marketing the software product line Brian had developed. As we worked on publicity plans and events together over many months, we became friends, and over long talks at lunchtime offered each other support and suggestions about our home life situations.

Suddenly, Brian disappeared from work. He wasn't responding to emails, and his boss could only reveal that there had been complications. My concern about him deepened. The more I worried, the more I realized all I could do was wait. When Brian did resurface at work, he found me in the courtyard outside the cafeteria. He delivered the news that Cathy's cancer had spread to a major organ and that her doctors did not expect her to live more than a few months. I remember feeling shocked, as if time stood still for several minutes.

The news represented the possibility no family member wants to hear, and I could see some of the ways it was affecting Brian. He went through the motions at work that day, moving almost robotically, as if in a daze. Some days he came into the office in sweatpants and a t-shirt, and some days he didn't come to work at all. When we did meet for lunch, however, he spoke realistically about his decision process regarding family matters. He felt that the care of his children was his number one concern. Brian felt caught between two opposite dynamics: the doctors' death sentence and Cathy's resolve to beat the recurrence by flying across the country to a well-known hospital for more treatments. He didn't know which road of belief to travel, but for the sake of the kids he felt he had to act and make decisions as if Cathy was going to pass away.

When Brian disappeared from work again several months later, I knew he must be heading to the East Coast where Cathy had been staying with her mom and sister. The next time I heard from him, Cathy was in hospice care at home and passed shortly thereafter.

I understood the pain of loss of a family member at a very real level, given my father's recent passing. But I didn't have any grasp of the ways that this loss would impact Brian and his children in the months and years to come. In the year after Cathy passed away, my relationship with Brian deepened. The closer we became, the more the life lessons my father had taught me flew out of my mind—especially the ones about analyzing pros and cons as one waits for the right time to take action. My mother's previous relationship advice suddenly didn't apply to me either. Only the song lyrics, "… the heart wants what it wants" seemed to capture my state of mind. I knew Brian's priority was the wellbeing of his children, and I had every intention to help. I didn't realize at the time that by focusing only on my new relationship with Brian, I was leaving Cathy out of the family equation. My life became a mixed-up ball of unrecognized naiveté rolled together with hopeful good intentions.

For better or for worse, I wanted to marry into this stepfamily, promising friendship and love with Brian and the ability to help him raise his children. Attitude-wise, I felt willing and even determined that I could make a difference in my stepchildren's lives. I do wish I'd been more aware that compassion and an understanding of the children's grieving and deep sense of loss could have softened my entry into their family.

Despite being raised in a stepfamily myself, none of us in my family of origin acknowledged by name that we were a stepfamily. Thus I knew nothing about the distinct nature of stepfamily formation—its undulations and patterns—coupled with the effects of grief and the possible ways grief can manifest over the years. It never crossed my mind or Brian's that we might need outside help to figure out how to grow our stepfamily and build healthy relationships.

Two years after Cathy passed, without much further study than snapshot observations of the children, I launched forward into "I do." Our union became one of husband, wife, and two children, ages eight and six, not to mention two dogs and three cats. At the time, I didn't grasp that Brittany and Ian's mom, though deceased, was and would remain an essential part of our new family. I can honestly say that I didn't fully "get" this crucial concept—one that could have made our stepfamily life so much more fluid—until I had a child of my own.

Brian and I had baby Amy when Brittany and Ian were thirteen and eleven. By observing how I felt while raising her, I gained tremendous insight into the strength and complexity of the love between a mother and her children. Experiencing what Brittany and Ian's mom shared with them awoke my heart to the pain and hurt I imagined Brittany and Ian had been feeling on and off throughout the years of our stepfamily togetherness. I finally felt how important it was for them to keep their mom alive in their hearts. I also finally realized why they had to find a different place in their hearts for me, which wasn't an easy task to accomplish. That growing empathy illuminated a distinct learning path for me as I began to see the beauty in a more organic stepfamily progression, complete with ebbs and flows of relationship dynamics.

Over time, blessed with the knowledge I gained from all my stepfamily and grief education, I became more comfortable letting my bonds with the kids develop on their own timeline, and I became grateful for any close moments we shared instead of trying to predict success points. Yet, it's obvious that in those early years, my actions were steeped in a more controlled progression of my relationships with my stepchildren—the only way I knew how to attempt and measure the progress of those relationships early on. I carefully orchestrated the stepfamily flow and activities, and I constantly sought out success markers instead of trusting that they were already there.

I'm still married to Brian. Somehow, through all the crazy phases of our family relationships and our gradual ramp-up to education about stepfamily life and about grieving, we've made things work. I can't say that the journey was ever easy. I can say that as Brittany and Ian have grown into adulthood, Brian and I have learned so much about the importance of honoring deceased family members and not taking the children's loyalties personally. I have no doubt, due to my

> Over time, blessed with the knowledge I gained from all my stepfamily and grief education, I became more comfortable letting my bonds with the kids develop on their own timeline, and I became grateful for any close moments we shared instead of trying to predict success points.

knowledge that grief doesn't have an end-point, that Brittany and Ian carry their own pain about their losses, and that it takes a community of support to bolster grieving children, no matter their age, so that they do not ever have to grieve alone or deny grief's existence.

Why I decided to write this book

On one level, my initial and blissful stepparenting optimism was healthy— as I moved into the role of stepparent, my positive and willing attitude helped keep the family mood on an even keel for a while. However, I learned that a cheery grin and a helping hand are not enough to sustain a grieving stepfamily. Even a year or two after our marriage, many family dynamics and behaviors remained confusing. For instance, why would Brittany come downstairs on weekend mornings and drape herself over the easy chair, hoping, it seemed, for the motivation to get through the day? Did she feel a lack of attention or did she need something she couldn't express? Why would Ian often check out into a world of video games? Was he, too, waiting for someone to pay more attention, or was he escaping to a place where he didn't have to deal with his feelings? Or was everything I observed just normal kid behavior?

Without any knowledge or research, I figured I should give the relationships time. On a daily basis, I bought into a common myth—one of the many that new stepparents encounter—that by giving our grieving stepfamily a little time it would start to feel loving and cohesive. I believed that by loving the kids hard enough with my words and actions—doing tuck-ins, helping with homework, making snacks and lunches—we would all "get through" the rough phase and bond to each other. I waited years for this miraculous transformation. My heart was in the right place, but I didn't understand that I had to become a more effective part of the solution if our family was to grow closer.

When I realized that our stepfamily didn't gel like magic, I dove into research. If I was going to give my stepchildren the help they needed, I first needed to help myself. I looked for a reliable resource on stepparenting after the death of a parent. To my surprise, I couldn't find one. I can still picture myself sitting on the floor of a beloved indie bookstore in Denver, Colorado, surrounded by various self-help paperbacks. Most of the books I found were devoted to stepparenting through a divorce; many were written specifically about how to get along with the ex-wife. But no book addressed the tough and inexplicable moments when grief re-surfaces all at once, or even how to recognize this phenomenon. What should I do when the panicked look in my stepdaughter's eyes tells me I can't wash that tightly clutched scarf that belonged to her mom? How can I address my embarrassment and frustration when my stepson cries because I didn't serve the butter sandwich open-faced, like Mom did?

I found some great books about grief education and stories about how children grieve, but not books about how to manage grief while building stepfamily relationships. I finally found two books about stepparenting that had *one chapter each* devoted to stepparenting when the former spouse has died. I took what treasures I could find, but two chapters didn't seem like enough. I began to think about the number of tips, insights, and observations that could fill a book about stepparenting through a child's grief.

My lack of education about grieving stepfamilies reminds me of the irony that we don't know what we don't know. The good news is that we can learn what we don't know. Once I began reading and talking with counselors and with other stepfamilies, I felt more equipped to try new ways to build relationships with my stepkids. I accepted confusion as part of stepfamily life, and I ramped back up to viewing stepfamily relationships with more confidence. This process led me to wonder, "Could my experience assist others searching for ways to connect more deeply with their grieving stepchildren?" I decided the answer was yes. I could create a companion guide for those stepparenting through grief and for those supporting grieving stepfamilies.

Who is this book for?

Many individuals touch the lives of grieving children, and in the spirit of the phrase, "It takes a village," many can help a child not only grieve but also thrive. The primary unit of care remains the natural (surviving) parent, if involved, along with whomever is in the role of the stepparent—usually the spouse or spouse-to-be. When the natural parent is unavailable for primary care, godparents, grandparents, or other relatives can fill the stepparenting role. Any of these parties can benefit from the insights in *Stepparenting the Grieving Child*. Grandparents in particular may be in a position where they have inherited the care of their grandchildren and are acting in a stepparenting role.

Additionally, teachers spend almost as many hours per day with a child as do the parents themselves. Teachers need strategies to help children cope with grief, as grief reactions may occur during the course of any school day. When teachers and parents are speaking the same language of support in the school-to-home connection, that commonality helps a child enjoy consistency between both worlds. School psychologists, counselors, and administrators, as well, can benefit by gaining familiarity with the needs of the grieving children in their buildings.

Finally, helping professionals of multiple titles may walk grieving children through their gardens of grief as well as through everyday activities. Psychologists, pastors, coaches, and other activity leaders make up a few of the many other adults who can provide a grieving child assistance and a loving base from which to grow.

How this book can help you

When I looked for a how-to guide, I longed for someone to talk "straight" to me about stepfamilies and grieving. Even though I was a bit afraid of discovering that I'd approached stepfamily life the "wrong" way, I had an overriding desire to do what was right for the kids and feel more secure in my role. Just as important, I wanted to balance how to take care of myself with how to provide help for my family.

I've designed this book to achieve similar goals and to help you feel encouraged as you open your heart and mind to gain any or all of the following benefits:

+ Support to know you're not alone in this situation
+ Relief and a more relaxed approach to stepparenting through grief
+ Permission to empathize with yourself, especially when you feel you've given your heart but family dynamics are still not smooth
+ Strategies to empathize with your grieving stepfamily members
+ Insights, ideas, and information to digest—for yourself, or to share
+ Direction when you feel stuck

I grew to the point where I could at least imagine the emotions my stepchildren have felt as a result of their losses. Yet, at the same time, I recognized my own losses, which are, I believe, representative of the types of losses stepparents go through. I realized that the love in my marriage couldn't magically make stepfamily life flow and that I needed help and direction to make sense of how to stepparent through grief.

Stepparenting the Grieving Child is a guidebook to keep you growing and learning through stepfamily abundance and storms alike. When you feel your optimism waning, you can access the wisdom and inspiration you need most, offered by a longtime stepmom to two grieving children. I learned that I *could* learn to stepparent in a more satisfying and gentle way for myself and my family, and so can you.

Stepparenting the Grieving Child roadmap

After many years of my best intuitive stepparenting, followed by many more years of research, my formula for successful stepparenting after a parent dies came to look closest to this:

What do I mean by sustainable stepparenting? This rich word "sustainable" has many meanings, all of which express the same thing: enduring and lasting, with an infusion of nourishment and encouragement. It's best to strive for a stepparenting approach that builds from the base you create with your partner. A sustainable approach involves many elements that keep you committed to developing stepfamily relationships *and* to enhancing your own well-being, through all the joys and sorrows. Such an approach balances your needs alongside a mission to advance the health and healing of your grieving stepchildren.

Stepparenting the Grieving Child mirrors my own process of discovery within the stepfamily. Part I, "Exploration: Engaging in Self-Reflection and Stepfamily Education," gives you a chance to process your thoughts and feelings about joining a stepfamily. How do you puzzle out *your* needs and *your* identity within the new family formation? This section also breaks down omnipresent stepfamily myths and presents instead a stepfamily development cycle that's relevant and illuminating, because it's based on the way real stepfamilies form and operate. Becoming aware of how stepfamilies develop and reflecting on where we fit into our families gives us the chance to take care of ourselves. This approach represents loving preparation in the process of developing empathetic responses to others.

Part II, "Empathy: Reaching Out to Your Family," shares meaningful ways to connect with grieving stepkids, with a focus on continuing bonds with the deceased parent. I share insights about how to nurture grieving children and teens, and how to recognize signs of re-grief even when the kids say they're fine. This section also sheds light on communication styles and empathetic responses within the stepfamily. We might take some of our most demanding stepfamily journeys when we encourage our stepchildren to keep their lost loved ones close. Although this process might bring up difficult feelings, honoring our stepchildren's needs ultimately builds the soundest, most trustworthy stepfamily relationships.

Part III, "Equilibrium: Finding Balance Day by Day," offers perspective and strategies to address the zigzags of daily stepfamily life, whether your stepkids live at home or have moved out. This section includes ideas to help you accept what is occurring in your stepfamily in the moment and to see stepfamily relationships as organic and growing rather than as static and unchanging. Part III also shares examples of the milestones and miracles that accompany long-term stepfamily living.

The order of these sections follows familiar airline advice: put on your own oxygen mask before you help children put on theirs. I believe you'll find it valuable to first explore your own feelings in this family situation and then to learn more about what to expect from being the stepparent of a bereaved child. These steps give us the chance to heighten our awareness as we turn our attention to our family's grieving behaviors and concerns.

At the beginning of each chapter, I share a short memoir—a poignant moment from my experiences with Brittany and Ian. The memoirs reveal my deepest hopes, frustrations, fears, or celebrations from the particular phase of the stepparenting journey that I discuss in that chapter. My observations may not match yours, yet my stories may trigger your self-discovery. You might want to first read through all the memoirs in one sitting to get a sense of my personal progression in my stepfamily. In each chapter, I also incorporate what I've learned from my own missteps and successes, along with insights other stepparents have shared with me during interviews. Additionally, I interviewed psychologists Mark Benn, Jean McBride, and Jennifer Aberle. All of their comments in this book derive from those interviews. I sometimes quote or paraphrase information derived from books by a variety of stepfamily and grief experts, and those books or articles in which their quotes originally appeared are listed within the narrative the first time they are referenced. They are then included in the Resource Guide at the back of the book.

> The order of these sections follows familiar airline advice: put on your own oxygen mask before you help children put on theirs.

I know that my views of the world color the way I express my thoughts, and therefore through "Reflection Prompts" in each chapter I ask questions to encourage you to consider your range of experiences alongside the stories I offer. Reflection time is time for you. While pondering these questions, go grab a soothing drink and, if possible, create some solitude. I recommend having a notebook, journal, or your phone's notes app handy to jot down your answers for each chapter's questions. Following the Reflection Prompts, each chapter concludes with its most salient "Points to Remember," which you may also want to capture alongside your answers. These points serve as great quick-reference reminders of the highlights within each chapter.

The final section, "Supplemental Materials," provides additional information for you to consider, including a chapter that covers common ponderings and questions based on what others have asked me through my blog and website, as well as a resource guide that is broken down by topics and provides recommendations to books and websites, both national and international.

What's so different about stepparenting after a death?

Before we move forward, there is one concept that seems fundamental to address—that is the acknowledgment that stepparenting after a death is distinctly unique from stepparenting as a result of divorce. Without the type of information provided in *Stepparenting the Grieving Child*, family members, family helpers, teachers, and helping professionals may not know the key challenges faced by grieving children after a parent's death.

Certainly, stepfamily members in both divorce and death situations experience various kinds of loss. Losses from the death of a parent—including the loss of a person and a presence— are not worse than divorce-related losses, such as the loss of a child's former home or the loss of living full-time with both parents. There's no way to quantify the severity of the losses suffered when marriages break up and families must find new ways to carry on.

My investigations reveal that stepparents of children who've lost a parent have some singular issues to consider. Most of those revolve around how this type of loss affects the children, while other issues grow out of some role confusion because the ex-spouse is not physically present.

Here's what I've discovered:

- Many children in divorced families have regular contact with both parents. Grieving children also need "contact" with both parents— a need that usually goes unsatisfied with regard to the deceased parent, because someone of that same gender is joining the family, causing some role confusion. I learned that I needed to encourage creative ways to keep the kids' relationship with their mom alive in addition to establishing my gender role in the family.
- When kids of divorce see both parents, they witness their parents' shining traits and their faux pas. When a parent dies, the children tend to idolize the dead parent with intense feelings of loyalty, which makes it extremely difficult and scary for them to bond with even the most loving, supportive stepparent.
- Bereaved children can have difficulty trusting others, especially trusting any level of permanency. They may be more hesitant about intimate relationships than divorced children. A natural question that bereaved children ask is, "Who's going to die next?" They question the surviving parent's mortality, and even their own mortality. I came down with pneumonia when Brittany was almost

eight. She immediately wanted to know if I was going to die.

- ♦ It's easy for the stepparent to want to step into the gender gap created by the physical loss of a parent. In contrast, when a child is moving back and forth between houses, or simply calling to speak to mom or dad on a regular basis, the stepparent/parent distinction is more concrete than when a parent dies and all stepfamily members live in one home.

As you move through *Stepparenting the Grieving Child,* you may identify additional differences between families formed after a divorce and families formed after a death. Depending on your particular circumstances, you may also identify experiences beyond those relayed in the stories you'll encounter in the following pages. Although we all share a common bond of having a relationship with a child who has lost a parent, we also honor our individual experiences. I invite you to acknowledge your unique story while using what is provided to help you navigate the ebbs and flows of life in this incredibly distinctive family circumstance. May you find validation, courage, strength, and compassion to continue to offer your heart to the family you've joined.

REFLECTION PROMPTS

1. What thoughts or feelings surfaced for you as you read my story?
2. What specific assistance would you like to gain from this book?

POINTS TO REMEMBER

- ♦ During stepfamily relationship building, neither my nor my stepfamily members' feelings were "wrong." Feelings are facts for each person.
- ♦ Stepparenting when a parent has died is distinct from stepparenting through divorce. However, both stepparenting approaches benefit from situation-specific education and empathetic responses toward the children and oneself.
- ♦ Love and good intentions are a great family base, but aren't enough to sustain stepparenting in a grieving family.

- Empathic skills and responses to grieving can be learned. These skills help us give back to our stepfamilies.
- By entering a grieving stepfamily, you become part of the team that helps the children continue their bonds with the parent who died.

The Stepparent Stories

WHEN I BEGAN SHARING MY SPECTRUM OF emotions about stepparenting—from hope for the future to feelings of frustration—with other parents, I found communities of adults who were also the stepparents of grieving children. When I chatted with these parents, we came alive with connection, as if we spoke a secret language that only the other understood. I interviewed several of those parents for this book, and their stories crop up throughout the chapters. Here's a brief introduction to each of these stepfamilies.

Adults: Ella and Walter
Children: Merle, Joanie, and Joel

   I interviewed Ella in the high-windowed atrium and café of the Denver Museum of Nature and Science. Overhead, an enormous dinosaur guarded the entrance to the museum exhibits, serving as a prehistoric symbol of the wisdom of the ages. A grandmother and stepgrandmother many times over, petite and lively Ella had very clear recollections of her stepfamily years and the lessons she learned.

Ella knew Walter's first wife, Madge, before Madge became ill. Ella worked as a private secretary to consulting engineer Walter in Walter's home. "We would all have lunch together. Madge made the most delicious lunches," Ella said. After Madge got cancer, Ella worked until Madge's health took the ultimate turn for the worse. What Ella didn't learn until years later was that Madge and Walter had already discussed Walter's potential remarriage. Madge, in fact, approved of Ella as a good choice for his second wife. "Walter was a strong man and a great provider," Ella said. "I had a son from my first marriage, and I yearned for a stable home for him. I went into it completely blind ... but living through it is the only way to know what it's really like. I gained the background to advise my friends who were thinking of marrying into a similar situation."

Adults: Marin and Rod
Children: Grace and Kiefer

Amidst the new growth of spring, sitting on park benches surrounded by plush grass, I interviewed the articulate Marin. Her soft tones and English accent sounded lyrical as she narrated her youthful entry into her stepfamily.

Marin had been Grace and Kiefer's babysitter for two years when Rod's wife, Wendy, got sick. Like our Cathy, Wendy died when she was only thirty-two. "Kiefer had just turned four and Grace was five when she died," said Marin. "I foolishly thought I had a foot in the door with the kids. When Rod and I told them we were getting married, things between the kids and me really changed." Marin also mentioned that she was very young—just twenty-two—when she and Rod married, two years after Wendy had passed. "I had the idea that I could go in and change the world," she said. "I couldn't. It was a very humbling experience."

Adults: Kit and Quincy
Children: Brad and Lana

The bold and outgoing Kit and I met at a coffee shop abuzz with activity and conversation, thus causing us to almost yell to be heard during the course of the interview. At the time we met, Kit was turning to her faith during a challenging new phase of long-distance parenting her young adult stepdaughter, who is also her niece.

Kit and Quincy took on the care of Quincy's sister's children after she died. Thus Kit and Quincy went from being Brad and Lana's aunt and uncle to also being their stepparents. At the time their mom died, Brad was seventeen, Lana was ten, and their birth father was just getting out of jail and wanted nothing to do with them. "When we went out for Sherri's funeral, we actually had on our counter an application for adoption, because we wanted a baby," said Kit. "When we flew out there, Quincy's stepmom said, 'There's no place for these children to go but with you guys.' It seemed like a match made in heaven—Brad and Lana got to have parents, and we got to have children." Kit said that although Brad, finishing high school, was "almost cooked" when Kit and Quincy brought the kids home, young Lana had a road full of challenges ahead of her.

Adults: Adam and Lily
Children: Rachel, Liz, Laurel, and Muncie

I interviewed the bearded, slight but strong Adam at a Barnes & Noble café, surrounded by the wisdom of a store full of books. As we sipped our hot drinks, this initially quiet man impressed me with his thoughtfulness and the amount of support he was providing his wife, Lily, throughout their stepfamily journey.

Adam had been married once before, and he knew he didn't want to live alone after his divorce. "I need the family support structure in my life," he said. "I wanted a wife and companion and I really enjoy home life and family life." Adam didn't have any children with his first wife, but he stepparented his first wife's children. Thus Adam had a head start on stepfamily wisdom. "Having lived in a stepfamily before, I knew some things to expect when I married Lily. We dated for two or three years while I got to know her girls," he said. Adam was willing to take it slow. This allowed the girls to get to know him over a longer period of time, while they still had a relationship with their own father.

Adam and Lily's situation changed dramatically when, after a year of being married, Lily's ex-husband died in an accident. Overnight, Adam became a stepparent of three girls grieving their father's death. Soon after, Adam and Lily had a child of their own.

PART I

Exploration:
Engaging in Self-Reflection
and Stepparent Education

It's an invaluable exercise to first explore your own
feelings in the stepfamily situation before turning
your attention toward your family's grieving behaviors
and concerns. We can learn what to expect from
stepparenting a bereaved child.
Becoming aware of how stepfamilies develop and
reflecting on where we fit into our families gives us
the chance to take care of ourselves. This approach
represents loving preparation in the process of
developing empathy for others.

ONE

The Dawn of Understanding

"All glory comes from daring to begin."
–EUGENE F. WARE

Brittany: Seven years old
Ian: Five years old
Years since their mom died: One
My relationship status: Engaged to marry in eight months
Season: Fall

I FELT AS NERVOUS AS A FOX at a hound convention. Brian's boss had asked him to visit customers in Japan for ten days, and Brian asked me to take care of his kids while he traveled.

Brian would be 6,000 miles away and a day ahead of us. Ten days alone with Brian's children seemed like an eternity for me; I could only imagine how the thought of it felt for the kids. Besides, the trip was over Halloween. What was I going to do for costumes? My sewing skills were limited to mending, hemming, and buttons.

However, with Brian and I recently engaged to marry the following year, I decided there was no time like the present to jump into the fire with a willing attitude. Though Brian's parents sometimes flew out and stayed with the kids, they weren't available this time. The alternative would have been for Brian to hire a nanny while I stood by. Why should I put off this opportunity? I wanted to help Brian, and sooner or later I would need to test-run more time with the kids. I said yes.

A few days into the stay, I wanted to know what the kids hoped to be for Halloween. Brittany had an idea right away—she wanted to be a unicorn. This magical horse with a horn seemed to fit perfectly with her early love of things equine. We found a unicorn costume kit … a skirt decorated with purple and pink tulle strips, along with a purple and gold horn-and-ears headpiece. This costume was shaping up to be easy; Brittany could wear the adornments over white clothing, add white "hooves" and gloves, and she'd be set!

Ian liked to dress up around the house at any time of year. A Ninja Turtle suit and a dinosaur costume represented his recent favorites. But he wore those around the house a lot, so they didn't seem very special for the upcoming holiday. Ian didn't know what he wanted to be for Halloween. The days ticked by, and he didn't grab on to any particular idea of his own, or of mine. One afternoon, we were watching the Scooby Doo cartoon, and the villain was dressed like a mummy. Together we came to the conclusion that the mummy idea looked pretty cool.

I hoped Ian would have a very specific idea about how to execute the costume, because he was a creative and out-of-the-box thinker. But he didn't seem to have any ideas for how best to devise proper mummy attire. We talked about using strips of old sheets, but we couldn't find any we felt comfortable ripping up. I thought about athletic tape but couldn't figure out how he would maintain his mobility.

I racked my brain. What was white, came in long strips, and was of reasonable width to wrap a five-year-old? I didn't want to admit how easy and obvious the solution seemed: toilet paper. Could we pull this off?

One evening, several days before H-Day, we staged a mummy dry-run in the house. I wrapped Ian's torso and one leg in toilet paper. He appraised himself *in the mirror, squinted and assessed, then approved. He wore the semi-costume around for maybe thirty minutes. It stayed on well, and then I removed it. So far, so good. I felt like we were on to something creative and cool-looking.*

I arrived at the elementary school on the appointed day and time, with rolls of TP in hand. Brittany had carried her costume to school in a bag and didn't need much help getting it on. Thank goodness, because despite the speed-wrap job I did on Ian, the project still took time. The mummy face proved to be particularly delicate. I took care to crisscross the nose and leave breathing orifices open.

When Ian's teacher announced that the kids could go out to recess before the parade, I cringed. I didn't know how perforated toilet paper would withstand the jungle gym and slides. The mummy looked a little ragged as he came in from the playground, but it wasn't until the parade started that I noticed little bits of toilet paper decorating the elementary school floors. Chagrined, I scooped up shreds and sheets of paper wherever I saw them. Teachers seemed amused by my attentiveness, and it finally dawned on me that I was probably doing the janitor's job.

As for Ian, he didn't care in the least that he was leaving bits of his mummy self around the school—he marched in the parade and headed back to his classroom to eat candy. Brittany, too, appeared to be a happy unicorn celebrating with her second-grade classmates. Relieved, I felt a welling up of satisfaction from our Halloween costume accomplishments.

By the first week in November, both Halloween and Brian's trip to Japan had ended. My fear was just a memory—I'd been able to handle the costumes and the stayover without any incidents.

The ten-day temporary stepparenting experience seemed like a good omen. Halloween gave our "family" of three a focus and a joint project. The weekdays flew by with a repeatable school routine, babysitting help, and a few phone calls from Dad. I'd mustered the courage to step into the job, and the kids reciprocated with their openness. Their dad was eons away and I was proud to be the "it girl," taking care of them.

In hindsight, I think it helped that Brian and I weren't married yet, so nothing about me was permanent in their minds. On one level, they might have seen me as another after-school nanny, of which they'd had a few in the last eighteen months. But in my mind, this was my first true foray into the role of stepmom, and I felt surprised and pleased by what seemed like relationship progress with the kids. Just as important, Brian was pleased that the stay went well, and he gave me a vote of confidence by sharing that he didn't worry much while he was gone. Still, I was relieved that Dad was back in business.

Stepparenting preparation: foresight or hindsight?

I'll venture a guess that you have ended up as a stepparent in a similar fashion to me—without much preparation. Even when I was testing out the stepparenting waters, I didn't think through how our family makeup would play out, or what each family member needed at the time. I jumped in and brought a positive and willing attitude. However, I still lacked knowledge about stepfamilies and grief.

Perhaps you're truly in the preparation stage, thinking over whether or not to marry someone with grieving children. You may even have kids of your own and are looking at blending families. If you are in contemplation, I have a few gems of wisdom to pass along. First of all, consider the ages the children will be when you marry. Every age and stage of childhood presents many developmental variations, including concrete versus abstract thinking, the evolution of confidence and personal power, and the stages of independence. Then, after a death, layer on age-specific ways kids process the concept of death and differences in grieving styles, from very internal to visibly acting out.

Marin, a veteran stepmom, leaned forward while expressing her reflections about marrying into a family with teens. "Maybe there is a point when the children are growing up that it's just better to wait to get remarried. It will be just a few years until late teens are grown and out of the house; consider waiting rather than expecting a sixteen-year-old to just slip into a new family and think it will all be wonderful."

Marin presents a thoughtful reflection. The obstacles of building a relationship with a teen may block, delay, or change the relationship you hope to create with your potential spouse. You may get more fulfillment out of dating and building an "off-campus" relationship. You could remain protected from teen-sized challenges. Why are we in such a rush to get married?

Consider also, when joining a family grieving a death, whether your beloved partner has had a chance to grieve. Sure, your partner has expressed love for you. However, he or she must also come to terms with the loss of the prior relationship and person. When faced with the excitement of a new relationship, we're only human. Our emotional vulnerabilities drive us to reach out and grab for someone to hold on to during chaotic times. Neither you nor your beloved may have the strength to stand up for individual space during a budding romance.

Brian was firm about needing at least one full year to prove to himself that he could raise his children. However, we started dating during that year, which in hindsight was still an impediment to his process of grieving his wife. He was afraid that I would give up and move on, so he wanted to keep our relationship going. Looking back, he wishes he had said the following words to me: "I want you *and* I need more time. How can we accomplish that?"

One last point to ponder in preparation of launching a new marriage is whether your presence will be perceived by the children as a parental replacement. Brian and I believed that the kids would benefit from having a female role model back in their daily lives. However, we missed a key point in leaping to that conclusion, as validated by psychologist, Colorado State University professor, and author Mark Benn. Benn shared his wisdom from the comfort of his counseling office at the university. "The kids absolutely need a female role model because they lost their mother. But you can't force a person into this role, because the kids will reject it," said Benn. "The thing about parenting is that the kids would rather have their own choice than be right."

To illustrate this point, Benn gave me a classic example about pre-teens and teens wearing the appropriate coat for the weather. The choice of wearing what they want is more important to them than wearing the right coat for the conditions. He also mentioned that this logic extends to kids' choices of friends, as well as whom they will choose as a parent substitute. Benn raised his dark eyebrows while delivering his conclusion. "Just like you can't choose kids' friends for them, you also can't choose their role models," he said.

Preparing for a Role

If you're considering getting married to someone with grieving children, perhaps you'll resonate with these reflections from one of my blog readers.

A divorced woman with a nine-year-old son, this woman had been dating, but had not yet married, a widower with three children, two of whom were teenagers. I was struck by how much thought she had given to the topic of blending families, whereas I, on the other hand, had come from the school of "jump in and keep your head above water."

"The one thing I have come to realize recently is that I will never be their mother or even a stand-in," she said. "When we first started dating, the woman in me thought I would be able to rescue them from a life without a mother and I would be able to fix this situation, which, of course, was naive on my part. So I'm in a stage right now of processing what my life will be like when we are blended, and I want to take the right steps and be prepared mentally as much as I can, though in saying that I know nothing will prepare me for the change in my life."

I thought this stepparent-to-be was right on track and that her intuition would serve her well in the blending process. She had already started the process of considering one identity in the family, that of a stand-in mother. She observed that this "replacement" identity wouldn't work, tossed that, and opened her mind to prepare for another kind of identity in the family—one to be determined as she grew with the family. Her thoughtfulness serves as a great example of the type of introspection that can help us sustain our stepparenting endeavors.

REFLECTION PROMPTS

1. How much preparation did you or will you do before taking on a stepparent role?
2. What are the ages of your stepchildren, and how could their stages of development affect your marriage?
3. If you are raising a grieving child in lieu of the natural parents, what changes to your lifestyle do you anticipate having to make?

POINTS TO REMEMBER

- You're going to survive the stepparenting role whether you prepare for it or not, but preparation can lend you a more thoughtful approach to your new family configuration.
- If you're thinking about partnering with a spouse who has older teens, consider dating and waiting to join households until they've graduated high school.
- Don't rush your remarriage—give your spouse-to-be and your stepchildren-to-be time to grieve.
- You can't choose kids' role models for them; thus your role in the stepfamily may evolve to be different than you pictured.

TWO

Your Marriage and
Stepparenting Mindsets

"You have it in your God-given power, the willingness to make
the years ahead of you become a brighter one."
–ISRAELMORE AYIVOR

Brittany: Seven years old
Ian: Five years old
Years since their mom died: One
My relationship status: Engaged to marry in seven months
Season: Late fall

*I TOOK SOME TIME OFF WORK JUST after Thanksgiving break. All four
of us had returned from spending the holiday in New York City with my
mom, aunts, uncles, and cousins. Now I was enjoying the space created by
being home alone—it would be one of the last times before my anticipated
post-holiday move across town to plan the wedding with Brian and the kids.
I curled up with a blanket and one of my journals, cozy in my dad's old ivory
recliner. I opened the journal to an entry I had written about two years prior,
after my first marriage was going awry, and before I got to know Brian. I'd
made a list of qualities I wanted in a husband and from a marriage.*

My ideal husband would be:

- Gentle and easygoing
- Non-violent
- Humorous
- Kind
- Outdoorsy
- Willing to have kids

My next marriage would be based on:

- Common values
- Mutual respect
- Shared financial responsibility
- Fun and adventure

I remember reviewing this list after Brian and I started dating and marveling over the matches I perceived. I read over these desired characteristics several times during the months that we dated, and each time I became more certain that Brian matched my wishes. Although Brian and I had discussed future possibilities during those early months of dating, we felt it was too soon after Cathy's passing to get married—certainly for the kids, and also for Brian himself.

Another journal entry was dated in the late spring of the current year. At that time, Brian and I had escaped to celebrate my thirtieth birthday. We were enjoying one of the most beautiful vacation settings I could imagine: an island getaway deep in the Caribbean, south of Florida. Little did I know that one of the packages in the hotel safe contained an engagement ring. In the middle of the vacation, we went out for a nice dinner on the ocean and he asked me to marry him. With all my forethought, I knew that my answer to that question would be yes, and I told him without hesitation. But then the journal related how, the day after his proposal, I found myself sitting on a rock in the ocean, crying. I had written: "The enormity and beauty of the sea triggered my vulnerability to all the changes I'd gone through in a very short time. My father passed away. My first marriage blew up. My job disappeared, which caused me to end up working in the software group where I met Brian. I watched him struggle through the hardest phase of his life, as his wife was dying. I had just turned thirty and was suddenly engaged to marry the kind and sensitive man of my dreams, who had a built-in family." *I guess the importance of these milestones washed over me along with the ocean waves—relief and happiness for the next phase of my life, and sadness for the relationships he and I had lost. The journal entry ended with those reflections.*

After the trial stepparenting endeavor over Halloween and the trip to have Brian and the kids spend time with my family that Thanksgiving, I felt more grounded about the new venture than I had while sitting in the sea. We'd set the wedding date more than one year forward from the engagement, hoping that would allow the kids and me some bonding time. Snuggled in the easy chair, admiring a harvest moon out my back window, I started a new journal entry: "This is it," *I wrote.* "I'm all in."

Over years of interacting with other stepparents, I witnessed that we marry and become stepparents for a variety of reasons. If marriage is part of your stepparenting equation, what makes your partner a fit for you? I believe that whether you're married or approaching marriage, your basic wants and needs drive you to choose an adult partner who's a fit, and your partner's children become part of the package. My story portrays my careful analysis of what I wanted in a marriage. That represented my marriage mindset. I found nothing in my journal that broke down the pros and cons of becoming a stepparent. My stepparenting mindset developed as a result of my marriage mindset.

Stepfather Adam reflects upon his thought process when he decided to remarry and take on stepchildren. He gathered his words carefully as we sipped our coffees. "The question becomes more of 'How do I handle this?' not 'Because of this, I'm not going to get married to this person.' The situation was an obstacle to overcome, not a prevention." Adam ended up a stepparent due to several relationship desires, including a need for family structure and wanting to stick with a woman he loved.

Regardless of whether you've already jumped in as a stepparent or not, reflecting on the roots of your marriage goals and desires can help crystallize the strengths you bring to your stepfamily. Just as important, here's another upside of studying your motivations to marry, enter a stepparenting relationship, or take on the responsibility of raising someone else's children: Your discoveries may reveal expectations or desires that, if unfulfilled, may manifest in your heart as emotional disappointments.

The mindsets

Where do you fit in among these possible reasons people end up in a stepparent role? Each marriage mindset will link to a stepparenting mindset.

- You wanted the company of a loving companion
- You wanted a parenting partner for your kids
- You needed financial stability
- You wanted to "get marriage right" this time
- You wanted to build a family nest
- You hoped you could or promised you would help this family
- You wanted to adopt children in your current marriage or a new one
- You're not sure why you became a stepparent

My relationship wants and needs represented a blend of reasons I ended up as a stepparent. I hoped to find a companion with whom I could share mutual trust and respect, and one who was also financially stable. My case was a mix of wanting an ideal companion with whom I could get marriage right and wanting financial stability. In addition, while not my main goal, I also didn't mind being part of an established family and was optimistic that I could help Brian and his children heal and thrive by being a good wife and a female role model for the kids. I definitely resonate with the marriage mindset of wanting to help.

Each of my relationship desires affected my stepparenting mindset. The combination of my desire for an intimate companion with my desire to get marriage right created a fierce willingness to accept and work with the "package deal marriage" to Brian and his children. In addition to a willing attitude, the strengths of my stepparenting mindset included a desire to help all parties ... after all, that was going to have to be a part of getting this marriage right.

The emotional traps present in my stepparenting mindset became more apparent to me over time. I was so determined—almost too determined—that I attempted to control and orchestrate what I hoped would be steady progress in building relationships with the kids. My willingness and my will almost became synonymous. Because I didn't understand that these relationships would grow best organically, I felt deep disappointments when I didn't see the results for which I was hoping. This personal emotional trap included a cycle of then trying even harder to make family dynamics smooth. Nothing changed as a result of my escalated endeavors, and I sensed that the kids could see when I was trying too hard as well.

Let's examine how each of your relationship desires might affect your stepparenting mindset, including each mindset's strengths and potential emotional traps.

You wanted a loving companion: If you married for the company of an intimate companion, which is a mindset in a lot of marriages, you are driven by love, intimacy, and companionship. Your related stepparenting mindset is likely to be one of coexistence and high tolerance of the precarious entry into the stepfamily. You'll find a way to navigate the highs and lows in your stepfamily, because that's what it takes to be close to your partner. You'll probably bring high willingness and motivation to the relationship. At times, it may feel challenging to share that companionship with the children. Remember that your partner's loyalties will be pulled between you and the children like a tug-of-war rope. You may fall into a jealousy trap as you crave your spouse's undivided attention. You'll become aware of the need for your spouse to spend time with his or

> My willingness and my will almost became synonymous. Because I didn't understand that these relationships would grow best organically, I felt deep disappointments when I didn't see the results for which I was hoping.

her children, but just the same, your heart may grow a moss of resentment when your spouse has less time for you.

When your own children blend into the marriage as well, you already connect with this dilemma from a different perspective. In the heat of new romance, you might compromise some of the stepchildren's needs in order to meet those of yours and your children's. This dynamic may make relationship-building with your stepchildren tricky. By way of recommendation, recognize that the old "Love will keep us together" prescription is not the sole tonic for making a stepfamily work. Stepfamily and grief education will help you build a more realistic view of what your stepkids need and how you can help them, while maintaining a close relationship with your spouse.

You wanted a parenting partner: When you desire a parenting partner, you've probably brought kids of your own into the marriage. You hope to be a team player in the blended family, with you and your spouse each taking on some parenting responsibilities. On some level, you expect your children to cooperate with and even accept discipline from your new spouse—their stepparent. Maybe you've been asked to provide—or you expect to provide—the same role in return with your new spouse's children.

The upside of this situation, in terms of a stepparenting mindset, is that you have high enthusiasm and commitment—a "we can do this together" spirit. You and your spouse also share common ground, facing challenges as you develop relationships with each of your stepkids. The downside is that collective wisdom reveals that the stepparent typically shouldn't step into the discipline role until accumulating years of relationship investment with the stepkids. Certain aspects of parenting—for example, coaching and discipline—may be received openly from the natural parent and fought when delivered by the stepparent. "Who disciplines whom" can grow messy and inconvenient. The kids may not accept the partnering approach you hoped would be there to help you, and that outcome may cause you to feel disappointed or frustrated.

Sharing of parental responsibility can succeed over time. With humor and patience, your marriage can grow closer through the upswings and the bumps alike.

You needed financial stability: Was a joint approach to financial security high on your list of marital expectations? If so, you may feel great relief after combining households, and therefore be more willing than other stepparents to ride the emotional rollercoaster of stepfamily life. Financial stability is usually not a person's only marriage mindset, but as you saw in my example, this mindset can accompany a main marriage mindset that you hold. If someone has been a single parent, for example, or has experienced other financial stressors, the desire for financial stability may be part of their marriage equation.

In terms of additional stepparenting mindsets, if you prioritize the business side of marriage first, you might maintain a certain level of emotional detachment from your stepchildren until you've put more structure in place. This can be a blessing, in that you might not feel tugged in several emotional directions at once. On the flip side, such a mindset may keep you distanced from stepchildren who are trying to figure out their relationships with you. The kids may see the marriage in black-and-white, perceiving that you just married in for the money. This judgment can be softened if you find time to prioritize some level of family relationship building along the way.

You wanted to "get marriage right": For those of you who have been married before, perhaps the new marriage is your chance to "get marriage right." Thus, your stepparenting mindset may be to feel driven to do everything possible to make your new family "work." Your motivation can be an advantage, because many stepparents who are equipped with a positive attitude and this type of determination find a way to make the stepfamily life flow for them.

Here are a few traps to watch for: You may take challenging times personally, seeing them as your own failures, as if you still can't "get it right." You may be too hard on yourself during a time fraught with the unknowns of building a stepfamily. You also face the philosophical debate around whether or not there is a "right" when it comes to marriage and stepfamily life. My recommendation is that you need to be gentler with yourself. You can still make your marriage and your stepfamily work, but that outcome most likely will not occur on your timeline. With further stepfamily education, you can draw some new conclusions about how to nurture your stepfamily's growth.

You wanted to build a family nest: Like Adam, who wanted companionship with Lily and a rich family life, you may have married because you prefer the comfort and security that comes from the structure and support of family. This marriage mindset relates to a strong stepparenting mindset: the family "package deal" won't baffle you, and you may even prefer the instant family environment.

Here's a pitfall of this mindset: Be careful not to expect the stepfamily bonds to occur instantly. Your stepchildren may not want to nest as much as you do. Like a good soup, stepfamily relationships need to simmer for a long time before achieving their full flavor. Author Ron Deal, in his book, *The Smart Stepfamily*, says that "...*time* and *low heat* make for an effective combination."

Another spin on this marriage mindset is that if you don't already have children, you might want to birth a family of your own. In addition to wanting to get marriage "right," I carried this aspect of the nest mindset into my relationship with Brian. I wanted to be a parent to Brittany and Ian, and I also wanted a baby with Brian.

The way stepchildren might view this longing never occurred to me until Ian, then fifteen, shared his conclusion while we were driving between his activities. "You just married Dad to have a baby," he said. Since Brian's and my joint project, Amy, was almost four at the time, Ian's statement came a bit out of the blue. I verbalized what I thought was an empathetic response, yet inside I was debating. *If this were true, why wouldn't I have married a guy with no kids?* Yes, the fundamental statement had some truth to it—I intended to have a child of my own and was not going to let go of that desire even though I married a man who already had two out of diapers. We did wait several years before attempting to add to the family, and we did communicate clearly with the kids. Even so, I could imagine Brittany and Ian thinking I was brushing them aside just to get to the "real" goal of the marriage—the new creation.

You hoped you could or promised you would help this family: What a blessing your marital partner must feel to have someone around who wants to help the family. This marriage mindset, and the willing spirit of the stepparenting mindset that accompanies it, can open up a lot of emotional possibilities in your stepfamily. For example, through your selfless approach to helping the children, you could soften their hard edges with regard to your motives in the remarriage. And if you're stepping up to the job of godparents, or you're related to the children or their natural parents, you likely share this willing stepparenting mindset.

An emotional trap here is one of trying too hard to help your stepkids, as if you're on a rescue mission. Your efforts may sap your energy and may not even be appreciated by the stepfamily members. Perdita Norwood, in her book, *The Enlightened Stepmother: Revolutionizing the Role,* said, "Your stepchildren don't want to be saved, least of all saved by you." Though that sounds harsh, I've learned that we can't push our stepfamilies through to the next phase singlehandedly, or through goodwill. My recommendations include asking the children how they would like you to help them. That sets up a positive tone for your assistance but allows some of the ideas to come from them. In addition, use stepfamily education to realize that the family's steps forward and slips backward can't possibly be attributed to one family member's actions or efforts. This cycle cannot be prevented and is part of the natural flow of stepfamily life.

You wanted to adopt children in your current marriage or in a new one: In this marriage mindset, a driving need or desire is wanting to expand your family or wanting to provide support for a close relative's or friend's children in the event that the adults pass away. Or you may become a stepparent without the factor of marriage woven in, for example, a grandparent raising grandchildren; another relative raising nieces, nephews, or cousins; or a godparent raising godchildren. In essence, your "marriage mindset" then is one of wanting to adopt the kids, legally or by another form of agreement.

The circumstances around families that adopt children vary widely. Is the child related to you in any way? Are you the child's godparents, grandparents, another relative, or a friend of the birth parents? In any of these cases, your stepparenting mindset is one of knowledge and high willingness. You bring the strength of a jumpstart in getting to know the child and his or her parents before any stepfamily formation even hits the radar. You may be more objective and in tune with the child's needs than you would be if you were stepping into the existing family as a stranger. Kit and Quincy, who are Brad and Lana's aunt and uncle, found themselves in this very situation when Brad and Lana's mother died. Their father was incarcerated and he was also unwilling to take the kids even when he got out of prison.

If you already know the children, the biggest emotional challenge of this stepparenting mindset is that you anticipate slipping into the family rhythm without a hitch. Stepmom Marin reminds us, in her lovely English accent, that knowing the kids beforehand does not always pave the way for smooth entry into the stepfamily. If a natural parent dies or disappears, the kids will see you differently than they did before. You'll still have to build your new role within the family.

If you're interested in adopting children but you don't know their natural parents, you run into a different trap: How will you establish a way for the kids to keep a place in their hearts for their parents? How will you carry the torch of memory in the new family? By way of recommendation, you can rely on other sources, such as relatives or friends of the deceased, or birth family research, to gather stories and memories when that person is not someone whom you knew well. In time, most adopted children crave to know more about their birth parents. They will appreciate any research you can do to share family-of-origin history with them. The stepparent/ stepchild relationship deepens when the stepparent works conscientiously to include the deceased or the unknown parents as part of the family.

You don't know why you got married: Admitting that you got married blindly is refreshingly honest. Without a clear sense of purpose and vision for the marriage, you might feel that love will get you through every conflict and will softly blanket even the hardest situations. You may believe that marriage has a way of working itself out. In terms of your stepparenting mindset, your positive attitude will take you a long way, but there are too many personalities and too many family dynamics involved to rely on love alone to solve problems. Marriage takes work, and stepfamilies take steady and dedicated education and effort. Your spiritual beliefs can guide and strengthen you *through* the difficulties, but won't prevent them. Your stepfamily will still go through its growing pains. To avoid the emotional traps of disappointment and feeling overwhelmed, ask yourself what kind of support you need to meet the challenges inherent in stepfamily life.

Develop your willing attitude

Now that you've taken a look at how you arrived in a stepfamily and at what strengths and challenges your mindset brings to light, let's shift our focus to the next important question. You joined the family, so how do you feel about being a stepparent? Positive and eager? Excited but fearful? Resistant? There is no wrong answer—I ask this question to encourage you to assess your current state of willingness and to become motivated to adjust it with the flow of your stepfamily life. Instead of just accepting stepparenting as part of the marital package or as part of a commitment you agreed to, give your disposition conscious thought. Does it move you toward the end goal of creating a sustainable stepparenting lifestyle? Look again at how our formula supports the premise that a willing attitude is a necessary element for sustainable stepparenting:

Willing Attitude

Acceptance   Stepfamily Education

Sustainable Stepparenting

Communication   Support

Grief Education

A willing attitude is not a figurehead in this formula. The kind of willingness it will take to serve a grieving family while still recognizing your own identity in the process requires a most delicate balance. Too much willingness, such as overcompensating, may lead to being a doormat or to sacrificing your own needs and desires. The other side of the coin represents an unwilling attitude or being overly self-centered. Children of all ages can pick up on either extreme of the willingness scale. Pushing back or pushing your buttons may be common responses.

Marin and Ella, stepmoms to two different ages of kids, explained their approaches coming into their stepfamilies. Marin was only twenty-two when she became stepmother to two young children whose mother had died. She ranked herself high on the stepparenting willingness scale and brought an idealistic optimism to the new family. "I had been their babysitter for years, including the time while their mom was ill, so I thought they knew me," she said, shaking her head while remembering how the kids distanced themselves from her after the wedding. Marin discovered that the kids took a completely different view of her when she married their dad. She had to start over and build a new relationship with the kids after she became their stepmother.

Ella, on the other hand, maintained a neutral or even distant stepparent role because her husband Walter's girls were in high school and college when they lost their mother. Confident in appearance and tone, she described her beliefs to me. "It was much too late to direct them," Ella said. "I never expected them to consider me another mother." Ella brought a willingness that scaled appropriately with her and Walter's view of what his older daughters needed. In contrast, Walter became a very active father figure to Ella's young son, Joel. Both Ella and Walter felt that Ella's son, because of his age, would be better off with two strong parental figures.

It's natural to maintain a high level of willingness when stepfamily life is clicking along without a hitch. But that's an ideal family state that few families of any type manage to sustain all the time. So, in addition to setting your intention to have a willing attitude, I suggest that part of your self-reflection include addressing how you deal with adversity. By identifying the ways you usually overcome challenges, you'll gain self-understanding that will serve you so that downswing dynamics don't deflate your willingness to keep moving forward. Consider the following as you take a look within:

- How do you deal with life's imperfections in general?
- Do you rise to the occasion when everyday challenges cross your path, or do these hiccups send you into a tailspin?
- Do you practice spiritual beliefs that bolster your resiliency?
- Do you practice hobbies that free you and relieve your stress?
- Do you have a strong network of family and friends to laugh and cry with you?

Your answers will give you some insight as to how you'll navigate the crests and troughs of stepfamily living. If you feel that coping with adversity is not your strong suit, take time to bolster your self-support before throwing yourself headlong into the work of stepparenting grieving children. This effort can happen in a less formal way through self-reflection and talking things out with your favorite support network. Or, if you sense a rise in your fear of adversity or fear of failure to cope in the stepfamily, you can seek out counseling.

Exploring your stepparenting mindset, expectations, and attitudes is a way of saying, "Here are the personal needs I bring into this family situation." Some aspects of those needs and wants, such as a desire to help and be a team player, are beneficial to stepfamily development. On the flip side, you may want to seek out support for personal expectations not being met in the stepfamily. The goal is to free the relationships you're building with your grieving children from any additional emotional burdens. That goal is easier said than met, because family members' emotional dynamics tend to get tangled up with each other.

> Exploring your stepparenting mindset, expectations, and attitudes is a way of saying, "Here are the personal needs I bring into this family situation."

What you can continue to control is how you take care of yourself. I suggest that at least once every new season of the year, ask yourself:

- How helpful is my attitude toward sustainable stepparenting?
- Do I need more self-care in order to refresh my willingness to help my stepfamily?
- Would I be willing to make some minor shifts if the ultimate outcome benefited our family?

These regular self-check-ins can bring you good reflection time that will boost the sustainability of your stepparenting efforts.

REFLECTION PROMPTS

1. How does your marriage mindset impact your stepparenting mindset? Consider the options we mentioned:
   - You wanted the company of a loving companion
   - You wanted a parenting partner for your kids
   - You needed financial stability
   - You wanted to "get marriage right" this time
   - You wanted to build a family nest
   - You hoped you could or promised you would help this family
   - You wanted to adopt children in your current marriage or a new one
   - You're not sure why you became a stepparent
2. What are your biggest fears as you proceed with your stepparenting journey?
3. How will you manage the adversity that's inevitable in any family life?

POINTS TO REMEMBER

- We marry into stepfamilies for diverse reasons.
- Each possible stepparenting mindset brings with it benefits and potential pitfalls.

- By flexing our attitudes and planning for some bumps in the road, we will sustain our stepparenting.
- If you feel you need help with your fears or coping strategies, take time to build that support.

THREE

Blood is Thicker than ... Everything

"Because you're not what I would have you be,
I blind myself to who, in truth, you are."
– MADELEINE L'ENGLE

Brittany: Seven years old
Ian: Five years old
Years since their mom died: One
My relationship status: Engaged to marry in seven months
Season: Late fall

WHEN CATHY WAS ALIVE, SHE AND THE kids started a summertime
tradition of traveling east and spending time with her family. Brian would
stay back in Colorado and work. The first summer without Cathy posed an
awkward decision: who would take Brittany and Ian on the traditional trip?
July melted into August and a lack of action from the Colorado side sealed the
outcome. There would be no trip this summer.

But when Mohammed doesn't go to the mountain ...

We expected the mountain to arrive today.

Cathy's mother, sister, and brother would ring the doorbell any minute. I hadn't yet met them and I heard from Brian that they weren't exactly thrilled about our engagement.

I knew that my only choice was to be myself. I thought I had launched a reasonable relationship with the kids and was hoping that the results would show. What I wasn't prepared for was Brittany and Ian's reaction to their relatives' arrival.

A foggy oval of Brittany's sweet breath on the front window marked her lookout point. Ian busied himself playing but startled at any loud noise.

No one had to ring the doorbell. As soon as the car pulled up, Brittany bolted out the door and into the crescent driveway. Ian scrambled behind her. I attempted to communicate something to them on their way out the front door, but it was lost in the commotion. Brittany took the shortest path across the driveway and into her grandmother's arms. Then she turned around, secure in a backwards hug, and looked at me as if to say, "Now I am home."

I remember feeling surprised by the kids' zeal for the visit from their grandma, uncle, and aunt. My reaction revealed how young and inexperienced I was in the stepfamily. I was under the illusion that in several short months of occasional contact, I had established a foundation with the children—one meaningful enough to breed some form of attachment between us. As that fall weekend progressed, I witnessed Brittany and Ian laughing, wrestling, and chatting with Cathy's family. Much of the time they were playing at the pool at their relatives' hotel, and the house felt empty. Instead of feeling happy for them, which I knew I should, I felt a bit hurt and increasingly unsure of myself.

What I didn't understand then is that the children needed these biological connections for nurturing and comfort. My reaction came from insecurity in my role and also from a misunderstanding about how stepfamily bonding works. The many myths of stepfamily life, as we'll cover shortly, include the belief that stepfamily members bond quickly.

The power of biology

Brittany and Ian continued their summer visits to the East Coast. However, it was not until many years later, on the heels of another "flight to family" event, that I processed this concept of the kids' need for biological connections in a productive way. This time, high-school-aged Brittany learned that a family member had died, a man who was related to her mom through marriage. Her uncle on her mom's side offered to fly her out for the funeral. As she finalized plans to take a 3:00 a.m. shuttle to the airport to catch an early morning flight across the country, I asked her if she was sure she wanted to do this. She spoke no words but gave me a slow affirmative nod.

Ian chose not to go, despite his uncle's pleas. At this point, the kids displayed two individual souls processing grief differently. Neither of the children really knew the deceased that well, but Brittany was willing to miss difficult-to-make-up days of high school, swim team conditioning, and a swim meet in order to go. I wondered why she wanted to go and why Ian didn't, but I supported their decisions.

When Brittany returned, I only had to observe her to gain understanding. She'd come alive and re-entered our family relaxed and chatty. She talked about how sad the funeral had been. She talked about how sorry she was for the widow, and she relayed that many people had commented about how much she looked like her mother. Brittany, at the tender age of fifteen, had needed to "go home" and be with those people who were closest to her mom.

With that sudden, middle-of-the-night trip I realized the all-encompassing and raw nature of Brittany's need to reconnect. Ian didn't share that need at that time, which could have been attributable to many different factors, including his grieving style, his age, and his gender.

After reflecting through these experiences, I'm convinced that stepfamily members help their stepkids by honoring the undeniable pull of biology. As we let ourselves move toward empathy for the children, we can be seen by other family members in a truer, more natural role.

Mother substitutes: relatives come close

In the book *Motherless Daughters: The Legacy of Loss,* author Hope Edelman's survey of "substitute mothers" sheds insight on the powerful role relatives can play after parent loss. Edelman asked women who had lost their mothers where they found female support and comfort after the death.

Of the 97 women who were asked if they found one or more mother substitutes, "33 percent named an aunt; 30 percent a grandmother; 13 percent a sister; 13 percent a teacher; 12 percent friends; and 10 percent a co-worker. Also cited, in descending order, were neighbors, friends' mothers, mothers-in-law, stepmothers, husbands, lovers, and cousins."

In this study, women who lost their mothers reached out to their aunts and grandmothers if available. Stepmothers were lower on the list, suggesting that the stepparent role is not the go-to relationship to fill that yearning for comfort. Instead, the stepparent relationship can provide other benefits, such as consistency and, over time, the possibility of friendship and support.

Another pertinent statistic from Edelman's study is that 37 percent of the 97 women interviewed said that "they hadn't found anyone and had learned to rely on their own resources."

Brittany's choices and Ian's too—although he is a motherless son—lined up with these statistics. Ian aligns more closely with the self-reliance model, which fits his independent personality. I didn't see any indications that Ian ever chose a mother substitute. He leaned more on the men in his immediate and extended family—Brian, my father-in-law, and to some extent Ian's uncle (Cathy's brother). Although articles exist about motherless sons, I have not found a book that focuses on that topic in the way that Edelman's book focuses on motherless daughters.

With Brittany, I always felt that when she still lived at home, she chose Brian's mother and my mother-in-law, whom we all called Nanny, as her mother substitute. This didn't bother me much, as I wanted to support the kids' relationships with their grandparents. Brittany's choice became even clearer to me after Nanny passed away and my father-in-law gave me what Nanny called "the Brittany book" to take care of until I saw a fitting time to give it to Brittany. The Brittany book contained lots of Brittany's pictures, school and music awards, drawings and poems, along with letters and later printouts of e-mails she had sent to Nanny during the years when my in-laws lived on the East Coast. The letters clearly expressed Brittany's admiration of Nanny, and they updated her grandmother regularly about how Brittany was doing overall. Although the written pieces were not deep and revealing—that is not Brittany's style—they expressed a fond connection with her grandmother. Within a month after baby Amy was born, my in-laws moved to our town and Brittany dropped by their house frequently, and even lived there for a short while during college when living at home didn't suit her any longer. I gave Brittany her special book on the one-year anniversary after her grandmother's death.

Brittany's aunt, Cathy's sister Anne, lived in the same eastern regional area as my in-laws and also acted as a mother substitute, especially after my in-laws moved to our town. Brittany continued regular visits to see her mom's relatives and had a lot of fun with Anne and her children, all of whom are just slightly older and younger than Brittany.

After reflecting on Edelman's study, an important question emerged for me. Can anyone fill the hole left when a parent dies?

Kit, who took in her nephew and niece, Brad and Lana, when they were seventeen and ten, concluded over time that the answer is no. Her speech slowed as she expressed her thoughts. "There is something biological that I don't understand—an attachment I could never quite fulfill especially for Lana," she said. "Nothing really fills that void."

Kit witnessed many behaviors of Lana's that pointed to the power of genetic bonds. For example, Lana adored her older brother, Brad, and felt lost after he graduated high school and moved away from Kit and Quincy's home. Brad was the only link to his and Lana's mother. Kit also noticed that Lana would fawn over her mom and dad's wedding picture. That alone is not unusual. However, Lana's parents were married for only three months, and her mom was an alcoholic. Lana's father had ended up in prison and then had rejected Lana by choosing not to take care of her when his wife died. Despite all of these circumstances, the biological pull and yearning remained for Lana. In essence, she had lost both parents.

Kit and I both felt a certain emptiness that came with the realization that our stepchildren would never feel about us the way they feel about their moms. But now, I say "*Of course* they wouldn't," because I've accepted, in my head and in my heart, that I can't fill that hole.

Yes, I yearned for a natural-parent style relationship. Yes, I wore the rose-colored glasses for years, even when those glasses didn't reveal what I wanted to see. But as Kit said, "It's okay that the biological mother still has those ties. You don't have to fight that. You have to get it in your heart. You are going to be something different—not better, not worse, just different."

Father substitutes: similar conclusions

The psychologists I have spoken to have not done pointed research on the comparisons between mother-loss and father-loss. Some experts believe that it's more difficult for a child to lose the same-gender parent; others think that either loss is just as complex. What we do know is that loyalty to the deceased parent is just as strong with father-loss as with mother-loss, which lowers the chances for the stepfather, no matter how kind or well-intentioned, to be a grieving child's go-to.

In my interview with stepfather Adam, who married Lily but then became the sole father role model after Lily's ex-husband perished, he related one of the ways he recognized his stepdaughter Laurel's intense loyalty. He had recorded an outgoing answering machine message that said, "You've reached the Jackson family," and Laurel, without telling him, re-recorded it to include her last name (her father's surname) as well. This action reminded Adam that the girls wanted and had to maintain an identity with their father, an identity separate from Adam's.

Resources in the forms of books and websites now exist for both fatherless sons and fatherless daughters. A stepparent can play a loving role by investigating gender-specific ways to help their stepkids.

The third set of relatives

If biological aunts, uncles, grandparents, and cousins make up a huge part of a grieving child's support network, how do you include these relatives in your family's and your child's lives? You may already have one set of in-laws—now you have two. How do you manage this?

I'll give you the bottom line: Keep the spotlight on the relationship between your stepchildren and their relatives. That doesn't mean you shouldn't develop a relationship with the relatives as well, but focus on the kids' needs to connect. Over time, observe who in their family they choose or don't choose for role models and confidantes. You and your partner can assess and balance how often and in what ways those relationships continue.

Stepfather Adam developed a very good relationship with his second set of in-laws, the parents of his wife Lily's late husband, George, based on steps he and Lily took to foster that connection. George's parents had already made a tradition of coming into town two separate weeks each year to visit with their son and granddaughters. Committed to a relation-ship with their granddaughters, they weren't about to stop visiting after George passed away. Lily provided the bridge to her continued relationship with her in-laws, and she helped facilitate their growing relationship with Adam. Adam was willing to step out of his comfort zone and get to know them—another step toward a successful relationship.

My own relationships with the third set of relatives are not as close. Nor are they terrible. They're simply civil, and that's all. Because I already acted as a support system for Brian when Cathy died, I appeared on the family scene quickly. Cathy's family members were of course in the throes of their grief and weren't in any emotional position to receive me non-judgmental-ly. Cathy's family and Brian never had as strong a relationship as Lily had with her in-laws, which impeded progress toward a smooth and produc-tive relationship. Additionally, Brian's family and Cathy's family, though they lived fairly close to each other, had a basic, civil relationship that didn't go deeper.

Thus, various factors affect your potential relationship with the third set of relatives. The relationships themselves are as complicated to form as they are to explain. I made a point to remain objective in front of the children when discussing their relatives. I was genuinely interested in their escapades back east, including fun outings like hide-and-seek in an extensive maze of raspberry bushes that they and their uncle's family called "gold mines." Gymnastics contests ensued at the adventure center owned by another aunt and uncle.

One year, Brian and I joined the kids on their trip to get a glimpse of their lives there. I appreciated how polite everyone was, treating us like any other guest they might have.

As I grew in my knowledge about how stepfamilies differ from biological families, I shared little tidbits with Brittany's and Ian's uncle and grandma on their mom's side—the two "third family" members with whom I dialogued most. Once when grandma came out for Ian's high school graduation, I shared with her a sincere epiphany related to raising my daughter, Amy, and how I truly understood now how close the kids had been with their mom and how much they must miss her. Her eyes softened a bit as she said, "We'll talk sometime." Neither of us went out of our way to create that opportunity for further closeness—partly due to geographical distance and partly due to the difficulty of the task, I'm sure. Sadly, I've now lost that opportunity forever, as she has also passed away.

I feel that certain principles remain the same across any human relationships on earth: if both parties open their hearts to work with each other, everyone will make some progress. In the meantime, keeping the spotlight on the child-relative bonds allows those ever-important relationships to flourish.

How to cope with rejection

It's not uncommon to hear stories like this: Kit shared a close relationship with her niece and nephew, Lana and Brad, before the kids' mother (her husband Quincy's sister) died. After the funeral, Lana and Brad moved to Kit and Quincy's and Kit experienced rejections that had never before surfaced, for the kids now interacted with her in the role of stepchildren and stepparent. Kit nodded, sharing her wisdom. "They wanted to have parents and to love us but they didn't want to betray their mom."

Similarly, we've already discussed how Marin, who had such a good babysitter relationship with little Grace and Kiefer, had to start over as their stepmom. "Knowing that their dad and I were taking the relationship to a different step *really* made a difference to the kids," Marin said.

Stepfamily professionals universally counsel: Know what to expect and be prepared for some form of rejection from stepchildren of all ages. Behaviors ranging from the silent treatment to non-compliance usually represent a temporary state of affairs while the kids work out their adjustments to the stepfamily transition.

If our parents remain part of our identities for life, then what is a stepparent to a stepchild? Eventually, we hope to become a guide and a friend. But at first, according to author Norwood, stepparents are occupying a place and space that rightfully belonged to their predecessor. "Dad's new wife" or "Mom's new husband" is the intruder, and the intruder becomes the butt of the negativity. It's like getting a new boss at work after you had a great relationship with the old one, except magnified many times over. Norwood also mentions that stepchildren initially distinguish the stepparent as a role, not as a person. While being parented, their only focus is on what the stepparent role represents: someone new, someone who is not the parent they wish was here.

Sounds grim, doesn't it? Think of it as a chance to polish your confidence to a brilliant shine. Every stepparent I interviewed found a way to bushwhack through the rejection and stay in the marriage. I took breaks from working so hard at the relationships, during which times I practiced what Sue Thoele, in her book *The Courage to be a Stepmom: Finding Your Place Without Losing Yourself,* calls compassionate detachment: caring and responding but not going out on a limb or forcing the relationships with my stepchildren. During one of these phases, I allowed myself time to focus on and enjoy my preschooler. During another phase, I went to several study groups at church and found fulfillment in the company of others, contemplating thoughts so much more expansive than the nitty gritty of day-to-day life.

Six schemes to depersonalize rejection

Here are a variety of approaches that might help you handle instances of rejection. These can range from a small rejection, like something specific your stepchild says or does on a given day, to longer phases of rejection, like when a teenage stepchild moves out of the house because he doesn't want to live any longer under your thumb. The overarching goal of these strategies is to help you continue to help the children, as opposed to fighting the relationships.

#1: Ask your stepchildren to describe or draw how a situation feels

Step back and view the situation as the child does. In fact, ask children older than about four years of age to describe how they feel, if they're willing to do so. Let's say a young child's statement of rejection was to throw a fit, yelling, "I don't want to have ice cream with you!" Later he might be able to say something like, "I just wish I could have ice cream with my mom," or "My mom liked chocolate-chip-mint ice cream." Clear statements like this may not happen at the moment they're expressing frustration, or when you're asking, but don't give up.

Expressing feelings in other ways than with words can be a powerful tool for young children, teenagers, and young adults alike. Slide a blank piece of paper and some markers their way and ask them to draw how they're feeling in the moment. You could steal away and create a drawing of your own to keep or share.

Older children might write their feelings in poems or essays that reflect themes of anger or sadness, and they might be willing to talk about what they wrote. The simple act of transferring feelings from inside to outside usually helps clear the air and opens the door for connection, even if only momentarily.

#2: Re-focus your energy toward the desired outcome of the situation

I could have chosen to feel devastated from one honest statement made by fifteen-year-old Brittany. She was resisting my motherly-like declaration that her boyfriend was acting like a jerk. Then she said, "I just don't feel like you're a mom in my heart." When I tell this story, most people's immediate response is: "Oh that must have hurt you so much." The truth is, yes it hurt, but by that point I had educated myself enough about stepfamily development to know how important that statement was to her and to our future relationship. I chose to look at the outcome of that statement instead of the statement itself: a girl who spent most of her time in the family keeping her deepest feelings inside had spoken out. I felt this to be more of a victory than a stab in the heart.

None of us want to feel hurt or frustrated, but I know I often ended up there. Much of what I dwelled on when I felt rejected by my stepkids was how much I'd taken care of them and how the rejection wasn't fair. This could be labeled as a "heaven's reward" belief: I've done good acts, so something good awaits me. This is a good example of dysfunctional thinking that doesn't help me feel better, nor does it help shape more productive family outcomes. I need to take care of myself by finding other ways to recoup when I've overextended myself rather than complain about how unfair a given situation is.

One way to re-focus is to reflect on the outcome you would like to experience in a given situation. To achieve this, modern psychology teaches a method called Rational Emotive Behavior Therapy (REBT), derived from the work of cognitive psychologist Albert Ellis,* a technique our family learned from a therapist we worked with. The premise of this theory is that people are not upset by the activating event itself. Our reactions and the things we say and do are compounded by our beliefs—our beliefs about the event, about any other person involved, and about ourselves.

The REBT technique diagrammed below forces you to explore your beliefs and decide whether you prefer the outcomes they are causing or if you would like to shift your thinking toward new (but still sincere) beliefs

---

* http://albertellis.org/rebt-cbt-therapy/

that cause a more desirable outcome.

Blank REBT matrix

EVENT:

1. BELIEFS	4. NEW BELIEFS
2. OUTCOMES	3. DESIRED OUTCOMES

Before we look at the specific example I've provided, let's take a look at how this technique works. First, the current activating situation is described under "EVENT." Then, starting in the upper left corner of the matrix, one's beliefs about the activating situation are outlined (1). Underneath those beliefs, the current outcomes of those beliefs are recorded—in other words, how is this thinking working out for the person (2)? In the lower right box, the individual then records some desired outcomes that seem acceptable and preferable (3). In the box just above the desired outcomes, the person then writes down sincere beliefs that would help achieve these desired outcomes (4).

During Brittany and Ian's teen years, the following vacation dilemma occurred in our family. Here's how I used the REBT technique to work through the situation.

EVENT: We purchased tickets for a Thanksgiving trip to California. Teenaged Ian later expresses that he wants to opt out of the trip. Brian thinks this is okay and responds, "I don't want to drag him if he doesn't want to go." I think Brian and I should be sticking up for the trip as "important to the family."

1. BELIEFS	4. NEW BELIEFS
I think it undermines the importance of family to give Ian the right to opt out and choose a new situation. I feel unsupported when Brian chooses what I perceive as the easiest way out. I also feel he's not supporting my point of view. This trip is to see my family, so I feel like Ian feels my family is not important.	I can express my desires, needs, and wants for the trip without being attached to the result. I want Ian to come on this trip. Ian doesn't prefer this type of relaxation and use of his free time on a school break. Teenagers are all about themselves. This is a phase and one day again they will want to join us on a trip.
2. OUTCOMES	**3. DESIRED OUTCOMES**
I feel hurt that Ian (and now also Brittany) don't want to go on this trip. I'm confused. Why is my perspective always "wrong" in this family? Why am I the one who always has to change my beliefs and expectations about the kids' behaviors? I'm disappointed, in Ian, in Brittany, in Brian, and in modern parenting psychology (our family therapist maintains that there was no point to force Ian to go).	I desire that I will not be bothered by Ian's choice with regard to the trip. I desire that Brian and I empower Ian to make the right choice. I desire that Brian and I relax and have a good time visiting my family.

By focusing on my new beliefs, I calm down and put this situation in perspective. I realize the situation and its outcome are not all about me, and I learn something about teenagers and about Ian in the process.

#3: Practice compassionate detachment

Though it's important to have good and loving intentions with your stepchildren, you will certainly experience times when you don't feel loving. By the way, this fluctuation of feeling is not just limited to your stepchildren but to your loved ones in general. How do you then step back to take care of yourself without having your loved ones perceive that you're abandoning them? Author Sue Thoele advises the practice of compassionate detachment previously mentioned, a position of stepping back without stepping away.

The philosophy of compassionate detachment is rooted in a broad view of love. Love is not just a feeling, but instead a set of kind, caring, and compassionate behaviors in which we participate. We are not necessarily feeling a surge of love when we have to wake up at 1:00 a.m. to pick up a teenager across town or when we mediate a sibling argument that is going nowhere. But we are demonstrating love with our actions. "Let me reiterate that the love I'm talking about does not require that we *like* all the kids all the time ..." Thoele says. "It simply means that we are willing to open our hearts and create a climate of love and caring."

Here are three ways to extend compassionate detachment:

- Set your limits and communicate what you're doing so there's no misunderstanding: "I need to take a time out right now. I'd like to talk with you some more later." Then make sure you follow up and at least offer your physical and emotional availability, knowing that your stepchild may be on to some other activity or state of being at that time.

- When you can't be physically present to extend love, set an intention that loving arms scoop up your stepchild or keep your stepchild safe, depending on the situation.

- Center around what Thoele calls a "ministry of availability." Be available when any of the children want to talk. Be willing to respond in a sincere way when they need something—even if that way means encouraging your spouse to rise to the call.

#4: Journal about times others took things personally based on your behavior

How many times have you turned to your spouse or your friend and said, "I can't understand why she reacted that way! All I said was ..."? We each operate from our centers of experience, which color the way we communicate and receive messages from others.

When I forced myself to journal about instances when my spouse or a good friend questioned my behavior, this exercise exposed my humanity. For instance, I once told my dear husband that I was disgusted by him. I had to revisit that undesirable comment several times over the course of two years before I could really communicate to him my real concern and emotion that had been driving that comment. In that context, it was also easier for me to understand that I can't expect dedicated adoration from my stepchildren.

Journaling about your own thought process is another way to take the focus off the current situation. Your journaling could also be done as a precursor or follow-on to REBT.

#5: Turn to your trusted relationships

Your spouse or partner is a huge player on your stepfamily team. Without the support of your spouse, friends, and the family members you trust, these rejections are going to be a tough road for you. Don't go this alone!

When Brian and I got married, Ian and Brittany were six and almost eight. My longtime childhood friend, Monica, flew from New York to Colorado to be my matron of honor. Among the various ways she helped before the ceremony were to hang out with Brittany and Ian and help them find things to do. Ian escaped her watch, and she had to search through the various rooms of the wedding venue until she found him.

Monica protected me for years from what she had seen in that room. Ian had taken off his corsage, and he was stabbing it with the pin, crying and saying, "I hate Diane." All Monica told me on our wedding day was that Ian was sad, missing his mom, and that he might need some extra care. She did tell Brian exactly what had happened but asked him not to tell me the details. Years later she retold me the whole story, including how she made sure to tell Ian that she'd known me for almost thirty years and she was 100% sure that I would take good care of him. Now that's what friends are for. In hindsight, I can hear that story and say, "Of course that was a horrible day for Ian, and probably Brittany too. It was the day that a ceremony forced a new mom into their lives."

Let your trusted relationships into your circle, and ask them to listen to your deepest feelings and to help you put things into perspective. There are times when our own understanding just can't explain something that's happening in our stepfamilies.

#6: Turn to a professional

If the above techniques or other methods available to depersonalize rejection are not working for you, please consider chatting with someone who is trained to help stepparents and blended families. It's especially important to discuss persistent feelings of low self-esteem, or even despair, with a psychological counselor, mentor, or spiritual advisor. Don't let these temporary relationship situations get the best of you. These rejections are all phases in the process of forming a healthy stepfamily. There's no shame in asking for help to build your resiliency in the process.

Ain't nothing like the real thing

The death or disappearance of a child's parent creates a hole in that child that no other person or people can *truly* fill. The good news in this situation is that you can relax—you don't have to compete or in any way compare yourself to the deceased parent. Your stepchild's journey consists of living with the hole, honoring the gap, and remembering the person who filled that hole. Through spiritual beliefs and bigger picture thinking, your stepchildren may be able to put their emptiness into greater perspective. Along this journey, your stepchildren can still thrive in their lives.

Your job as a stepparent is to find ways to accept your stepchild's needs for biological connections. At first, you may only acknowledge these needs conceptually, and you'll still feel hurt when the needs lead your stepchildren to choose to confide in someone other than you. By learning more about stepfamilies and about grieving, and by giving your stepfamily relationships more time, you'll reach a point where your heart will melt when you understand what your stepchildren really crave, and why. Eventually you may even be able to joke about the differences between blood families and new families, which shows you're accepting those differences in your heart. When your heart cracks open to your stepchildren, you invite them to open up more to you.

NOT the Mama!

Do you remember that cute little dinosaur from the TV show, *Dinosaurs*, who would quip quotable quotes from his high chair? He'd occasionally whack his dad, Earl, over the head with a frying pan and shriek, "NOT da mama!" When Baby wanted Mom, he made no bones about it.

If you're a stepparent trying to fit in with a new family, you might be smarting from the bruise of a figurative frying pan. In one way, it would be better if your stepkids were as clear as baby dino, though admittedly that would hurt too. Instead of a whack on the head, however, you may get furtive whispers just loud enough for you to hear, sideways glances, lack of cooperation, or any one of a list of more subtle frying pans.

What the kids are trying to get across (though sometimes not delivered tactfully) is right. You are not the mama (or the dada, as the case may be). It doesn't matter if their mom or dad lives around the corner, across the country, in jail, or in heaven —you are still not the natural parent.

With regard to the mama, though more than one fine woman can play the role of mom as needed by the family, think of the kids' perspective. For them, the woman who bore them—their blood—will be *the* woman they crave in that role. No bones about it. "But wait," you say. "Why is she laying this on me so heavy?" Because this seed of knowledge could change your stepparenting life. I wish I'd figured this out sooner. It might have changed my relationships with my stepdaughter and stepson. I spent a very long time thinking I could eventually be another mother to them, and I think my expectations resulted in disappointment for me and confusion for them.

The good news is that, as usual, we are doing more right than we know. Even with my misunderstanding of my role, I remember that the kids and I would watch *Dinosaurs* together, and occasionally Ian (smiling) would pretend to whack me on the head and squeal, "Not da mama." We all had some good laughs over that.

The role you'll play in your stepfamily will be something fresh and new, something that's yours to own. Don't spin your wheels trying to be the thing you cannot be—think of that as wearing a clothing style that just doesn't suit you. Create your own style in the new family, and expose your stepchildren to it bit by bit, one tiny step at a time. Then they have the chance to know who you really are. And, guess what? You may learn more about yourself too.

REFLECTION PROMPTS

1. When your stepchildren say or do something that shows they need a biological connection, how do you feel? Be honest; this is for you.
2. Identify some times when you've needed to reach out to your own biological connection/s to feel better. For example, my parents are no longer alive, so I often reach out to my brother and cousins on holidays.
3. Which of the rejection depersonalization schemes will you try first, and why?
4. Name one or two ways you can begin to honor your stepchild's biological connections.

POINTS TO REMEMBER

- Your stepkids' need for biological connection is not a personal assault on you, but it will feel like one. Be prepared for rejection. Focus instead on how to depersonalize that rejection.
- The sooner you can transition to honoring, not fighting, biological connections, the more likely your stepchildren will be able to find a place for you in their hearts and in the family.

FOUR

Debunking Stepfamily Myths

*"I therefore claim to show, not how men think in myths, but how myths
operate in men's minds without their being aware of the fact."*
– CLAUDE LEVI-STRAUSS

Brittany: Eight years old
Ian: Seven years old
Years since their mom died: Two-and-a-half
Years since our remarriage: Almost one
Season: Spring

*SPRING COLORS BLAZED THROUGHOUT THE YARD OF a new home
for our stepfamily of four, a home that felt like a more neutral place to grow
a family. We continued to settle in as the earth sprouted and seasonal rains
glittered the lawns green.*

*Even in the midst of beauty and a new start, I wrestled with an uneasy
feeling about the way our family related and with the way I felt in the family.
I couldn't find words to describe what troubled me, so I just pushed forward.*

One evening, in the changing light of a northern Colorado dusk, I became frustrated while interacting with Ian. He couldn't say on the outside what he felt on the inside, but he could show me. Because of this dynamic, his emotions peaked in a full-body outburst, which he was now having on our front porch. My attempts to talk him down didn't work. I tried something new that I'd been taught—to physically scoop him up with love—and it too failed. Ian writhed in my arms and let out loud wails, reminding me of the nighttime coyotes that roamed the nearby prairie open space. He broke loose and ran back into the house.

I confronted my own internal tornado of pent-up frustrations. Why didn't anything work in these situations? What was wrong with me? Would home life ever feel smooth? When my psychological cyclone touched down, the swirling adrenalin forced me into action. I whirled into the backyard looking for something to relieve the pressure and spotted Ian's orange plastic bat—a streak of fluorescence in the green grass. Some primal need to wield the bat took hold. I surveyed the yard for something to swing at and my eyes stopped at the chaise lounge that had come from Brian's old house.

"It's not fair!" I screamed, giving the cushion a good hard whack. "Why isn't this working?" giving it another wallop. I glimpsed the first cirrus-like wisp of stuffing pop out of a time-worn rip in the cushion. Yelling and sobbing now, I let the four corners of my small backyard nation know that my life wasn't right. A cavewoman in the fleeting dusk, I grunted and heaved from the deepest part of my lungs until the pounding pulse in my ears gradually slowed. Sinking into the tattered chair, I asked myself, "What just happened?"

As I flash back to this moment I think, "Why didn't I just let Ian have his outburst and talk to him later? Or why didn't I get Brian?" The answer is, I have no idea. Neither of those strategies occurred to me. If I was having trouble putting words to my feelings during this time, imagine young Ian's struggle. I needed to get my feelings out without hurting anyone. And isn't that what Ian was doing too?

The early period of stepfamily formation can be just plain confusing and hard. We experience a creeping infiltration of what Mary Ann

Emswiler, in the book she coauthored, entitled *Guiding Your Child through Grief*, calls "a vague sense" that the stepfamily doesn't feel or act like a "real" family, like a family related by blood. You and your stepchild don't share the same sense of what stepmother Marin calls "genetic kinship" as compared to the prior family who developed inside jokes, traditions, and even quirks all their own.

The undercurrent of uneasiness is not completely conscious among stepfamily members, and it clashes with beliefs we want to hold about our families. We enter stepfamilies held hostage by the belief systems we've learned about natural families, including the most important one: that there is only one type of ideal family. Whether we have gotten our model family from the media or from comparing ourselves to other families whom we think are "perfect," carrying this ideal into our stepfamilies lessens our chances for stepfamily authenticity.

I craved connection with Brittany and Ian, yet I had no idea how to attain it. So most of the time I had trouble relaxing and acting like myself. This artificial way of relating demanded an enormous amount of my energy. In the backyard at dusk, almost a year after Brian and I got married, I felt the real me cry out for help.

My list of family-related questions kept growing. Why couldn't I just be myself with the kids? Did they even like me or appreciate me? Why couldn't my husband just pull our new family together? What fueled my insecurities and frustrations? I had not yet educated myself enough to know that these are standard musings in the early stages of stepfamily life.

Common stepfamily myths

Sustainable stepparenting totals a sum of so many pieces and parts: attitude, stepfamily education, support, grief education, communication, and acceptance. With regard to stepfamily education, learning more about stepfamily myths and about how real stepfamilies develop can help you take a huge leap forward in your understanding of this family form.

In the mid-1990s, the organization then known as the Stepfamily Association of America (now the National Stepfamily Resource Center) posted a list of stepfamily myths on its website.* The original myth I'll bet you are most familiar with is that "stepmothers are wicked." Those of us who grew up reading fairy tales or watching Disney movies got exposure to multiple stepmothers who were not nice, kind, or fair. The fallout from this myth doesn't jumpstart female relationships with our stepchildren on the proper footing. Stepfathering did not carry such a reputation wallop.

> With regard to stepfamily education, learning more about stepfamily myths and about how real stepfamilies develop can help you take a huge leap forward in your understanding of this family form.

Five additional myths strike me as particularly vital to making sense of stepparenting after a child's parent has died.

MYTH #1: Stepfamilies formed after a parent dies are easier than those formed after divorce.

MYTH #2: There is only one kind of family: the ideal and original family.

MYTH #3: Adjustment to stepfamily life occurs quickly.

MYTH # 4: Love occurs instantly between the child and the stepparent.

MYTH #5: Children of remarriage are forever damaged.

Remember my blissful belief that, because I had good intentions, and because Brian and I loved each other, our family would magically coalesce?

---

* http://www.stepfamilies.info/stepfamily-myths.php.

There's nothing wrong with love and good intentions, but a little knowledge about these myths would have gone a long way for me.

MYTH #1: *Stepfamilies formed after a parent dies are easier than those formed after divorce.*

Reality: Stepfamilies formed after death and stepfamilies formed through divorce have an equal number of, but very different, challenges. When a parent and spouse dies, loss usually leaves surviving family members yearning for the family they once had with no chance of a redo. Just as important, grieving family members don't want to let go of the threads of connection they still feel. When widows or widowers remarry, they may want a bond similar to the one before, especially if the relationship was good. It's possible, then, that new partners may find themselves competing with a memory. Grieving children are holding on to their memories as well, and the stepparent threatens their loyalties to the deceased parent.

In contrast, when people remarry after a divorce, they are usually looking for something very different from the characteristics of their previous life partner. The children will yearn for "the way things were" when mom and dad were together, but they will hopefully still have personal access to and visitation with their other parent. The stepparent may have a better chance of being viewed as a "bonus" parent in this configuration, although the stepparent still exists in conflict with the children's deepest wish that the original parents will reunite.

Widows and widowers need time to grieve the loss of a loved one, and many don't take that time. Statistics show that widowers tend to remarry more quickly than widows. Remarriage usually activates unfinished grieving on the part of your spouse and the children. These emotional issues may cause resentments that weigh down the new partnership.

By way of an example, Ella told about how high-school-aged stepdaughter, Joanie, would find ways to engage her dad, Walter's, attention by drawing comparisons. Ella furrowed her brow, remembering that she felt Joanie did this in a non-inclusive way. For instance, Joanie would launch a discussion about how Madge's cooking had made life so much better.

Ella would become frustrated with what she perceived as competition and confrontation—as opposed to everyone working together to improve family meals, something that seemed to concern Joanie. Walter wanted to give his daughter time to express herself and felt that Ella didn't understand his goals. The individual who loses a spouse may feel that the new partner is not supportive, and the new partner may resent that the grieving family members are not ready to move forward.

This story leads to one more difference between stepfamilies formed after death and those formed through divorce. Another behavioral characteristic of stepfamilies after death is the natural family members' lack of ability to think realistically about the person who has died. The deceased exists in memory, not in reality, and sometimes this person gets elevated to sainthood. Subconscious attempts by the surviving parent and children to live up to that "perfection" may cause them to feel pressured without knowing the cause.

Finally, the physical absence of a parent often causes role confusion. It's easy to think: "I'm the only parent of that gender; am I really a stepparent?" This thought obscures the important point that the person who died is still part of the family, even though that person can no longer have an earthly influence in day-to-day life.

MYTH #2: There is only one kind of family: the ideal and original family.

Reality: This is the myth that says your new family will feel and be just like a biological family. A logical look at today's families shows that kids grow up in so many different kinds of families: biological, single parent (even after a death), same-sex parents, foster parents, and stepfamilies, to name a few. Each is valuable, and each can provide a loving environment. Yet each family form displays its own set of characteristics. When we attach ourselves to some particular family ideal, we may be frustrated when we don't achieve it. And remember that idealizing "the way the family should be" may hamper your ability to be yourself and show your family the gifts you can provide.

The children may fantasize that the new family will feel and be like the natural (first) family. Know that the children will need to experience the truth in their own time and on their own terms. A turning point will eventually shatter the fantasy. In *Guiding Your Child Through Grief*, coauthor Jim Emswiler tells how his second wife, Mary Ann, couldn't sew her stepdaughter Kate's Halloween costume, whereas Kate's deceased mother, Mary, would have whipped out a home-sewn, professional-looking product. "Kate had remained in the fantasy stage for a long time. After that costume discussion, the fantasy began to unravel. Mary Ann was not Mary, and never would be," said Emswiler. Mary Ann and Kate could then begin the work of moving from myth to reality.

MYTH #3: Adjustment to stepfamily life occurs quickly.

Reality: Most of us are optimistic and hopeful when we remarry. We want life to settle down so we can feel fulfilled. If your expectation is that once wedding vows are spoken, life will return to your definition of normal, you may be—take a wild guess—disappointed.

My reaction to Ian that spring evening on the front porch turned into an overreaction due to my pent-up expectations and frustrations. Brian and I had been married almost a year, and I'd known the kids for nearly double that time. I wanted so much to be able to comfort Ian, yet he couldn't accept it from me. That triggered an outpouring of all the insecurity and disappointment I felt about what I perceived to be a snail's pace of our stepfamily's development. I'm sure that my views were influenced by the family belief systems mentioned under Myth #2. I expected that our family members should at least be able to support and accept support from each other by this point.

Marin felt humbled when she realized the big differences between being a babysitter and being a stepmom. "There is a distinct difference in the caretaking," she said, looking to the bright blue sky to collect her thoughts. "Often I felt left out because they didn't want to confide in me. They would tell their dad and want to do things with him but not with me ... I didn't have the maturity to know that was pretty normal."

Because stepfamilies are full of complex relationships, it takes significant time to get to know one another, to create positive relation-ships, and to develop some family history. According to foundational work accomplished by psychologist Patricia Papernow during her studies of the stepfamily lifecycle, stepfamily formation can take six to ten years, or more, even continuing through the time your stepchildren become adults. Papernow published her findings in her first book, *Becoming a Stepfamily: Patterns of Development in Remarried Families.* We will explore Papernow's stepfamily lifecycle in great detail in the next section.

MYTH #4: Love occurs instantly between the child and the stepparent.

Reality: Because we love our partners, we assume that eventual love for his or her children will transfer, as if by osmosis. With the same logic, we also expect that our stepchildren will come to love us. I believed this love would grow naturally, because I see myself as a pleasant person who is, on occasion, pretty thoughtful as well. We forget that establishing loving relationships takes time; it does not happen overnight or via silver bullet.

When challenging this myth, we also run across the differences be-tween the adults' expectations and the children's expectations of the step-family structure. Adults usually view the new stepfamily arrangement as the best family structure for a child who's lost a parent, as opposed to be-ing orphaned or raised by a single parent. Children, however, experience life differently from adults. They are more focused on what they want, or what's right in front of them. Prior to late adolescence, children aren't sit-ting around pondering what is theoretically best for them. If left to their own, they act purely from a place of needs and wants, and at first they want biological connections and a return to the way family life felt before their parent died.

Even if we do recognize that relationships take time, it may be hard to accept that sometimes we want to have a relationship with someone who is not willing to have a relationship with us. That can hurt deeply. When we feel pain, we may become resentful and angry.

Stepfamily adjustment progresses when we come to the new relation-ships with minimal and more realistic expectations about how the rela-tionships may develop—organically, with some growth spurts and some delayed development as well. Think of all the words that describe cycles in nature, for example, ebbing and flowing, waxing and waning. When we allow a natural progression of our stepfamily relationships, we can be pleased when respect and friendship bud and blossom.

MYTH #5: Children of remarriage are forever damaged.

Reality: Researchers have hopeful news about children of remarriage.[**] Although it takes some time, most children do recover their emotional equilibrium. Five and ten years later, with time and steady support, most are not significantly different from kids in first-marriage families.

Driven by this myth, however, parents often respond to their children's pain with guilt. Somehow adults feel they can "make it up" to their kids, trying to fill that emotional hole with material things, trips, relaxed boundaries, or other types of Band-Aids. None of these solutions respond suitably to our children's hurt. Armed with new or refreshed learning about grief education, you can dive deeper than these surface fixes.

Perdita Norwood relates the story of Brandy, whose mother died of breast cancer when the little girl was five years old. "She was raised by her single father and his parents, who fulfilled Brandy's every wish— toys, clothes, trips ..." When a woman named Lucy considered becoming Brandy's stepmother, Brandy's father and his parents were getting ready to buy Brandy a pony. Norwood explains, "… Lucy was expected to be an indulgent stepmother because Brandy, now fifteen, had grown up without her mom ... Lucy decided she couldn't live in that environment and decided to have a heart-to-heart talk with everyone separately."

Lucy found that each person was protecting someone else: Brandy's grandparents thought she needed indulging, Brandy was allowing the indulgences to occur because she thought her dad needed to give to her in that way, and Brandy's father thought that everyone else needed this behavior in order to be happy. By unearthing all the underlying agendas, Lucy set a new precedent for communication in the family and created a family spot she felt she could step into.

** http://www.stepfamilies.info/stepfamily-myths.php.

The Stepfamily Cycle: what to expect as your stepfamily grows up

Building on your knowledge about and liberation from stepfamily myths, how do you transition from a place of weakness—insecurity, desperation, and lack of information—to a place where you feel powerful, individual, and more authentic? When you emerge from your metamorphosis, imagine how much better you'll feel, and how this change could rub off on your family members. Further stepfamily education advances your role in the stepfamily lifecycle.

If first-family-style closeness is unrealistic, what family feeling can one hope to attain? Author Mary Ann Emswiler says, "... because the possibilities for stepfamilies are different from that of a first-time biological family, so is the path to getting there. That's why your stepfamily needs a different road map." The "road map" many stepfamily educators and professionals have come to rely on is Patricia Papernow's Stepfamily Cycle. This cycle explains the stepfamily member journey from fantasy to reality—a journey that is definitely not a myth.

In the 1990s, a few notable psychologists studied stepfamily formation and came to this stunning conclusion: stepfamily development has its own cycle and rhythm. In *Becoming a Stepfamily: Patterns of Development in Remarried Families*, Papernow says, "What is most striking in my own work with members of stepfamilies is that they do not see themselves as members of a special kind of family facing unique challenges. Rather, they regard themselves, and are often viewed by helping professionals, as members of poorly functioning biological families."

The Stepfamily Cycle gives us a developmental map that explains how stepfamilies form and specifies which hiccups block our stepfamily development. You may have watched or experienced parents of newborns voraciously consuming articles and books to know when to expect their infant's first smile, steps, and words, or to predict when their child might toilet train, read, and write. Similarly, stepfamilies can track what they might expect and encounter as the months and years of family life unfold.

Here is an overview of Papernow's Stepfamily Cycle, which is divided into three main parts:

- The Early Stages, which I call "Fantasy to Reality."
- The Middle Stages, which I've affectionately dubbed "Slogging Through the Communication Quagmire."
- The Later Stages, which I like to think of as "Finding a Rhythm."

I've devoted the most space to explaining the Early Stages, as these tend to be the longest and most confusing times in stepfamily development. Average-paced families may take about six to ten years to experience characteristics of all stages of the Stepfamily Cycle, and four or five of those years in the Early Stages is not unusual. Take to heart that no amount of time spent growing as a stepfamily is wrong as long as family members are working on relationships. I'll never forget one of my stepparent counseling sessions, in which Dr. G. informed me that after five years I was still in the relationship-building phase with my stepchildren and I shouldn't yet be taking on any disciplinarian role. He burst my pride balloon that day, but I felt better knowing the facts.

Learning the stages of stepfamily development helped me feel like I wasn't crazy. Real stepfamilies grow through different phases than biological families. Several times, as I read through these stages I thought, "Real stepfamilies have gone through these stages and survived!"

As you read through the descriptions of a stage and the stories related to that stage, I hope you'll recognize where you and your stepfamily fall along the development cycle. At the end of each stage you'll find a summary of helpful tips to persist through that phase and transition to the next phase. The lines between the phases aren't black and white. You won't transition on a certain day or time; this is not like a graduation ceremony between phases. Rather, you'll sense shifts in the things that people in your household say and do, and see new patterns of how your stepfamily members relate to each other. For example, when all of our family members began to look forward to contributing during our family meetings, I felt that our stepfamily behavior mirrored more of the Middle Stages than the Early Stages. When your stepfamily interactions most closely match the descriptions and stories in the next stage ahead, you can follow the tips for that stage.

As you discover that your stepfamily has moved to a new stage, it's important to keep in mind that a zigzag phenomenon is common in the Stepfamily Cycle. During zigzag, any family member at any time can take two steps backward. These setbacks are temporary and are usually triggered by some form of re-grieving the big losses—the substantive loss of a parent and spouse, or fallout from that loss, or in the case of the stepparent, the losses of feeling close and making the family progress you imagined. Thus the Stepfamily Cycle may not have a definitive endpoint; your stepfamily will continue to evolve naturally as the years pass.

The Early Stages: Fantasy to Reality

The Early Stages of stepfamily life are the most confusing and disjointed. This period of adjustment can feel unfulfilling for all stepfamily members. Stepparents may feel like they are trying to find places for jigsaw puzzle pieces that they haven't yet realized actually belong to a different puzzle. The family remains divided along biological lines. Most of the nurturing, discipline structure, traditions, and easy social connections happen among the biological relations, while those not related may feel increasingly like outsiders. Papernow says that children's identities remain "inextricably tied" to the parent who died, which helps explain why many dynamics, including interactions with new family members, don't feel comfortable at first. Insecurity naturally infests step-relationships, especially in the Early Stages when stepparents are sitting outside the genetic power center.

Roadblocks in the Fantasy to Reality stage include:

1. Lack of awareness that stepfamily relationships have their own development cycle, and
2. Hesitancy to let go of an ideal view of how a stepfamily should feel and operate. Some solid and sometimes solitary emotional work can boost family members through to the next development phase.

When a stepparent joins grieving family members under the same roof, life may feel surreal. Each party in the household has a different point of view, but it's rare that anyone is talking about their feelings. Meanwhile, everyone thinks they're moving forward as usual, thinking something like, "Okay, now this is my new family," but not feeling a sense of family solidarity deep within.

The stepparent may not be aware how much the grieving family members hurt. The stepparent does not feel this pain unless he or she was close to the deceased parent. Instead, we hold out hope to provide what's missing in the family and also to be appreciated for our efforts.

In another layer of the fantasy comes stepfamily myth #4—that love occurs instantly between the stepchild and the stepparent. The deceased's children often crave the single-minded attention of their remaining parent, searching for an exclusive relationship with that parent. One reaction the kids may have is to wear blinders in their new stepfamily, limiting their view of reality to the surviving parent. On some level the kids are worrying about whether that parent is going to die too. Another possible reaction from grieving children might be to stick to the parent's or stepparent's side like your shadow, as if clinging to someone will fill the enormous emptiness left after the parent's death.

If the children are young, they may expect the stepparent to exhibit characteristics of the parent who died, as was the case with Kate, Mary Ann, and Kate's Halloween costume. In any event, it's too early in the relationships for the children to see you, the stepparent, as an individual with positives to contribute to the family. Instant love remains a myth.

Over time, the realities of the stepfamily structure begin to hit home. If the biological family remains intensely connected, which is the norm, then the stepparent starts to feel that he or she is occupying an outsider position. It's quite normal for the stepparent to feel strong waves of jealousy, resentment, confusion, or inadequacy. Stepparents who bring their own children into the new family may, without realizing it, transfer this outsider mentality to their children, and the new family may operate like two families living in one home.

I remember a time when Brian and Ian had been playing games for hours. Brittany was gone at a playdate, and I was roaming the new house, uncomfortable in my own skin. I finally came by and exclaimed to Brian in frustration, "Do you have time for me now?" Brian gave me a stone face and said, "Right now I'm taking time with my son." My fear of being an outsider was blocking my ability to accept that Brian wanted to interact with his boy.

Unless the surviving parent is also a stepparent in the new family (that is, both adults have brought kids into the relationship), he or she may not understand the stepparent's rollercoaster of emotions, which can cause the stepparent to feel even more isolated. On some level, however, the natural parent may fear that the stepparent will leave the relationship. Brian sometimes compromised his time with his children in order to make sure I was getting what I needed from the marriage. Some nights we sat up in bed, neither of us able to sleep. He would confide that he thought I would give up and leave; I would reassure him. Yet that didn't change my uneasy feeling that something just didn't feel right, comfortable, or what I perceived as normal. Nor did it change Brian feeling torn between my needs and those of his kids. He was caught in the middle of the entire scene.

Figuring out *what* doesn't feel right in a stepfamily can be a futile effort. The devil does live in the details: your stepdaughter doesn't want a tuck-in from you, your young stepson challenges you with a plastic sword and shield, or your step-teenager won't speak to you. The details represent symptoms that may heighten the uneasiness. Time is passing and the stepfamily should be progressing, but it doesn't feel like things are coming together.

In hindsight, I feel the most helpful mantra during this stage is this: *Stepfamily development is different and it will not feel like first-family development.* Recall the term "genetic kinship," that Marin coined. A "first family" has a subconscious library of history, actions, jokes, and traditions that even the family members would have a hard time naming. But the genetic kinship exists, and one (or more) of the members who shared that kinship is gone. In addition, we are plagued by aspiring to some made-up family ideal influenced by media and seemingly ideal families around us. Thus believing, I remember feeling extremely embarrassed when I couldn't think of an image for the "What do you see in the clouds?" game Brian and six-year-old Brittany were playing one afternoon when I came to visit. Brittany looked pretty smug about my lack of response. I imagined I knew what was going on inside her head—"My mom would have seen something." or "We can see something, why can't you?"—and I felt even more like an outsider.

The mantra, "stepfamily development is different and it will not feel like first-family development," requires a leap of faith that involves a lot of introspection and acceptance on the part of the stepparent. Open communication about this dynamic among all stepfamily members would be a healthy bonus. You could say something to the children like: "I realize that this family is not the family you wished you had. You're missing an important person in your lives, and I'm sorry for that. Eventually, I want to help you remember that person and get to know me as well." I hadn't learned to say that to my stepkids, but I feel as if this would have been such a valuable first step toward expressing my feelings while also considering and acknowledging their feelings.

Eventually, the fantasies of an instant, harmonious family will fade. Stepparents can gain increasing clarity about the "way it is" with the biological connections, that there is a biological family comfort and rhythm of which the stepparent is inherently not a part. Surviving parents are also shedding their fantasies of an easy-care, instant rela-

> You could say something to the children like: "I realize that this family is not the family you wished you had. You're missing an important person in your lives, and I'm sorry for that. Eventually, I want to help you remember that person and get to know me as well."

tionship between stepparent and stepchildren. It's appropriate for surviving parents to step up and assist the developing stepfamily relationships by repeating their versions of the aforementioned open statement to the children; something like: "We've been through a lot and we are all missing the person who died. I want you know that as we move forward as a family, we will not forget that person. We also have someone new in our family who wants to help us, and who is already helping me so that I can help you."

When I recognized I could not occupy an insider position, I stopped being so hard on myself for falling short. A glimmer of hope appeared on my horizon as I realized that I must carve out my own special role in the family. *Truly accepting* this is a complicated process and often lengthens the time spent in the fantasy stage. I didn't want to suffer the loss of my fantasy, and all I had hoped for, to start the hard work of re-cultivating the foundation of our stepfamily relationships. Bridging this gap took me about seven years, although I had earlier flashes of insight along the way.

One sure sign of emerging from fantasyland is when you become aware that it feels more genuine (and frankly better) *not* to live like an ideal family. I had one of these epiphanies on a ten-day beach vacation that Brian and I took alone. As the hard edges of days blurred and time slowed, Brian continued to plan the next phone call to the kids, who were safely in his parents' hands. I, on the other hand, had less of a need to talk to them while we were on vacation. I was able to admit to myself that I needed a break from trying to build relationships that were so slow in coming.

After the first half of the trip, Brian would get on the phone, and sometimes I would as well, but at other times, I chose not to do so. I got on a call when I felt sincere, and I let myself off the hook when I didn't want to make the effort or had nothing to say. I acted authentically, instead of forcing myself to engage with the children through the phone lines.

Tips for Balancing the Rope Bridge to the Middle Stages

Although transitioning between phases of stepfamily development is a tenuous position, these tips based on Papernow's findings can help you.

- Bear the confusion and disappointment of early stepfamily life *without giving up*
- Have patience, and then some, with this stage
- Recognize and speak out about the different experiences each family member has in the new stepfamily structure, especially the insider versus outsider dynamic
- Acknowledge how crazy hard this stage is for you, and seek support from friends and/or counselors
- Relinquish fantasies enough to be willing to learn about how to build a family out of strangers

The Middle Stages: Slogging Through the Communication Quagmire

In the Early Stages, the stepparent's journey is usually more solitary than in the Middle Stages. In the Early Stages, a stepparent is still trying to figure out how to fit into the family and may not be bold enough to speak the truth or start an argument to determine a fit solution to a challenge. A stepparent's focus may be more on how to be liked and accepted, and then when that is not working, on how to feel supported and cared for.

In contrast, the Middle Stages are a time when stepfamily members speak up with greater confidence, and the entire family restructures itself to strengthen all relationships, including step-relationships. Children need clear direction about new boundaries from their natural parent, who may be giving over some of the every-day care and guardianship-style discipline to the stepparent.

Roadblocks in the Middle Stages boil down to these:

1. Chaotic, unresolved communication or unproductive arguments, and

2. Opposition or unwillingness to make changes.

Communication is a huge theme in the Middle Stages. With more strength and energy than before, stepparents start voicing their needs and concerns to spouses. Children too will feel more comfortable speaking out and participating in family discussions, first with the natural parent only, but then eventually with the full stepfamily. Children should be encouraged to share their feelings and frustrations about how the family is changing and growing. All this vocalizing of needs may make the parent's insider position more painful as he or she is tugged even more between the spouse's needs and the children's needs. Arguments over such trivial household tasks as who cleans the dishes may be rooted in larger control issues among family members. You'll begin to recognize real power struggle dynamics in your stepfamily, because everyone is lobbying for what they think they really want. The Middle Stages present an ideal opportunity to start or continue a family meeting tradition, a regular forum during which meeting guidelines allow each stepfamily member a turn to be heard.

In our stepfamily, Brittany and I fell into power struggles over choosing the family Christmas tree. Neither one of us was willing to give the final decision over to the other, each of us likely trying to control *something* in the family. Nor could we seem to agree on the same tree. During our tree-shopping expedition right after Brittany turned twelve, Brian and I split our stepfamily into two teams. At the tree farm, Brittany and Brian chose three possible trees. Then Ian and I picked the one from those three that we would chop and haul home. That strategy worked to break up the power struggle. Over the years, Brittany and I got to the point where we could either trade off who had the final say or simply agree on a tree. This type of creative negotiation and cooperation is one sign that a stepfamily has planted itself in the Middle Stages.

Through facilitated communication, stepfamilies become ready for action. According to Papernow, the main developmental task of the Middle Stages is to "negotiate some new agreements about how the family will function." Family members' behaviors in this stage move away from the roles of insider and outsider and move toward seeing each other as real, dimensional people with personalities and feelings.

During the Middle Stages, some form of personality sorter can be a helpful tool to aid the process of understanding each other as family members become more open and receptive to sharing information and disclosing feelings. A tool like this can serve as an objective way not only to learn new things about each other, but also to figure out why family members do things the way that they do. Many different self-help quizzes and personality portraits exist, such as Myers Briggs, the Keirsey Temperament Sorter, the Enneagram, True Colors, and Wilson Learning's Social Styles, making it easy for families to choose a favorite or two, get profiles, and discuss the results. Successful movement through the Middle Stages, especially with the aid of tools such as these, can bring understanding to family activities and individual personalities so that family members start to recognize and reduce power struggles. Hopefully, this type of activity would also expose the personalities that have a more difficult time accepting changes and lead to techniques to make those family members more comfortable. Strategies, such as providing more advance warning that a change is coming and offering more hand-holding to walk through the change, will help to alleviate unnecessary duress for everyone.

Author Mary Ann Emswiler says that through the processes of communication and cooperation, "you increasingly find common ground with others in the family: shared interests, shared expectations of roles, shared assumptions about how the family 'works,' and so on." A glimmer of normalcy, which is really the hope that life might proceed with less stepfamily challenges, appears on your horizon and infuses new energy into your stepfamily relationships.

Tips for Balancing the Rope Bridge to the Later Stages

How do you make the power struggles and communication sessions during the Middle Stages productive so that you can move to a more peaceful and relatively more unified family dynamic?

- Set times for facilitated communication opportunities, such as time spent in family meetings or counseling sessions
- Help family members identify the challenges they're most willing to fight for
- Negotiate new agreements about these challenges
- Emphasize the value of honesty in communication, especially with regard to feelings about the deceased parent
- Learn more about one another as individuals, for example through personality tests
- Practice building relationships in one-on-one pairs, including stepparent and stepchild
- Do something new altogether: get a pet, complete a project, or volunteer together

The Later Stages: Finding a Rhythm

The transition from the Middle Stages to the Later Stages is more subtle than from Early to Middle. The Later Stages reflect a period of sound family structure. The main clue that you've reached the Later Stages is that the family can often function as a family without constant attention to "step" issues.

The biggest roadblocks in sustaining the Later Stages are:

1. The zigzag phenomenon, which predicts temporary setbacks for all stepfamilies, and

2. Lessened communication opportunities with adult stepchildren as they pursue their own lives, especially if the children moved out during the Early or Middle Stages.

Family members can find relationship success by continued practice in one-on-one pairs: parent and stepparent, stepparent and one child, or parent and one child. Finally, a greater level of intimacy becomes possible in the step relationships.

I can remember a time when Brittany was turning fourteen and she really wanted to go to Disneyworld. Although she didn't insist on the trip being just her and me, she did drop some hints. My decision felt complicated: Brian and I had a baby girl who was only nine months old. Could I leave her? Was Brittany craving attention from me that had been refocused to baby Amy? Brian played the pivotal natural parental role in this situation by assuring me he could take care of Amy and encouraging me to go with Brittany. We had a blast, and we were even able to meet up at Disney with my friend and former matron of honor, Monica, her husband, and young daughter.

Ian and I found common ground first through playing cold-weather indoor volleyball tournaments in our living room, using a small beach ball and some rope to outline the court. After Amy was born, Ian was the kid who enjoyed playing on the floor with her and her toys, and he provided me many cumulative hours of laughter with his high-pitched rendition of "Elmo's World."

In the Later Stages, family members increase signs of accepting the relationships for what they are in the moment. They continue to be more comfortable speaking their minds. The marital relationship becomes more of a sanctuary, source of nourishment, and support for all issues, including step-issues.

Here, the stepparent is solidly established as what Papernow calls an "intimate outsider." The stepparent is "intimate enough to be a confidante and outside enough to provide support and mentoring in areas too threatening to share with biological parents: sex, career choice, drugs, relationships, remaining distress about the [death]." If a stepparent joined the family when the children were teens, it may be well into the children's adult years when the family feels it has arrived at the Later Stages. Ella, whose stepchildren were high school-aged and college-aged when she married, said, "It wasn't until Joanie and Merle were married and having children of their own that they saw when I put myself out for them. I had the feeling, then, that they appreciated me."

When stepchildren no longer live in your home, the burden falls upon both the adults and the young adults to continue the family relationships. Usually the adults end up continuing holiday and other celebratory traditions at the home base, or at least taking some ownership for those traditions. Because young adults are developing their own lives and pursuing their own passions, they may not be the initiators of family events for a time to come. It's important for you as a stepparent to reach out in ways that feel sincere and authentic, so as not to slip back into any trap of trying too hard and feeling resentful.

> If a stepparent joined the family when the children were teens, it may be well into the children's adult years when the family feels it has arrived at the Later Stages.

Calling the Later Stages final is misleading in that it may imply the Stepfamily Cycle is complete and will not slip backwards. Certain events or crises may very well trigger a portion of the cycle, or even the entire cycle, to repeat. At this stage, however, the dynamics happen in ways that shouldn't threaten the couple or stepparent-stepchild relationships. You're now a family of your own making—not anyone's ideal family, but rather, the one you all chose to shape over the years.

REFLECTION PROMPTS

1. Which of the stepfamily myths spoke most directly to you, and why?
2. Based on the descriptions of the stages, where does your stepfamily sit in the Stepfamily Cycle?
3. What would you and your family need to do to move toward the next phase in the cycle?

POINTS TO REMEMBER

*   Stepfamily myths, often reinforced by media, are omnipresent in our world—yet they are truly myths.
*   The Stepfamily Cycle is a researched explanation of a typical stepfamily growth curve. The cycle has no specified development time, but a period of ten or more years is not uncommon.
*   A stepfamily is not a poorly functioning biological family.
*   An undercurrent of uneasiness is felt but not consciously understood by stepfamily members. The uneasiness—often just a sense that something is "off"—clashes with ideal beliefs we want to hold about our families.
*   Given time to blossom, stepfamily members can move beyond the original family roles and power struggles to see each other's individuality.

FIVE

Your Identity in the New Family

"Every oak tree started out as a couple of nuts who stood their ground."
– ANONYMOUS

Brittany: Nine years old
Ian: Eight years old
Years since their mom died: Three-and-a-half
Years since our remarriage: Two
Season: Summer

ON THE SUMMER SCHEDULE, I HAD MORE opportunity for outings with the kids. At their ages, Brittany and Ian showed more independent thinking and even played together better than during their younger years. I still struggled with my connection to them, and I'd gotten a new idea in my head that if I asked them to come up with a fun name for me, that could make us closer. I dreamed up a world where a more affectionate moniker than my first name, which is what they called me, would soften their path to loving me.

One June day, the kids and I were hanging out in our newly finished basement, where it was cool, and I popped the question. I asked Brittany and Ian to come up with a name that was neither Diane nor Mom; something of their own creation that they thought would fit me. If they had been teenagers, this exercise could have been either very fun or very tragic for me, depending on the name. I guess I was asking too much of them for their ages and for our stage of relationship building, because neither one could come up with another name for me.

Later that summer, a sunny July day found us at the city's outdoor pool, swimming and snacking the afternoon away. I felt excited to ask them one more time about a naming idea. I had come up with a name of my own, one that I thought was a great middle ground. The name was non-threatening to their mom, but represented something special to their dad. Brian's favorite cartoon character was Snoopy, from the Peanuts *comic strip. I had considered this very carefully, and I was ready to be Snoopy with their buy-in.*

They didn't bite. Brittany continued to call me Diane, explaining that she cared about me no matter what she called me, but that she just couldn't call me anything but Diane. Sometimes she even called me "my Diane," which was cute. I had to admit that she was clear about her intentions.

Ian, in a surprise move, decided that he was going to call me Mom. I was not angling for this name switch at all; however, he started up overnight. So now I had two different names from two different children—the exact two names I hoped to avoid. The lesson? Do not try this at home.

Many psychologists agree that part of our identity is wrapped up in what people call us. I was fascinated with the idea that a name change could work some relationship magic. In hindsight, however, I spotted something deeper going on with my naming initiative. At school and out in public, I definitely felt that "Diane" could be a babysitter or nanny (family outsider). I wanted them to call me something fun that they picked, something that was more reflective of an insider role. Fear of staying a family outsider definitely drove me to persist with the naming discussion. Not to mention, my ego was looking for strokes from the children, in the form of a bonding sort of name. Instead of strokes, I got status quo from Brittany, and a name change from Ian that would later come back to haunt us both. In the end the whole exercise turned out to be confusing to the kids, thereby not helping us bond or helping me become a family insider.

Mission identity

As psychologist Mark Benn mentioned, no one can choose the children's role models for them. Since you can't own whichever gender role you fit in the stepfamily, and you're not supposed to replace the parent who died, where does that leave you in terms of role and identity in the stepfamily?

In considering identity in our stepfamilies, it's important to address our own sense of loss. Grieving stepfamily members are experiencing some obvious deprivation—a parent or spouse died, and supportive adults make time to pay attention and help. It's less obvious to the world that stepparents suffer our own set of disappointments, frustrations, and heartaches, including:

- Loss of our identity as we enter a new situation and environment
- Loss of the possibility to start a family from scratch
- Loss of the hope to feel like a family insider
- Loss of the expectation that we'll be called Mom or Dad
- Loss of the fantasies of an instant family bond
- Loss of constant, intimate access to our spouse or partner, who needs to share love and attention with the children
- Loss of being recognized by the children as a real, dimensional person

I know on some level that I felt my losses were nothing compared to those my family members felt. But we're not trying to compare the losses. We must recognize our own heartbreak in this family situation. It hurts to be an outsider, in an entirely different way than the children are hurting.

What release could you feel if you acknowledge your losses? What could happen if you recognize the high energy and low results involved with trying to become a family insider? Could you forgive yourself for not being the oil that makes the family gears engage more smoothly? Taking some pressure off can open up the possibility of visualizing your special role in the family. To quote the old television series *Mission Impossible*, "Your mission, should you choose to accept it," is to identify the parts of yourself you will retain, cherish, and be proud of as you move forward with your new family. Let's call this collection of traits the "you that shines through." Allowing this "you" to emerge is a crucial part of your journey from the fantasy of stepfamilies to their reality. At some point, the fog is going to clear enough that you look in the mirror and see yourself again.

Reclaim the authentic you

I've found the following motto useful for my stepparenting life: Stepparents are the "and," not the "instead." The stepparent role is not meant to be better or worse than any other, but it's a different role than most of us think we will play. Though you can, over time, contribute to the well-being of your family, always remember that the deceased person is still part of the family identity as well.

> Stepparents are the "and," not the "instead."

If you suspect you are filling the gender-role gap and scrambling to patch family fissures, redefining the stepparent role could actually be very freeing for you. What if you didn't have to do all the discipline, run the family, or orchestrate every spare minute with your stepchildren? What could happen if your main objectives became those most often recommended by stepparenting experts?

- To support the surviving parent in his or her centerpiece role in the family
- To learn about your stepchildren a little bit at a time instead of taking it all on at once
- To allow the deceased parent to surface in the family whenever it is important for the children to keep connected

◆ To continue learning about grief and about stepfamily development, independently and with your spouse, so you two can discuss
different perspectives and share helpful information and strategies
with the whole family

Would refocusing on these concerns release you to feel more natural
with your stepchildren? Could you then devote more time and energy to
your own children, to your spirituality and self-care, to a favorite hobby or
sport, or to your career?

Adam communicates what I feel is a healthy perspective on his role.
He says, "I see my job as more to help Lily and her girls build a bridge for
communication, especially when I see there's a rift." Rather than take over,
he jumps in and gets things going again when there's a stall-out between
one of the girls and their mother.

If you have agreed to embrace grieving children unrelated to you, consider yet another perspective. We know that bereaved children crave connection with blood relatives. It might make sense to ask some of the child's
blood relatives if they could act as resources for you from time to time. You
can also call upon your own support network, such as trusted friends, relatives, spiritual leaders, or counselors, for help. Although you want to find
ways to keep your kids connected to the deceased parent or parents, it's
important not to take an exhausting, 24/7 approach to the daily parenting
work and the memorializing tasks.

A relevant question at this point is: *What* is going to help sustain you
through your losses in order to carve out a special place in your new family? Exploring the following concepts can help yield the "you that shines
through":

◆ Build your support network
◆ Invite the natural parent to claim his or her role
◆ Reframe yourself in a larger identity picture
◆ Manage your ego
◆ Connect with your confidence
◆ Weave traditions side-by-side

Each of these concepts offers space and the opening you may need to allow your heart to shine through. To better understand them, let's take a deeper look at each concept separately, and wrap up with some special guidance when children have lost both parents.

Build your support network

The support portion of our sustainable stepparenting equation is key to coping through stepfamily challenges. Support remains a fundamental building block toward the unwieldy yet exciting prospect of crafting your identity.

How do you go about building a support network? Help can come in many different forms, including formal or informal support groups, counseling, prayer, self-education through books and media, or combinations of these resources. Some stepparents wait and eventually hit the wall (or, in my case, the chaise lounge) before they reach out for help. Try some of these support strategies instead:

- ♦ If you have a spouse or partner in this endeavor of parenting a grieving child, that person should be your most important support resource. Author Norwood offers some collective advice from stepmothers: "Recognize that if your marital relationship does not hold together, you won't have a stepfamily to worry about. Commit to it … preserve it, and above all enjoy it."
- ♦ If your spouse or partner is not supporting you in the ways you need, explore help for that roadblock while seeking out other

forms of general support.

- Have a career, hobby, or tradition you can call your own. Examples might be your work, a sport you play, hobby-related retreats and events, or even regular girls' or boys' nights out.

- Get in touch with other stepparents. If you have access to the Internet, search stepfamily support. Many websites will pop up, including that of the National Stepfamily Resource Center (NSRC). Some of the websites have chat forums available. Look for chats or threads that seem positive and solution-oriented, and avoid those that feel like complaint sessions.

- Talk through your challenges with non-stepparent friends—they can identify situations that are challenges for all parents, not just stepparents.

- If you have a spiritual mentor or advisor, request a discussion. He or she may have additional resources to share.

- You may have counselors in your community that specialize in re-marriage and stepfamilies. Seek them out.

Your support resources will help you feel that you're not alone, but moreover your network will encourage you to look outside yourself and your own situation. Your supporters may offer the fresh perspectives you need to see yourself emerge within the stepfamily you are creating.

Support and Step-mountains

After a radio interview with Barbara Bue, a reverend and the former talk show host of KRFC radio's *Creative Living*, I was struck by how little she and I knew about each other and yet how much we had in common as stepmoms. I left the interview feeling satiated. We had shared some joys and challenges and had also laughed about some of our ridiculous moments as stepmoms.

With other stepparents, we may have instant camaraderie. The only caution I hold dear is not to be pulled down into a whine fest (a wine fest might be okay in moderation, however). I hold out the hope that when stepparents support and mentor other stepparents, we attempt to keep our kvetching to a minimum and instead really problem-solve and get productive suggestions flowing.

Another great source of support is the general universe of other parents. Why? I call it a reality check. I can't tell you the number of times I have ... well ... whined a little about a situation or relationship with my stepchildren, only to have someone who has never had stepchildren turn around and say, "My son or daughter does that too!" Two distinct examples I recall are when my tween stepdaughter asked me to stop walking to school with her and when my elementary-school stepson wouldn't finish his homework in the timeframe I asked. Some issues are just not stepfamily issues, and I think it's healthy to recognize we don't have to make every challenge in the stepfamily into a step-mountain!

Invite the natural parent to claim his or her role

The support portion of our sustainable stepparenting formula is integrally dependent upon the role the children's natural parent (the partner whom you, the stepparent, live with) plays in the family. As a family builds itself and creates a new identity, the surviving parent remains the key link between past, present, and future.

In the best of possible family dynamics, the natural parent will be the oak tree in the storm. I've researched, witnessed, and been told stories about three steadfast ways a natural parent can strengthen the stepfamily and enhance the children's self-esteem. It's essential for the natural parent to:

1. Be the central hub of the stepfamily.

The natural parent acts as a bridge between you and the children. The natural parent should facilitate communication, direct traffic, ward off accidents, and manage any crises that occur. Jean McBride, therapist and Executive Director of the Colorado Center for Life Changes, has a long history of working with families who are blending due to divorce and death. As we sat at a local park one sunny fall morning, she told me that the natural parent provides the equilibrium in the family, "like a stabilizer on an airplane." It's a lot to ask the natural parent, who is only human, to perform all of these roles at the same time as potentially working, grieving, and maintaining sanity. Therefore, it's not uncommon for some of these tasks to slip through the cracks, creating gaps. McBride, speaking with a growing smile on her face, paints a picture of the messiness that natural parents can face: "Since they are often in their own grief, it takes them a while to regroup … they will often look like a deer in the headlights and they don't know what they can contribute. They are holding up a lot! They have to eat their Wheaties!"

Over time, a stepparent who has worked on building some trust with the stepchildren can take turns sitting at stepfamily central and filling some gaps. Having been a stepparent for twenty-plus years, I can say that our kids still look to their father for an overall sense of stability, but I see that they also recognize some of my strengths. For example, when a family event needs organization and drive, Brittany will usually turn to me. The trick for the stepparent is to let the natural parent keep the majority of facilitation, authority, and control.

2. Be the main disciplinarian in the stepfamily.

Your stepkids can miss out on the chance to grow a trusting relationship with you if you are doling out the discipline. Adam (the stepparent) and Lily (the parent) embody a wonderful example of handling stepfamily discipline. Lily takes the lead. But Adam will step in to help mediate conflict, with the goal of making sure the girls respect their mother ... *not* to make them listen to his rules.

Over time the parent can direct the children to follow the stepparent's discipline in certain situations. For example, if Lily is going to be away for the weekend, she makes sure to tell the girls that Adam is in charge and they are to respect him.

3. Be physically available (present) and emotionally available (interested).

Work with your spouse to reach agreement about the following recommendations regarding availability: Spend time with the kids. Make sure the kids know when to rely on the natural parent being around or at least available electronically and by phone. Listen to what the kids have to say. Share feelings about family difficulties, as long as those feelings don't betray the stepparent.

If you, as a stepparent, share the three natural parent guidelines with your partner, and you still feel as if he or she is not behaving like the steadfast oak, what should you do? First of all, please don't rush. A natural inclination is to step in and fill the gaps you feel the surviving parent isn't covering. You might reason, "That's not replacing the deceased person, is it? Don't the children need these holes sealed up?" Recall author Sue Thoele's comment that filling a gap is a "tender trap" that can lead to real pain and frustration when the children don't respond in receptive ways to you, your authority, or your structure.

Take the time to evaluate why the natural parent might not be willing or able to claim the role. Our three guidelines represent an *ideal* for the natural parent role after the death of the children's other parent. Given the load I know the natural parent carries, I can think of a few issues that may factor in:

- A lack of confidence in parenting skills
- A lack of availability (physical, emotional, or both)
- A personality style not conducive to the steadfast oak
- Ongoing grieving

A lack of confidence in parenting skills may be the easiest to address. Education and practice remain the best solutions to fortify parenting skills. Parents can find a wealth of parenting expert information in the form of websites, podcasts, and all forms of books (printed, audio, and eBook). The natural parent must of course be willing to study up, hopefully with our support as stepparents. Practice opportunities present themselves every day in family life; however, we must have follow-up discussion about what went well and what requires a new approach.

Another solution I can recommend as a supplement to education is a little trickier but can work in tandem with daily parenting practice. If you have clearer parenting strength and skill than your partner, you can coach your spouse from the sidelines (in private, please, not in front of the kids) or help your spouse find coaching from a mentor or counseling profes- sional. Remember that it is not until well into the Middle Stages of the step- family cycle that a stepparent should be taking on a lot of direct parenting responsibility. Thus, an advisement role is best.

When the natural parent is out of town, working, or otherwise physi- cally unavailable, encourage your spouse or partner to set boundaries. If my husband were speaking to our children, it might sound something like this: "I may not be here physically, but you can be sure that everything Diane asks you to do or talks about with you, she and I have discussed and I agree with. She is in charge for this period of time, and I'll be more avail- able on the weekend." This approach covers situations we as stepparents are thrust into, feeling compelled to act in the natural parent role. I can't emphasize enough how helpful this type of support from the natural par- ent is when the natural parent is absent.

McBride conducted some interesting studies with Japanese stepmoth- ers and found that they, not the natural dads, spend the bulk of time every day with their stepchildren. Japanese men are usually employed outside the home and the work ethic is intense—the men are often gone ten to twelve hours per day. When a Japanese man remarries, it's not a cultural norm for him to adjust his work schedule. This leaves Japanese stepmoms in charge of the children for very long hours. In addition to supporting the stepmoms by giving their children boundary statements, Japanese fathers must work hard at creating times they are physically and emotionally available to their children.

When a natural parent is emotionally unavailable to the children, for example through substance abuse, a chemical imbalance, or a psychological problem, that is a larger challenge—potentially beyond the scope of what a couple can handle without professional help. This can be a scary situation for the stepparent and the stepchildren alike, so I encourage professional involvement sooner than later.

The natural parenting gap created from personality differences is difficult but not impossible to address. In Brian's and my relationship, this gap definitely tempted me to step in to a disciplinarian role too soon. At the time my husband was widowed, he didn't consider himself to be much of a parenting expert. Rather than book study, Brian learned so much about parenting skills from years of hands-on experience. From a personality perspective, Brian also happens to prefer harmony to confrontation and laissez faire to boundaries. It's just his style. I like the harmony part, but I definitely prefer structure and closure to open-ended evolution. And, I'm a very firm believer that kids not only need but also want boundaries. Instead of stepping aside for a while, which would have been the healthiest thing for the stepparent to do, I often took the helm I felt was not being manned in the way I would do it. More than once, this tender trap door opened and I fell in.

Therefore, I humbly add a fourth guideline for the natural parent:

4. Work alongside the stepparent, who has good suggestions and a more objective view of the family dynamics.

Because it's in the children's best interests, whenever possible, have the parent be the main gig. My guideline, number four, can help satisfy both parent and stepparent. If the natural parent can listen to the stepparent's observations and insights about the family, the couple can take its time and work together to set up new structure and boundaries in the family. The delivery of the message about the new structure or boundary, however, will come from the natural parent. For example, I recognized over time that young Ian had a hard time transitioning from one activity (let's say playing on the floor), to another activity (let's say getting dressed to get in the car for day camp). Sometimes he didn't know how to cope with the change and would break down in tears or just curl up on the floor. Working through that behavior oftentimes made us late. I relayed this observation to Brian in private, and he and I ended up working with a counselor to come up with a new system where Ian got three "countdown" alerts before he had to shift activities. Brian explained the system to Ian, but either of us could carry it out and have it work.

I urge you to keep on communicating with your spouse when you feel strongly that the kids should be parented a different way. In the end, the most important reason to insist on a change is when a behavior of theirs affects you negatively or disables your productivity. If the teenager's summer curfew is too late because you stay up worrying and can't function without sleep, renegotiate that with your partner first rather than going directly to your teen and changing the curfew. Stand up for your beliefs when they matter most. Choose these battles wisely, and be willing to let the rest go so as not to create constant control clashes in the household.

With regard to personality style, other stepparents might voice complaints that their spouses are too passive, too quiet, too busy, too distant, too stubborn, etc. to meet the three guidelines. Here's the summary of the lesson: When your spouse's personality style isn't conducive to striving for the steadfast parent's role, I think you have a few choices. Your first is to see how it goes without you running interference. Give your spouse a chance. There isn't only one way to raise children. Trust me on this—the kids really, really want their own parent to take the lead. The stepparent does not get hero or heroine points from the kids for stepping into stepfamily central. In fact, a stepparent's commandeering approach can delay the progression of

The stepparent does not get hero or heroine points from the kids for stepping in to stepfamily central.

the stepparent-stepchild relationship. Since taking control is not a choice, the remaining choice is to work behind-the-scenes to partner with your spouse.

Ongoing grieving can from time to time impede the surviving parent's ability to carry forth. I am going to split this topic down gender lines.

Boys and men, at least in American society, are often chided by other boys and men when they cry or "get soft." It is a rare and difficult behavior for a man to let himself experience the full range of emotions around grief. The heartfelt McBride said, "Sometimes the dad isn't very good at helping the family grieve and he just wants to move on and replace." But what we know about grief is that it's a lifelong process and thus it will continue to come out whether we allow it or not. So even though a high percentage of widowed or divorced men remarry within a few years, their grief will still go along for the remarried ride in some way, shape, or form.

Women, especially those with children, are less likely to remarry as quickly, but about half of widowers or divorcees eventually do. With either gender, stockpiled feelings of grief can prevent parents from connecting emotionally with their children. Sometimes parents subconsciously view the children as reminders of the loss, which is an unfortunate misplacement of emotions that could leave the children wondering if the state of the family is their fault.

Grief can also enable parents to overcompensate out of feelings of sorrow or guilt. For example, a parent might shower their child with material things. "Poor dear—she lost her mom. This would be a good time to buy her that car." Or some parents let boundaries slide. "Awww, don't be so tough on him for staying out too late—his dad died only a year ago."

What can you, the stepparent, do in situations such as these? You can choose again to coach your partner—this time through grief. When you practice what you'll learn in the upcoming grief education chapter, you'll be encouraging your spouse to talk about and talk through the losses, to experience feelings instead of stuffing them. However, you probably don't want to take on that initiative all by yourself. Support and encourage your spouse to engage in either a self-study or a group study about grief and loss. Hospice organizations, for example, often host these types of groups. Finally, you can help them connect with a therapist who specializes in grief and loss.

If nothing else, don't underestimate the ripple effect of either pushing grief way down inside or pushing it off to the future. Grief has a way of seeping through our insides out into real life in the most unexpected ways.

Reframe yourself in a larger identity picture

Many times over the years I forgot that my stepparent role (or any other life role) is only a fraction of my overall identity. I do have a strong faith that gives my life a bigger picture frame than just that of my here-and-now family; I just have to remind myself to tap into that bigger picture. Many stepparents have commented about how their spiritual beliefs make them feel connected to something larger than their daily struggles. During Lana's most difficult teen years, Kit reflected, "Who was I to think I could protect her fully? My faith is the only way I'm getting through these years."

Your beliefs—along with your work, your passions, your hobbies, and your dreams— all line up to create a bigger picture of the authentic you. Your life is not one-dimensional as a parent or stepparent. Notice what drives you. What makes you want to get out of bed each morning? Although your stepkids may not appear to care what makes you tick at first, your steady dedication to your passions will eventually make an impression. I remember when Brittany was about ten and I was preparing flipcharts and slides for a corporate workshop I was facilitating that week. She watched me as I worked and wanted to write up some of the flipcharts for me. We decided which ones she could do, and she loved working with the fat, fruit-scented markers to create her giant flipchart pages.

Manage your ego

Because we are human, and despite our security in a bigger picture, many of us still struggle with our stepparent identities. Ultimately, my identity gave in to ego many times along the way, prompting me to ask such self-serving questions as:

- "Why can't the kids call me something other than Diane?"
- "Where do I fit in?"
- "Don't the kids need a female role model?"

Look at the difference between those questions and the following queries that focus on taking care of myself rather than feeding my ego:

- What do I need to feel more peaceful?
- What character traits do I claim as my own?
- How can I be at my best when my family comes to me for help?

Marin was able over time to see the difference between feeling sorry for herself and taking care of herself to be a more heartfelt stepparent.

"I realized that I'm not helping anyone, including myself, if I don't take care of myself so I can see things more clearly," Marin said. "That shift made a big difference and helped me be able to get past my 'it's all about me' phase."

Author Thoele tells the story of how much she worried about her kids, stepkids, and husband when she was flat-on-her-back sick for ten days. When everyone turned up just fine, she had to face the fact that she was not the indispensable mother or stepmother.

My early crusade to get Brittany and Ian to call me something other than Diane is my shining example of ego at work. I don't consider myself egotistical, but I suppose that even to deny that part of myself is egotistical.

Naming success stories do exist, however, especially when driven by the children, not the stepparent. McBride's eyes sparkled while she told me about a stepmother client who agreed to the suggested name Wick—short for Wicked. McBride said that even the sound of that nickname brought a touch of humor to the family's otherwise tense situations. What a clever way to defuse all the fairy-tale build-up around the evil stepmother!

Ego is no friend, but it is ever-present. The best we can do is to be aware of those times when our egos are talking and manage them. Don't be afraid to run situations by trusted friends, family, and mentors. They can provide a checks-and-balances system for your ego.

Connect with your confidence

The Early Stages position of family outsider can generate feelings of inadequacy and insecurity that hold over to other stepfamily stages. People handle insecurity in a variety of different ways, depending on personality. Some stepparents might compensate by becoming more domineering and aggressive, which helps them earn the tag of mean stepmother or stepfather. These styles may not show that they feel insecure. Other personality styles might shrink away and retreat, obsessing over every detail of the relationship—contemplating questions like, "Who said what today and how was it delivered?" or "Did we make any progress in the relationships today?"

Marin suggests that part of her insecurity came from not knowing if all stepfamily members loved each other. "With your natural children you generally all know you love each other, so even little spats can heal up more quickly than the transgressions they become in stepfamilies." Marin, whose stepchildren are now grown and out of the house, spent a lot of their child-hood time second guessing herself. "I always harbored the fear that if I told the children to do something like a regular mother would say it, they wouldn't like me for it."

My insecurity sometimes led to feeling a lack of empowerment as a mother figure. Brittany was very good friends for years with neighbor girl Jersey (one year younger, who attended a different school). When Brittany was invited to join the popular crowd at her middle school, she left the neighborhood girl out of the picture for get-togethers. Jersey's mom came to me, expecting me to tell Brittany that what she had done was wrong. Although this was a clear opportunity to help Brittany grow in her charac-ter, I didn't feel empowered to play out that discussion with Brittany. I could ask Brittany questions about her relationships, but I didn't feel I could tell her what to do, for example, to include Jersey or even to apologize to her. Jersey's mom couldn't understand my point of view, and I couldn't explain myself any better than that—I felt certain limitations to my influence with Brittany.

No doubt, developing your confidence in the midst of your stepfamily will challenge you. Daily stepparenting life can be enervating, and the grind of working the insider/outsider dynamic does not make a fertile bed from which to grow confidence. I had to turn to outside support sources and to a bigger picture to connect again with the confidence and optimism I had before I entered the stepfamily. If you suspect that your insecurities are bubbling up in the forms of constant irritation or depression, for example, it's time to take a temporary step away from the stepfamily grind in order to figure out what you need to regroup.

Weave traditions side-by-side

In a blended family, all members risk losing traditions that were precious to them prior to the new family formation. Traditions tell stories about one's family, and therefore play an important role in shaping a person's identity. For example, Marin grew up in England, where she never saw her Christmas stocking before Santa filled it for Christmas morning. Here in America, her new family hung stockings over the chimney weeks before Christmas. Marin felt outnumbered and gave up her English tradition. Later, she noticed that it made her feel disempowered in a family where she already battled the outsider status.

In contrast, Ella retained a tradition through circumstance and compromise. Ella was used to working outside the home, whereas Walter's first wife, Madge, had, in recent years, stayed home. Ella continued to work but shifted to working from home—for her, an empowering solution.

When considering the children's needs, it's important to also honor their first-family traditions, but I would strive for creative solutions that don't require you to sacrifice all of your traditions. You can accomplish this by identifying the traditions that are important to you, while asking the natural parent to help identify the first-family traditions important to all. For example, putting up a live Christmas tree was not a tradition I was willing to sacrifice. Thankfully, this didn't clash with anyone else's attachments … no one cared if the tree was real or artificial. However, what adorned the top of the tree represented a meaningful tradition for the children. If the navy-and-white crepe angel disappeared forever, the kids might have felt like a piece of themselves was missing.

Special guidance when children have lost both parents

If you're in this group of stepparents, you face some special challenges. The loss of both parents is a devastating situation for the children. Stepparents, godparents, and grandparents may notice increased fear and sadness that stems from abandonment, which is sometimes expressed or acted out in ways that would benefit from the assistance of helping professionals. In your home, apply the age-specific strategies for helping grieving children cope, and be prepared for older teen stepchildren to be tempted to separate and want to forge out on their own.

If you are related to your stepchildren—for example if you are their grandparents—you at least have a link to the family history and can find ways to easily honor the deceased parents with the children. I recommend that you research discipline strategies, but many grandchildren who knew their grandparents growing up do honor their grandparents' rules.

A grandparent might be parenting when the children's parents have died, but may also be co-parenting with their adult child, or protecting grandchildren when they come out of foster care. No matter what the situation, this group of stepparents will be helping the children overcome feelings of abandonment.

If you are not related to your stepchildren—for example, you're unrelated godparents—you have two main tasks to which you want to pay special attention. The first is to gather stories about the children's parents so you have a repository to draw from to help them connect to those memories. The second is to do research or gain professional advice about how to stay empowered to discipline the children. As much as a young child or teenager may have enjoyed you as their parents' friend, remember that your role has now changed, like Kit and Quincy experienced when their roles grew from aunt and uncle to Brad and Lana's stepparents.

As author and stepfamily educational specialist Ron Deal likes to say, stepfamily life is *not* the Brady Bunch. Building a new stepfamily *and* finding your identity within it is not an easy or quick task. The journey won't mesh like the Bradys, but it can be done. Find the resources you need—be that your spouse, your faith, your career, or your therapist—and rediscover your identity. You can create your approach and move forward with confidence.

REFLECTION PROMPTS

1. In your stepfamily, do you feel you sit back, do your thing, and wait for the stepkids to come to you? Or do you take charge with them? What benefits could the first approach yield? If you have taken charge, what setbacks have you witnessed?
2. What role do you hope the natural parent will take on? What might be blocking your partner's ability to help the family gel and how might you facilitate the changes?
3. How will you build your confidence in the midst of all the stepfamily dynamics?
4. When you think about taking action to rediscover your identity, which ideas feel like they're right for you? Consider our list, or add your own:
   - Build your support network
   - Invite the natural parent to claim his or her role
   - Reframe yourself in a larger identity picture
   - Manage your ego

- Connect with your confidence
- Weave traditions side-by-side

POINTS TO REMEMBER

- Stepparents are the "and," not the "instead."
- It's normal to feel torn between the role you hoped to play in your stepfamily and the role it's most healthy for you to play.
- We might believe that the kids need the missing-gender role model to come to the rescue. Reality shows that you can't choose the kids' role models.
- Your losses as you join the stepfamily are very different from the grief your family members suffer (unless you were close to the deceased). Your loss is one of identity and family expectations. The two loss processes are not in sync, however, both sets of losses need to be supported.
- If you were close to the deceased, you can share with your stepkids your own feelings of grief and your fond memories of the parent who died. This can help them process their own feelings and develop a bond with you.
- You can help the natural parent recognize how to remain a strong family centerpiece through discipline techniques and good communication about availability and boundaries.
- Watch for ego rearing its head as you work to establish your identity.
- Don't forget to talk to non-stepparents about your concerns. You may find out you're worried about something that's "just a kid thing."

PART II

Empathy:
Reaching Out to Your Family

We might take some of our most demanding family
journeys when we encourage our stepchildren to
continue a relationship with the parent who died.
Although this process may bring up difficult feelings,
honoring our stepchildren's need to keep a lost
parent close ultimately builds the best stepfamily
relationships. Know that your efforts and actions lay
the groundwork for future milestones: rites of passage,
celebrations, and the weathering of other losses.

SIX

The Lifework of Grief

"... suffering, no matter how multiplied, is always individual."
–ANNE MORROW LINDBERGH

Brittany: Ten years old
Ian: Eight years old
Years since their mom died: Four
Years since our remarriage: Two
Season: Early Fall

DURING BRIAN'S AND MY PURSUIT OF GRIEVING *stepfamily support,*
we met our new family therapist, Dr. G. He wasn't just any garden-variety
counselor. He had a goofy grin and a way of making us laugh hard at least
once during a session. At one of the get-to-know-you appointments, he met
with me separately.

"So how's it going with the kids?" he asked.

"Pretty good, most of the time," I said. "But there are times when I feel
none of us are comfortable being with each other."

"How long have you known them?"

I sat up a little straighter in my chair. "Going on five years now."

"So, you are still in the relationship-building phase," he said.

I nodded my head in the affirmative until his words caught up with my ears.

"What?" My eyes popped. "I said five years."

"That's right," he said. "The relationship-building phase goes on for a very long time, even ten, twelve, fifteen years."

I couldn't believe what I was hearing. All those rooms shared during vacations, school lunches packed, and hot-pretzel-and-cheese snacks baked after school—didn't these little traditions mean we had created a solid relationship?

Dr. G. proceeded to tell me about guidelines I'd only heard of recently, but didn't yet believe. "You shouldn't be disciplining the kids during the relationship-building phase, because you haven't yet earned their trust." Oh dear, I thought.

"And it would be good for the kids if you thought about ways to remember Cathy's birthday and death day anniversaries," he mentioned.

The chagrined look on my face caused Dr. G. to take a gentler tone. "Maybe we should start at Grief 101," he said.

Once again, I received the message that stepparenting in a grieving family might require some additional homework. This time I needed to learn more about grief. No matter what the circumstances, we adults seem to barely understand how to grieve and have an even lower comfort level helping others who are grieving.

The good news is that we can tap into ways to understand grief and loss. First, we can examine our own loss experiences. I've lost loved ones, pets, competitions, and possessions. When I reconnect with the feelings I've had about these experiences, then it's easier for me to express empathy for others who are in the midst of grieving. I remember how helpless and angry I felt when I received the call that my father's doctors in California couldn't do anything more for him. *Surely they've missed something,* I thought. I felt violated when thieves broke into my car and stole my purse, which was loaded with everything from credit cards to pictures. After my dog died, I panicked at the thought that I would have to give up the intense feeling of connection she and I had and replace that intensity with some other way to remember her.

Beyond connecting with our own feelings of loss to shed understanding toward others' grieving, we can also educate ourselves about loss, grief, and mourning.

Grief education is a vital piece of our sustainable stepparenting formula. Investing time to learn about grief and loss will serve us throughout our lives as we address the myriad of losses we'll inevitably suffer along the way. Tapping into all available resources to understand grief helps us and helps our stepkids and spouses grieve as well.

Understanding loss

Across the span of our lives, we experience all kinds of losses, from small to very intense. Earl Hipp, in his book for teens and adults called *Help for the Hard Times: Getting Through Loss*, says that loss is an "event that changes the way things have been ... separation, missing something that was there before, going on without, no longer having something you loved, letting go."

The same event for two different people may range in intensity from small to huge, and we cannot assume how intense any loss is or will be for another person. For example, one adolescent girl may shake off not making the school play as a small loss and easily move on to some other passion or hobby. Another young lady might have been counting on participation in the school play as an experience she could list on her resume for college. She may have already set aside the time for all the rehearsals. To the second girl, this loss will feel bigger.

In our stepfamily, we eventually sold "the big red van" that the kids had enjoyed during many road trips with Brian and Cathy and then with Brian and me. Ian was more attached to that vehicle than Brittany, and at the age of eight or nine he'd even talked about the van being his first car. But we'd found a great deal on a station wagon that was more practical to drive and park, and it still fit all of us and our gear. After adding the wagon, due to our homeowners' rules, if we kept the van, we would have had to pay to store it away from our property. Brian and I decided we couldn't keep the big red van around. The sale was much harder on Ian than on Brittany, and for sure a bigger loss for him than for her.

While loss does not have to mean death, the death of a loved one is almost always a high-intensity loss. But what happens when we layer a high-intensity loss on top of life's usual range of small- or medium-intensity losses?

Author Hipp uses a visual concept called the "loss pot" to address this question. Everyone has a loss pot with some level of "loss stew" inside it. As losses of all intensities mount, the pot can overflow. Imagine how anyone, but especially a young person, might have trouble coping with any loss-related events when his or her loss pot is already brimming.

About six months after Brittany and Ian lost their mom, Brian brought home two cats. Ian chose the crazy black one, and Brittany chose the calmer grey one. While visiting their house, I observed Ian's cat, Blackie, streaking through the house at top speed, randomly darting under furniture and sometimes losing Ian in the chase. In contrast, Brittany's cat, White Sox, would sit atop Brittany's bed while she petted him.

Brian called me one night about a month after the arrival of the cats. Blackie had done his crazy run out the front door and into the street in front of a moving car. He died instantly. Brian said Ian wailed and took out his anger on the car, saying "stupid car" over and over. Little Ian's loss pot likely overflowed during that time, such a short while after his mother had died.

A full loss pot carries a wide range of consequences, including:

- gloominess and associating with others who also have dismal outlooks on the world
- anger and potential associated random acts of violence
- the shutting off of all feelings, positive and negative
- oversensitivity and crying at the smallest offense
- a giving-up attitude
- substance abuse

By comprehending more about the reactions to losses—what we call grieving—we can help our stepfamily members steer away from these possible consequences.

Understanding grief and grieving

If loss is the event that happens, grief is how you feel as a result of the event. The ways in which you let your feelings out in order to heal is called grieving. Individuals who don't grieve their losses pour even more "loss stew" into their pots.

There is no "right way" to feel or process a loss. Ways of feeling during grief are as individual as the perception of the intensity of the loss. Hipp says that it is normal to have "a tangled mix" of many grief feelings at the same time, including:

- Sadness
- Confusion
- Anger
- Hopelessness
- Fear
- Loneliness
- Crabbiness
- Relief

- Hysterics
- Embarrassment
- Fatigue
- Guilt
- Worry
- Disappointment
- Helplessness
- Resentment
- Low self-esteem

Looking back, Brittany and Ian expressed their own tangled mix of such feelings, including worry, fatigue, resentment, confusion, and low self-esteem. At the time, I was not tuned into their grief—I focused on doing things for them in the hopes of building a relationship and getting them to like me. Now I see the mismatch between my intentions and my stepkids' feelings. By taking the kids' lukewarm responses less personally, and by learning more about grief, I could have been more helpful by encouraging them and Brian to take time to grieve.

With a tone both pleasant and firm, therapist McBride said, "Stepparents want to provide the missing-gender role model. I think it gets out of sync with what the kids and the family need to do in terms of grieving. I do think kids benefit greatly from having both sexes as caregivers ... I think sometimes it happens way too soon."

> At the time, I was not tuned into their grief—I focused on doing things for them in the hopes of building a relationship and getting them to like me. Now I see the mismatch between my intentions and my stepkids' feelings.

When I joined my stepfamily, I knew that grief was a normal and inevitable human reaction to loss. It took me years to realize that grief doesn't go away. Grief just changes, as we change, over time. Therefore, nothing about the way we handle grief makes grief disappear. Someone who stuffs their emotions or numbs out with substances only postpones grief, instead of healing. No matter what, grieving never ends.

Additionally, we sometimes don't factor in all the details about the extent of a young person's loss situation. Lana, for example, not only lost her mother to disease, but also lost her father to rejection. He didn't want to take care of her after her mother died. Kit said about Lana, "She had terrible, awful feelings of rejection, and it's something Quincy and I have never been able to fulfill. No matter how many times we say, 'We love you so much … we're so glad we got to pick you as our child,' nothing really fills that void."

The only way to heal is to grieve. No one likes to grieve, so we ignore, postpone, or otherwise thwart the grieving process. You may have heard the expression, "Give him time, he'll get over it." My biggest lesson about grief over the years is that our family members will never get over their losses. They'll just confront the losses differently throughout the rest of their lives. Accepting this concept actually frees you from looking for the breakpoint between your family members' sadness and happiness. Their emotions will cycle, and the re-processing is their work to do. You can help directly if your family members want your help, or behind the scenes if they resist.

When Brittany was a child, I observed that she was very internal about her losses. Throughout her young adult years, Brittany became more communicative about impending losses. Two of Cathy's immediate family members on the East Coast—Cathy's mother and brother—became terminally ill within a short time of each other. Brittany shared the facts with us about what was going on with her grandma's and uncle's illnesses and care, showing growth from her childhood communication. When asked, she also shared realistic feelings about the status of each individual.

Brittany visited her relatives as often as she could, given the distance between her home in Colorado and the two different Eastern cities. Sometimes she traveled with her fiancé and later husband, and sometimes Ian went along as well. Brittany and Ian eventually lost their uncle and their grandma within a year of each other. I sensed that Brittany had been preparing for this along the way by enjoying them while they were alive and by talking about the progression of their illnesses. Perhaps her processing didn't make the losses easier, but by grieving more openly she faced the losses instead of running from them. In comparison, Ian remained more stoic and private about these losses, and we suspect that Ian's loss pot to this day remains more full than Brittany's.

Displaying a similar pattern of openness, Brittany also discussed with us her fears about having children of her own, given her genetic predisposition to breast cancer. Grief sometimes shows up as a mountain of fear, and Brittany's conversations are helping her climb over the top. While she hasn't yet resolved her concerns, I've seen her move from a position of "I'm never having kids" to a softer "maybe" stance.

Grief-avoiding patterns in your stepfamily might include:

- Pretending everything is "fine"
- Attempting to handle big problems alone, as if asking for help demonstrates weakness
- Remaining tough in the face of obvious tragedy or trauma
- Wanting to and thinking they can "get over" the grieving
- Being willing to substitute and move on quickly (for example, with the loss of a pet)
- Minimizing the loss, as if it's "no big deal"

The key to emptying our loss pots is to embrace the temporary discomfort of grief. Revisiting your loss pot and reopening your feelings about the losses can't be done in a three-hour block on a Saturday. This process takes time. Stepmom Marin says, "We can only understand what's in our realm of understanding at any one time. Over time that realm becomes bigger. The kids just have to keep reliving the things that make them sad … it's a protection, and you can't do it all at once."

Grief and Mourning Differ by Culture

Just as each individual grieves in his or her own ways, different cultures also approach and handle grief in various ways. The "Toolkit for Nurturing Excellence at End-of-Life Transition" (TNEEL) course created by the University of Washington School of Nursing identifies three types of societal responses to death: death-denying, death-defying, and death-accepting.

In North American culture, we avoid talking about death and dying, like it's some musty family secret. This is an example of a death-denying culture. Therapist McBride says, "The way American culture looks at death and dying is to either ignore it and bury it or to want to process it quickly and move on." A death-denying culture refuses to confront death. One could argue that certain aspects of American culture are also death-defying: the inevitable outcome of death is often prolonged through youth-extending and life-extending treatments—such as plastic surgery, Botox, and hair dye—along with heroic end-of-life measures.

The textbook characteristic of a death-defying culture is the belief that people can overcome death and be equipped to continue into the afterlife. Egyptian pharaohs were buried with supplies of food, oils, clothing, and even furniture. Mummification preserved the deceased's remains as well, so the soul could continue into the afterlife.

A death-accepting culture views death as a natural and inevitable part of the lifecycle. Mexican culture celebrates "Dia de los Muertos," or Day of the Dead, by incorporating joy with mourning. Families decorate their cemeteries with flowers and candies and sometimes hold parades. They build altars for their loved ones with pictures of the deceased and prepare foods and baked goods, often in the shape of skulls. This culture recognizes and accepts death by inviting death personified into their rituals and by going face-to-face with death, using symbols to integrate death into life.

No matter what the culture, the rituals in that culture help its citizens and families to know the first things to expect and do during a time of high-intensity loss. That familiarity helps those individuals address the enormous event of a death through meaningful, somewhat predictable steps.

Understanding mourning and its four tasks

We use the word mourning to classify the outward behaviors used to express grief. Our family traditions and our cultural backgrounds influence how we mourn personal losses. For example, we may meditate, wail, sit in silence, wear black, or tell stories among family members. Bi-cultural families will oftentimes integrate mourning traditions from both backgrounds. A family may honor its history through important mourning traditions.

Many religions have specific rituals for mourning a loss. For example, Jewish families suffering a loss practice a ritual called "sitting Shiva." For seven days after a death, many friends and relatives visit the grieving person(s) at their home to listen, cry, laugh, tell stories, deliver and serve food, or just sit in silence. Hindu families in India work quickly to prepare the body for release of the spirit of the deceased from this earthly life.

Regional infrastructures demonstrate mourning as well, with rituals that bring meaning and some form of honor to a publicized loss. In the midst of a national or world tragedy, our country lowers its flags to half-mast. We experience outpourings of grief in the wake of mass shootings and terrorist attacks. Some cities around the world post large billboards or screen-print banners that display pictures of their deceased leaders. Citizens may gather in common areas like city squares and plazas to memorialize the loss of a public figure.

According to Jennifer Aberle, Assistant Professor and Director of the Human Development and Family Studies online degree program at Colorado State University, "We all have work to do when we experience death and dying. This comes in the form of different tasks." Sitting in her university office that resembled a small library, Aberle's statement came as a revelation to me. I was not taught that grief and loss require work. For some losses, this work happens naturally. For example, when I've lost or resigned a job, I start the process of hunting for a new job. When thieves stole possessions out of my car, I made a police report and went about replacing certain items that I lost. But when a loved one dies, I don't know what to do. I never thought of consciously attending to grief work when I've lost a loved one.

The four tasks of mourning related to grieving a death evolved from the work of J.W. Worden in his book, *Children and Grief: When a Parent Dies,* including major findings from the late 1990s Harvard Child Bereavement Study. The tasks do not have to be done in any particular order as long as families continue to work on each task.

- *Accept the reality of the loss.* The significance of this task is to believe the death has occurred so that you're not denying it. Some basic ways one can accept the reality of a loss include going through the rituals of a funeral or memorial and beginning to speak about (and think about) the deceased person in past tense. On a more complex level, mourners move toward accepting the significance of the loss. In my situation, I believe that Brian's and my wedding heightened the significance of Brittany and Ian's loss of their mom. The act of the ceremony made their mom's absence official. Brittany, almost eight, appeared calm. She even made us a clay snake, which she gave to us as her wedding gift, a gesture toward accepting her father's remarriage. Six-year-old Ian, being younger, had a harder time accepting the reality of the loss, which is why my matron of honor found him off in a private room, attacking his boutonniere with the pin that was supposed to hold it in place.

- *Work through the pain of grief.* This task requires taking time out periodically to experience grief. Important to this task are acknowledging, talking about, and understanding these complex emotions in order to work through them. Let's face it, who wants to feel pain? This is a very difficult task, and most of us need coaxing to allow the feelings to wash over and through us. Sometimes children, in particular, don't get enough of this type of encouragement and help. As a result, their grief spews out in random, unexpected moments, or they stuff away their grief. We already know that escaping or ignoring grief doesn't make it go away. Thus, for healthy stepfamily living, stepparents have to take part in telling the kids, "We are going to take time out to grieve." Aberle says that this is a "fundamental step that parents and stepparents can initiate in the family."

- *Adjust to your life and environment in which the deceased is missing.* This adaptation happens over an extended period of time and can require emotional adjustments, lifestyle and skill-based adjustments, and spiritual adjustments. It may take a significant period of time to begin to realize the different roles a loved one performed and how those gaps show up in the new daily life. The new environment for a stepfamily is usually "fine" until something obvious reminds your spouse or kids of the deceased. These reminders could be something such as that sandwich made "wrong," a favorite game you try to play with the family but don't know how, or the football game on TV that makes your spouse tear up because one of the teams is his former love's alma mater. Stepparents can be blindsided by these reminders, since most of us are not also grieving the deceased. With our support, however, everyone has the best shot at adjusting over time. Aberle told me it would be ideal if my stepchildren could eventually say, about their mom's death, "Yeah, my mom died and that's been hard. I have another kind of mom who can help me with the fact that my mom died, and my new mom is going to take care of me." The kids haven't said these words directly to me, but some of their actions have shown confidence in me as a mom figure.

- *Relocate the person within your current life while embarking on a new life.* The importance of this task is for those grieving to contemplate how a *meaningful*, ongoing connection with the person who has died is going to look for them as they continue on with their lives. We each have a certain amount of emotional energy we give to our loved ones. We use special words and phrases with our dear ones—think of the funny names we end up calling our pets, or the nicknames we coin for our family members. We share rituals and traditions, and we invest energy learning the rhythms of how to live with and around each other. This emotional energy needs a place to go, and it should not be dismissed. Aberle suggested that a good conversation to have with my stepkids would go something like this: "You can still have a bond with your mom, and she will remain important to you. How would you like her to be important to you? Where do you think your mom is? When do you feel her during the day? Let's give her a place." This type of conversation was not easy for me to have—it always felt clunky, and my comfort level has only improved a little bit over the years. I believe in the purpose of a conversation such as this, which is to explore what memories feel meaningful to those who are grieving. This could have been an easier conversation among us if the kids had chosen me as their confidante, and if they had ever invited me to talk about their mom with them. Without that initiation, my broaching this conversation rings a bit insincere and forced. Even so, I've found it helpful to have a model of what to strive for, and I use parts of the model at times. For example, I can look at pictures of Brittany in her mom's wedding dress and comment that I feel happy for her and for that connection. I can imagine the raw smart of the loss both Brittany and Ian feel when another family member passes away, as I know it connects with their task of placing all of the deceased in their hearts and lives. Both kids have heard me acknowledge the hardship of these multiple losses. In the end, the beauty of this task is to help your family memorialize their loved one and make meaning of that person's life and death. Cathy's brother, sister, and mom worked very hard to convince our city to dedicate to Cathy a natural area that she had fought to preserve. Now her pictures, her story, and her name grace the signage at the natural area's trailheads. Cathy's family used this memorial act to make meaning of her life and their new lives without her.

Continuing bonds

During my research about grief and loss I learned from Aberle that while family members find places for the deceased in their current lives, it's also important that they find ways to continue the bonds with their loved ones. Around the time I learned about the concept of helping the kids carve out a dedicated place in their hearts for their mom, I also participated in a one-day artists' retreat at a local church. The retreat gave me the opportunity for uninterrupted creative work. I spent part of the time contemplating the kids' dilemma of losing their mom, and my own dilemma of not knowing how to help them. Some imagery took shape in my mind, and I spent the rest of the retreat getting that picture down on paper and writing a poem to go with it.

To an uninformed eye, the picture looked like a flower garden with rays of light coming down. Each piece of the picture held meaning to me. The entire scene represented our stepfamily. The rays of light represented Cathy's presence in our family. Of course light is not always present, but when it is, it's important to maximize, not block, the light. I decided that the stepparent role is the gardener, the person who weeds the garden and plants something new. No gardener would ever block the source of light for his or her new flowers, which represent the children. Nor would a gardener let weeds of selfishness and resentment take over the garden. Thus a gardener has to work hard to clear the weeds from the garden. The natural and surviving parent is the soil, the fertile base, the foundation for the garden. The soil is nurtured with the support that comes from water and other nutrients passed along through a variety of natural and manmade sources. Growing something new is the goal of the garden and the stepfamily.

Stepfamilies in Bloom

Clear the weeds
Plant the seeds
Embrace the light:

Watch what grows.
Cultivate the ground
Add water
Plant again.
You can't control the garden.
You can always
Clear the weeds
Embrace the light
and
Plant the seeds.
–DIANE INGRAM FROMME

With the garden analogy, I could visualize what the kids' continuing bond with their mom would look like. I knew that they would have to develop their own contexts for continuing bonds, but I did share this creative vision with Brian first, and then with them. Brian liked the analogy, and though I received a minimal reaction from the kids, I was content with having communicated that I was working on this process of embracing their mom's presence.

This exercise also helped me see Cathy's positive place in our family. I hoped I was modeling the "placement" task of mourning for the kids. Aberle leaned forward in her office chair and said, "Their mom is there, nurturing them every day. She's not giving them their peanut butter or going to PTA meetings, but she can be in their hearts in certain ways. And you're honoring that by being their stepmother in this way." My family garden seemed to be a concrete expression of the phrase, "Stepparents are the *and*, not the instead."

The theory of continuing bonds rejects Sigmund Freud's previous notion that we need to cut off our energy from the person who died in order to be healthy. Continuing bonds also underscores the teaching that we don't "get over" a loss. If we tell our stepkids to move on, it could be interpreted as "forget him or her and move on." This could result in alienating your stepchildren's feelings. As stepparents, we have to watch for the delicate balance between, on one hand, keeping the status quo and, on the other hand, moving forward. The healthiest strategy remains to encourage forward motion, in partnership with the natural parent and the presence of the deceased.

We stepparents can learn the facts about loss, grief, and mourning, but what is our role in pulling the family together to accomplish healthy grieving? How will we contribute to that goal? If you felt close to the deceased, you'll share a heart-level connection with family members' grieving, which will help you better understand and have compassion for their grieving. If you did not know the deceased well, your objectivity can serve family members as you remain detached but mindful of ways for them to work through the tasks of mourning. A stepparent may not be the children's confidante but can certainly be a catalyst for action or an organizer of events that the parenting team believes will help the family. Sharing ideas within our stepfamilies about how to support each other can move us to new levels of trust and communication.

REFLECTION PROMPTS

1. Choose one of the high-intensity losses in your own life. For example, this could be a loss from death, the breakup of an important personal or business relationship, or a hardship loss. What was your grief reaction to this loss at the time? How has your grieving changed over time?

2. Which traditional mourning rituals or expressions did you

experience in your family of origin or culture of origin? If none, what mourning rituals have you or could you establish in your own life? Would any of these bring meaning to stepfamily members' grieving?

POINTS TO REMEMBER

- Grief and mourning expressions vary from person to person, based on age, culture, upbringing, loss intensity, and other factors.
- Grieving does not occur in a right way or wrong way.
- A key guideline about grief is to face it.
- One good question to ask grieving family members is, "How is your way of grieving helping you find a place for your loved one?" For a younger child, ask, "After you have time to feel sad or angry about your loved one dying, do you feel better for a while?" Then, "What makes you feel sad again?" These are merely conversation starters.
- Stuffing grief, running from grief, and masking grief only postpones healing.
- Healthy grieving means addressing the four tasks of mourning: accepting the reality of the loss, making time to work through the pain, adjusting to a life and environment in which the deceased is missing, and relocating your loved one while also embarking on a new life.

SEVEN

Is Everyone Really "Fine?"

"No one ever told me that grief felt so like fear."
–C.S. LEWIS

Brittany: Ten years old
Ian: Eight years old
Years since their mom died: Four
Years since our remarriage: Two
Season: Fall

WHEN EVENING TEMPERATURES REQUIRED HEAVIER JACKETS AND *the golden leaves turned to brown, Cathy's death anniversary crept closer on the calendar. I knew enough about grief now to sense I should do something to honor her memory, or at least work with Brian to initiate a family remembrance. Brian and I brainstormed a bit, but he reminded me that the kids would have to agree with our ideas.*

Although I felt proud of my awareness to memorialize Cathy, the topic still seemed awkward to discuss with the kids. I didn't know what to suggest as a suitable memorial act and I felt shy to raise the subject when the kids seemed fine and the days rolled along. The demands of daily life took over as usual, leaving this conversation unfinished. November 16 dawned without any further discussions.

The anniversary date fell on a Saturday, which left us with the opportunity for more options of things to do and time to do them. I woke up that morning and worked through some ideas on my own. With a clear weather forecast for the day, I thought we could do something outside. I went out front and looked up into the overcast sky, as if searching for an answer from Cathy herself. Against the white backdrop, I visualized balloons traveling higher and higher until the sky swallowed them. A balloon release clicked with me. A ceremony like this represented something I could believe in and do.

Even my enthusiasm around this idea didn't grab Brian. He was likely going through his own grieving process and didn't want me dictating what to do. His slow ramp-up to mornings also made it difficult for him to commit to something this important this early in the day.

While the kids watched cartoons and played Legos, I asked them if they wanted to come with me to release balloons to remember their mom. They looked at me, blinking, and then looked at each other, perhaps waiting for the other to respond first.

All around, our lack of planning combined with the difficulty of the topic was not working in favor of doing something as a family. Brian jumped into the conversation and said that if they didn't want to go, it was okay and that he would take a walk with them.

With balloons entrenched in my head, I felt the familiar drive to action that shows up when I believe in an idea. I concluded that I needed to do this with or without Brian and the kids. I told them, "I'm going to think about your mom today while watching the balloons until I can't see them anymore." At that point, I didn't expect they would come with me. I figured they would opt for the time with their dad. Because of my new sense of mission for the morning, I held no grudge.

After picking out a multicolored balloon bouquet at the local Party America, I headed to Troutman Park just a few miles from our home. The *milky sky waited above, a contrasting backdrop to the forest green, silver, and light-blue orbs in my hand. Forest green connected with the earth, silver symbolized the proverbial cloud lining, and blue would be the color of the sky beyond today's clouds.*

I let go of all the balloons together, uttering the words "for you," and contemplating Cathy as they rose, spun, and drifted upwards. As they took their course, I added assurances:

"I'm helping take care of Brittany and Ian."

"Your kids are healthy."

"Your kids miss you."

I watched until I saw tiny dark dots against the greyish-white sky and then scanned and scanned until every dot was gone. Despite no one else joining me, I sought peace, reaching out to the kids' mom in spirit. Happy to have made the time to experience that connection, I didn't feel slighted or left out of the family's activities for the day.

Brian and the kids did go for a walk, on their own time. That afternoon we informally shared a few words about each of our experiences, but the kids were not comfortable or ready to talk about their feelings. No matter; I knew I had done what I needed to do that day.

I had helped myself recognize this anniversary, but the question remained: Could I and should I continue to help my family members grieve? Was there a "best way" to memorialize Cathy?

My experience on that Saturday captured many nuances of the challenges to navigating grief and loss in a stepfamily. I didn't want to ignore an important anniversary, but I also couldn't tell my stepkids how to grieve. As I faced memorializing their deceased parent's birth date and death date each year, I knew these days felt awkward to me—only slightly outdone by Mother's Day, which follows closely after Cathy's birthday and my birthday.

My awkwardness stemmed from:

1. Not knowing the person I was celebrating, and
2. Not knowing how to celebrate these days. What actions were sincere? Meaningful? Enough? Too much?

That year on the morning of November 16, the kids did seem fine. They engaged in activities they normally do on a Saturday morning. Why break the day's peace and stir the emotional pot by interjecting "forced grieving time"? It would have been easy to rationalize that it's better not to ask the family to engage in a remembrance. However, then I would have been enabling the family to skip over one of the tasks of mourning: to allow time to grieve.

Even Brian couldn't easily communicate with his own children about the significance of the anniversary. Brian struggled with ways to connect to his own grief. He had already committed to our new relationship, and neither of us understood the importance and timing of the grief work that could have been done before I joined the family. However, what was done was done, and we needed to find ways to move forward and help the kids continue their bonds with Cathy.

Creating memory-keeping opportunities

Over many years, setting up times to memorialize Cathy within our family got a little bit easier for all of us. From the time we figured out that anniversaries demanded attention until the kids were teens, we offered them choices of ideas. I have to admit that for the longest time we still didn't plan very well. We wished the kids would come to us with ideas, and when they didn't, we sometimes waited until the day of the anniversary to figure out how to honor that day.

Starting around ages sixteen or seventeen, Brittany and Ian accepted our suggestions, whether in the form of looking at pictures, bringing a small candle out to a family lunch, or placing the paper angel on top of the Christmas tree. However, they still didn't come to us with ideas of their own, so the memorialization continued to feel somewhat forced. Linked to the idea that you can't choose your stepchildren's role models, perhaps I, and even Brian, were not the right people to connect the kids to memories of their mom. If you feel this is true in your own stepfamily, look outward to the circle of love that surrounds your stepkids. Who, besides yourselves, could help them keep the memories going? Are your stepchildren starting to express their own ways of keeping connected with their loved ones?

During their young adult years, Brittany and Ian's styles of memorializing began to surface through putting up special pictures, visiting with Mom's relatives, Brittany trying on Mom's wedding dress, or Ian keeping a special baby blanket close. Cathy's relatives cultivated more memories, including having both kids spend the night in Cathy's "growing up" room, visiting a special memorial on their uncle's property, and discussing Mom in casual conversation.

With the kids living their own lives now, Brian and I aren't the initiators of any memorial acts but often light our own candles to recognize the anniversary dates or sometimes text the kids to check in on how they're doing. I hope they've continued to find private ways to celebrate that are truly meaningful to them.

Something I did learn along the way was to never take a child's statement, "You don't have to do anything," as bait to ignore memory keeping. I encourage you to let your stepkids know that you as a family choose to honor, in some visible way, the continued bond with their mom or dad. An internal clock is ticking in the subconscious during these anniversaries, and marking the date gives kids a way to integrate that ticking into the rhythm of their day.

What happens to people on anniversary dates? McBride, recalling her own mini-altar rituals to honor her parents, says that anniversary dates are "encoded in our brains, really at a cellular level ... they're like time-release capsules." Anniversaries link directly to a concept called re-grief, a word that says exactly what it means: a re-grieving of the loss. Sometimes we feel the encoded message physically in our bodies, feeling tired or achy, for example. Other times, we feel more emotional than usual, perhaps irritated, angry, or sad.

Never take a child's statement, "You don't have to do anything," as bait to ignore memory keeping.

It's also possible not to feel anything unusual or different on an anniversary date, but that definitely doesn't mean we've forgotten our loved one. The time release just didn't fire at those moments, or the brain's wiring didn't yet pick up on the anniversary messages. One morning on November 16, Ian was playing in our basement while Brian and I made breakfast upstairs. We hadn't yet made the time to head downstairs and connect with him about the anniversary. Cathy's mom called from New York and caught him cold, unaware of the anniversary date. She became very angry with Ian, an example of her own re-grief. Ian was placed on some sort of blacklist that day, and he suffered some emotional punishment and lowered self-esteem due to the withdrawal of favor from his grandmother. This incident went right into Ian's loss pot along with so many other losses over the years.

Fear and guilt can play right into a person's grieving experience. Fear shows up in a few ways. Not only do we worry that other loved ones will die, but we also fear losing memory of and connection with the deceased. The latter type of fear could have been dominating Ian's grandma's feelings on her daughter's death anniversary, and she was probably on edge when she initiated that phone call. Her fear and anger prompted a young boy to feel guilty for an anniversary he didn't mean to forget, and probably sparked new fears and guilt that he had indeed forgotten about his mom.

This story heightens the importance of our stepfamilies recognizing death and birth anniversaries in some way. As you read through this list, consider which celebration ideas would work well in your family:

- Light a candle that represents the loved one's presence and keep it burning as long as you are around the house that day.
- Write cards or letters to update the loved one about goings on in the kids' lives. Keep the letters, or burn them if that seems healing, or send them to a relative who would understand.
- For birthdays, take a birthday cake to a place that was special to the loved one. Hold the birthday ceremony with that person's presence there.
- As I did, release helium balloons to the heavens. Choose colors symbolizing something special to the deceased.
- Frame pictures of the loved one with his or her children. Give one to each child to keep.

- Go out to eat at the loved one's favorite restaurant, or cook a favorite recipe together.
- Put an empty chair and place setting at the table for special meals.
- Go around your table and share a favorite memory of the loved one. Stepparents who didn't know this person can learn more about him or her through the other family members' reflections.
- Plant something in your garden in honor of the deceased.
- Visit the grave or memorial site for the loved one. Bring something from your garden or another type of special decoration.
- Make a donation together to a charity or organization that is meaningful to the loved one.

Adam let Lily and her daughters figure out these celebration days. "The girls usually didn't go to school on their dad's death date, and the sisters went off to do something together," Adam said. "Sometimes Lily participated as well. It was a time for our daughter Muncie and me to do something on our own and the others to do something on their own."

I believe that this separated approach can work well as long as the stepparent and natural parent work together to determine that this is what the children prefer. When we stepparents still express caring and empathy, our stepchildren hopefully won't perceive our non-participation as a lack of interest. Perhaps they'll even be relieved that they can grieve openly with each other and with their natural parent, without the participation of the stepparent, whom to them remains an outsider to their grief.

My balloon experience reminded me that expressions of mourning must be individual. Even what Brian, as natural father, wanted to do in Cathy's honor might not have matched up to what an eight- and ten-year-old would find meaningful. Finding meaning seems to be the ultimate key to effective grieving—meaning in the memorializing actions and meaning in the timing of the actions. Only time and persistent communication will help peel away the layers of awkwardness around this topic so that your family members can discover how they can accomplish the "time to grieve" task of mourning.

Beyond anniversary commemorations, regular memory-keeping activities take memorializing one step further and help integrate the deceased mom or dad into daily family life. Giving the parent who died "a place" was another important task of mourning for those grieving a loss. We stepparents can help our families tackle this task by thinking through how to make the implicit (what's going on inside) explicit (visible).

Psychologist and author Mark Benn acknowledges that this technique will be difficult for most stepparents. "Of course it's hard. It seems like a personal affront," Benn said. I explained that it took me the longest time to understand why it was important to put up a picture of Cathy in our home. I finally did it one day when, rummaging around in the basement, I found a lovely framed picture of Cathy, Brittany, Ian, and their cousins—one I'd never seen before. I got the idea to put a picture of my baby daughter and me side-by-side in our main hallway with this portrait of Cathy and her kids. I liked the symmetry of the idea. As I was getting out the hammer, stud finder, and nails, Brittany came up from the basement into the hall. "I just thought I'd hang these pictures," I said to her. She disappeared into her main-floor bedroom and soon I heard her chattering on the phone. I believed she was excited.

"The reality is that Cathy's still there, with or without the picture. The picture helps make the implicit explicit," said Benn.

Besides pictures, what memorial elements could you consider to bring into your home setting? For example, you could find items sentimental to the deceased and make them visible in your home. One family I spoke to periodically rotated and displayed quilts in their home from their mom's collection. Helping the kids start a memory scrapbook could be another great family memory-keeping project. Or you could gift the kids the supplies, space, and know-how to begin, and then they can add to it when they find a special picture or want to journal about a special memory. Many scrapbooking kits have pockets for memorabilia as well—perfect if your stepchildren have concert tickets, greeting cards, or letters they want to keep and preserve in one place.

A question to always ask yourself is: What can I *sincerely* contribute toward honoring my stepchildren's loved one? What gifts can I offer toward that memory-keeping; what feels right to me? The answers will range from the ideas themselves, to the organization of resources, to full participation in the activity or event.

Additional examples of regular memory keeping include:

- Create a slide show or video using still photos.
- Organize a family athletic team and make a memorial competition shirt. Enter events together, such as local runs.
- Pray, alone or together as a family, for the parent who died.
- Document and share treasured advice from the loved one. Ask the kids, "What would your mom/dad say about that?"
- Cook a favorite recipe together.
- Finish a project that the parent who died started.
- Make a memory quilt or some other ongoing craft that builds on itself.
- Encourage the kids to write in a private journal, or older children may want to try a blog. The blog could be private or could encourage grieving children to connect with each other.
- Write letters to the person who died.
- Write poetry, prose, song lyrics, or music.
- Take a trip the loved one would have enjoyed.

By adding continual memory-keeping opportunities to your family mix, the birth and death anniversaries may not feel so big and awkward. Rather, those special days can become a natural progression of taking time to grieve and helping your family members find a place for the parent who died.

Age-appropriate ways to cope with grief and loss

Children process the concept of death differently depending on age and therefore differently during each phase of their lives. Psychologist Aberle advises giving accurate yet age-appropriate information about the death during each phase.

Ages four or younger

Before five, kids don't understand that death is irreversible. After five, children grow toward the concept that death is universal. Aberle said, "A four-year-old may have to ask eighteen times in one day, 'When is Mom coming back? Where is she?' The perception of how Mom died is not concrete. But at ages five through eight you have the thought that death does happen and that people don't come back."

Let's say the death occurred from a fatal car accident. Aberle advises that to a four-year-old you might say, "Mom died in an accident between two cars. This is something that hardly ever happens. People don't usually die until they are very, very old."

Possible interventions for grieving children under five include:

♦   Repeat your short, honest answers
♦   Provide lots of reassurance and nurturing
♦   Help kids maintain a consistent routine
♦   Create opportunities to play as an outlet for grief

Ages five through eight

At ages five through eight, the phenomenon of magical thinking can kick in, and children fantasize that they caused the death. Aberle said the script might go something like this: "I was bad. I didn't listen to him. He died because I didn't listen to him." Here's another magical thinking statement: "When she told me I couldn't have that toy, I got mad at her. She died because I was mad at her."

Kids also transfer their fear of death to the next closest adults in their worlds. The logic is, "Mom died, so you're going to die." I experienced this directly with Brittany when she was almost eight. About one month before Brian and I got married I got pneumonia. I was running a 105-degree fever and I couldn't get out of bed for a few days. When Brittany visited me on the second day, she climbed onto the bed and asked, "Are you going to die?"

My mother-in-law used to find out what Brittany and Ian worried about by getting down on the floor and playing with them. Whether the activity was Legos or Calico Critters, she found that the kids were more likely to talk to her when they were engaged in play.

I had noticed behaviors during ages five through eight that pointed to the kids' grieving. In our old house, I would sit in the main-floor master bedroom and read. The kids' tinny voices drifted down the hall as they played with Barbie and Ken.

"I want my mommy!" one doll would say.

"I want my REAL mommy!" the other doll would say.

Brittany brought home, from elementary school art class, beautiful collages and pictures of mommy and baby animals together, including one piece for which a child's art collector actually offered money. She declined and we put it up in our bedroom for the rest of her school-aged years.

Ian, an out-of-the-box thinker who had not yet mastered all the motor skills of his sturdy body, was occasionally bullied at school for his lack of coordination. The agitation from this loss of respect from his friends probably triggered some re-grief in Ian. In reaction, he would act out, fight back, and get in trouble with both school staff and soccer coaches. But then he would come home and calmly build amazing, intricate Lego worlds with multiple characters and levels.

For ages five through eight, the following strategies may help children grieve more effectively:

- Talk with the kids while they are engaged in quiet play
- Initiate symbolic play using drawings and stories
- Continue the child's regular physical outlets
- Encourage expression of a range of feelings
- Answer questions factually with an added level of detail for these ages
- Explain various ways to grieve and allow them to make choices

Ages nine through thirteen

Pre-teens understand that death is universal and irreversible. Pre-teens still have fear of death and need ongoing open discussion and reassurance. Kids nine through thirteen are thinking more concretely and can therefore handle more details in the description of circumstances leading to the death. With regard to the car accident, for example, describe how mom got projected from the vehicle and was found outside the car. Then a helicopter airlifted her to the nearest hospital where doctors tried to save her life but her blood oxygen level was too low to keep her heart and brain alive. Pre-teens (and teens) appreciate these types of facts surrounding an accident.

Supportive adults can help pre-teens too, with the following strategies:

♦   Reinforce that death is a natural part of life and give examples of various life cycles in our eco-systems
♦   Have patience
♦   Be available to listen, to talk, to nurture
♦   Encourage verbalization and self-expression
♦   Help children separate the facts from their feelings about the death
♦   Plan family activities as requested by the kids, within reason

Teens

For teens, death has a social dimension. Teens need to relate and connect death to other important aspects of their lives, such as relationships with peers, relationships and resources on social media, artistic expression (music, writing, fine art, performing art, etc.), and current views of spirituality. Teens need encouragement and healthy diversions so as not to cover up grief with chemicals, anger, bitterness, isolation, and other death-denying behaviors. Teens have the opportunity to learn more about themselves and their own feelings through their grieving experiences.

Pre-teen interventions also apply to teens. Additional support for teens includes:

♦   Ask what kind of support they would like from you
♦   Encourage teens to talk to each other within pairs or groups
♦   Provide reminders that denying death through risk-taking behaviors won't make grief go away
♦   Help teens find a creative outlet for grief and self-expression, such as painting, music, journaling, etc.

Adults

Adults may have the most difficult grieving process because they are not necessarily being encouraged to grieve like we encourage our children and stepchildren. Fear of death still applies when adults have lost someone close to them. Brian became ultra-sensitive to possible cancer-causing agents in our home environment and paid special attention to updating or installing radon and carbon monoxide detectors. Because Cathy got breast cancer, Brian made sure I was doing my self-examinations and that I started mammograms promptly at the age my doctor recommended.

Some time-tested strategies to help adults grieve include:

♦ Just be there for them—your loving presence may be in silence or through verbal or physical exchange of love

♦ Let your spouse talk about their loved one

♦ Ask about the fears you perceive they're displaying

♦ Let your spouse be angry or sad

♦ Provide the type of pampering your spouse desires

♦ Don't give up on your spouse

♦ Don't criticize the person who died

♦ Don't offer platitudes such as "she is in a better place"

♦ Engage professional help if severe grieving persists or if your spouse doesn't respond well to your assistance

Because teens and adults have the advantage of more developed abstract thinking than other ages, they may be able to see some of the gifts in loss. Helen Keller said, "… we would never learn to be brave and patient if there were only joy in the world." As a departure from the face and pace we maintain for the world around us, teens and adults may find beauty in being broken. Deeper discoveries about self, love, faith, humanity, priorities, and relationships can all occur during times of grief.

If we reach inside ourselves to once again connect with our own loss processes and what has helped us, we can bless others with our thoughtfulness. Author Hipp said, "By supporting someone else who's experiencing a loss or by taking good care of yourself as you grow through your loss, you are giving the world a gift. Because others are watching and learning

> As a departure from the face and pace we maintain for the world around us, teens and adults may find beauty in being broken. Deeper discoveries about self, love, faith, humanity, priorities, and relationships can all occur during times of grief.

from your experience, you are a teacher, and you're changing the world in small but important ways."

An angel's child faces special struggles

A deceased parent is often memorialized as perfect or sainted; he or she is an angel. A child who's lost a parent has no frame of reference anymore for what that angel wanted for them or expected from them. Kids feel a pressure to live up to imagined or fantasized desires that now cannot be clarified. Subconsciously, our stepchildren may feel they have to live up to that perfection. This self-imposed pressure stems from the circumstances that the kids do not see their deceased parent's greatness *and* foibles. "When someone is dead, you just don't say anything bad about them," said Adam.

McBride points out that having a deceased parent also magnifies loyalty issues. "With mom passing away, the kids never know if mom would have approved of the new mommy. 'Not knowing' factors into so many things about the way they grieve and the choices they make."

The angel dynamic conflicts with a child's knowledge that nobody is flawless. Marin pulled her fingers through her short, blonde hair as she reflected, "You know, the angel mother never did anything wrong and she was perfect. People who are well-meaning will say to the kids, 'Oh, you look so much like your mother, and you're wonderful and kind like her too.' That's an overwhelming legacy to live up to. It's not healthy to be told that you're just like someone else."

Adam saw the angel dynamic in his first marriage to a woman with children from her first marriage. The kids' natural dad was alive but in jail. "Here was someone not paying a dime of child support, beating his wife, and ending up in jail, yet the kids just thought he was the greatest. You just couldn't say anything negative about him," said Adam, shaking his head.

Author Hope Edelman said that after allowing a certain time period of memorializing, "It's best if family members can get some of the reality back into the picture to ground the kids and release them from this self-esteem trap." Otherwise, the internalization of unmet expectations may turn into the thought pattern, "If I can't be perfect, what's the point of being good at all?"

Kit saw this dynamic throughout Lana's high school years. Her eyes flashed as she told me the story. "All through high school she followed the wrong crowds. She had periods of lucidity where she really wanted to do good, and she would. Then, she'd go back off track with some drinking, and the promiscuity was awful, especially given the death of her mother combined with the rejection from her father," Kit said.

Adam walked a fine line when he felt tired of stepdaughter Laurel saying "I miss Daddy" whenever she wanted to be let off the hook for questionable behavior. "How long do you allow a child to say, 'I can't finish my homework or clean my room because I miss Daddy'? I don't know what the time limit is," said Adam. "I try to stay out of that and let Lily handle that, but it's difficult. A stepparent has to walk carefully. I finally said, 'We all understand that you miss your dad, but that's not an excuse for your behavior in this situation.'"

When Brittany at sixteen and seventeen was struggling with some of her own grief-denying behaviors, she and her dad went to some counseling sessions together. She declared to him, "I'm not my mom. I'm my own person." The child of an angel experiences a regular struggle to stay bonded with the deceased without letting the connections define them.

Allowing and encouraging re-grief

Re-grief demands additional examples because it's such a powerful factor in the moods and flow of grieving stepfamily life. You could feel as if your stepfamily has transitioned to the Middle Stages, past the Early Stages chaos and into the phase of sharpening good communication, when something will trigger a re-grief episode that feels like a setback.

Connecting with some of your own re-grief examples helps you better understand the re-grief episodes in your stepfamily. That understanding may allow you to feel compassionate instead of frustrated, for example, and may spur you to respond with empathy instead of focusing on the pain a setback can cause. Here are a few examples of re-grief from my own life. In hindsight, one was predictable and the other completely blindsided me.

My mom passed away when I was forty-seven. For ten years before her death, we enjoyed extra family time together when she moved to my city. I was also able to attend to her hospital bedside daily during the three weeks while she was ill and before she died. I mourned losing her before she passed, during the weeks leading up to her hospice care, and of course after her death. I grieved as I cleared out her house and possessions, responded to sympathy cards from friends and family, and wrote an essay about the difficulty of accepting an intense loss. As one year without her turned to several, the severity of the pain of the loss lessened. I knew she wanted me to go on with my life, so I did.

One year, in early September, I woke up with headaches a few days in a row. I felt a reduced appetite, irritated, and "off." I realized that the fifth of September is my mom's death anniversary. My body was remembering and re-grieving her death. That is a simple example of re-grief, one that is able to be forecasted—an important anniversary triggering big feelings. I just needed to make the connection with the anniversary date, and then I could decide how I wanted to observe the anniversary.

During that same year, fifteen-year-old daughter Amy showed a loss of interest in her treasured sport of eight years, and in the same period of time declared that she might not believe in any higher power. While I wasn't attached to her following, in a cookie-cutter fashion, the faith in which she had been raised—a faith which was also my mother's faith—the idea of her denying a higher power cut me to the core. A herd of big and illogical feelings stampeded right past my brain and into my heart. I felt despair, and failure as a mother, which led me to wonder if my mom felt the same way when I went through my rebellious teen days. This link to my mom led me to feel devastated that I couldn't talk to her about Amy *and* that I had put my mother through my own rebellious time … and piled pain upon guilt upon sorrow. With re-grief in full swing, I sobbed on and off for most of a day. I cried for all my losses, including the current loss from my daughter's declarations of her identity at the time. I could not have predicted that this re-grief would happen, or when. Additionally, I needed my spouse to listen to me that day—just to listen and not necessarily come up with any solutions. I needed to cry, talk it out, and have him hold me. The next day, I felt better.

Kit said that Lana re-grieved her father's rejection on every single one of her birthdays. "Lana would wait, wait, and wait for her dad's present to come, and it almost never came—sometimes cash or a check, but never a present, and never on time. The cards weren't even signed by him; they were signed by his girlfriend," Kit said. "Once, when we were walking into Sam's Club about two weeks after Lana's twelfth or thirteenth birthday, she said, 'Maybe my Dad's card will be there when we get home.' When I said 'Maybe, but let's not count on it,' she broke down in the parking lot and wept and wept for that."

Marin's sister passed away, leaving her children behind. "My niece was in a high school boarding school. When she had a crisis, the staff sometimes said, 'Your mother died six years ago. You should be over this.' And I think they just didn't get it. People just don't get how a grief experience is woven into your very being."

Please understand that your stepfamily members might hit some tripwire that spins them off into re-grief and their reactions may not seem logical. Your family members may not accept you being a part of their feelings-related work, yet they still need help. The rare amazing communicator can hint at what's going on during re-grief, but more likely it's a scenario where the person doesn't know what hit them.

One way to handle this situation is to tell them you are aware of the re-grief phenomenon and that you believe it's possible they are re-grieving their losses. Using this approach acknowledges that the grieving person is experiencing something monumental and out of the ordinary. Offer help and support, yet don't be surprised if they don't take it. Even if you are only the catalyst for your stepfamily member's awareness of their re-grief, what a gift you have given to them. Just hearing that someone was willing to help may be enough, or they may come to you later, or they may choose someone else to help them. Keep in mind that all the age-appropriate grief-support strategies described earlier in this chapter apply during re-grief, so be sure to utilize those that feel "natural" to you and your stepfamily member.

Despite having a heart to help, we stepparents may feel hurt and left out during family member spikes of re-grief. One fall, when Brittany was still in college, she contacted only her father for a few months. I don't know what caused that behavior to start or stop, but I remember thinking, "Here we go again." I had to regroup and steel myself through what seemed like a hiatus in our relationship. My strategy boiled down to being patient and letting her reach out when she was ready, which she eventually did. We stepparents must, if we're going to help others, find other ways to address our hurt when re-grief seems like a personal attack. Consider that your stepfamily member in re-grief likely hurts much deeper from loss of a loved one than you smart from the ego attack.

> Even if you are only the catalyst for your stepfamily member's awareness of their re-grief, what a gift you have given to them.

Is grief counseling necessary?

As discussed previously, our spouses are in a special grieving category, where they may have "moved on" to be with us and so did not address their grieving to the fullest extent. This may be a case where, in order to process grief in a healthy way, as opposed to stuffing it or lashing out, adults need to seek help with grieving. In my opinion, help can come in the form of counseling, conscientious self-study, or a support group.

The first step involves giving yourself permission to grieve. Men, especially, must buck gender stereotypes to allow themselves to process grief. This permission-giving can occur as part of a self-study program, or counseling may be needed to activate the grief process. In other words, awareness of the need to grieve becomes the initial focus of an effective self-study or grief counseling program. A support group, such as those offered by hospice organizations for those who have lost loved ones, can help draw out this awareness as well. Any of these three forms of suggested assistance can zero in on the specific strategies outlined earlier for grieving adults. The goal of any program will be to move an individual through the tasks of mourning:

- Accepting the reality of the loss
- Working through the pain of the grief
- Adjusting to life and an environment in which the deceased is missing
- Relocating the person within your current life while embarking on a new life

Those family members with a willing spirit, or at least the core knowledge of "I need some help," will find themselves well positioned to allow counseling discussions to take root. The same premise goes for self-study endeavors. If you and your loved one choose the self-study route, you'll find many grief-related books to explore. If you want to locate a grief-support organization near you, contact your local hospice provider or check out the list of organizations at the National Center for Grieving Children and Families, operated through the Dougy Center in Portland, Oregon.

What do I do when family members won't seek help?

What happens in a stepfamily when grieving loved ones don't want to seek help of any form? If a family member older than about fourteen is opposed to seeking help for their grieving, then any mandated help will be and feel forced and will likely not do its job. There are two life forces that motivate people to action: pleasure and pain. For example, pleasurable motivations in life might include feeling in love, wanting a raise, hoping for praise, winning a race, or meeting a goal. Painful motivations might be threats of any kind (such as the threat of a spouse leaving), loss of a job, hitting an extreme and distressing place in one's life, ruining a relationship, or chronic physical pain. Someone unwilling to currently receive help may have to wait until one of these powerful forces, or some other, becomes a motivator.

In an attempt to encourage a family member to seek help with grieving, it's important to avoid offering input such as, "*You* have a problem." Your willingness to partner with your family members speaks greater volumes. You can strongly encourage your spouse or teen stepchild to read a book, attend a class or workshop, or try counseling. It's possible that they will "do it for you" initially and then discover some truth that strikes at their core, which could motivate further exploration of feelings of grief. If the children's parent models this behavior, the children might follow. You could also offer to participate, showing your support at a deeper level.

Whether or not your stepchildren attend grief counseling is a decision their parent needs to make. If the parent is not creating a healthy grieving climate, it can result in heartache for you, or enough pain that you decide to take action. Here's a hopeful note: time and any combination of events could lead to a parent's or child's new threshold of pleasurable or painful motivation toward getting help.

Are the Kids Really Fine and What Do I Do?

The simple answer to the question, "Is everyone really fine?" is no. No one's feeling fine, especially if no one is addressing feelings of grief. Author Hipp said, "Consider the ocean's undertow. The surface of the ocean might look calm, but at the shore can be powerful below-the-surface currents ..."

Assume that your stepchildren are, in the big picture, always grieving. They are not grieving every single day, but reminders of the loss of their parent could come up at almost any time. Your spouse is probably also grieving. Neither your spouse nor his or her children are exempt from that task of mourning, which states, "Take time to grieve."

Special times to watch for include:

1. Anniversaries – the death date, the birth date of the deceased parent, and your marriage anniversary.

2. Holidays, or any time of year the deceased parent was a key part of traditions (an annual fundraiser, for example).

3. Mother's Day or Father's Day. Especially watch for Mother's Day in the elementary schools, where kids are making gifts and cards for their moms.

In an email dialogue with a concerned stepmother, I learned that she was stepparenting three elementary- and middle-school-aged children whose mother died several years earlier. Her husband worked a lot, which left her to be the primary parent most times of day, except evenings, when her husband was often too tired to deal with discipline issues. As great and caring as this stepmother was, those kids needed their daddy. They needed the surviving parent to be involved, especially with their discipline.

She mentioned that the two youngest (boys) seemed to be taking to her structure and boundary-setting well. Her stepdaughter at thirteen was a different story. The relationship was rough, further complicated by such early teen behaviors as eye rolling and verbally snapping back. After trading multiple messages, it seemed as if this stepdaughter did not have any females she looked up to in her life. Layered with having a busy dad, she was in a situation where she neither accepted love from the woman available to her in her home, nor received the support she needed from her father.

This astute stepmom, only married one year, also recognized that no one was talking about Mom. "It's almost as though the subject is taboo," this stepmom said. That statement carried a personal sting for me, as I knew our stepfamily had difficulty integrating Mom into our conversations in the early years. Thankfully, I didn't shut down references to Mom when they did come up.

The dad in this family believed everything was going "fine," both in the family and with his daughter. In fact, he was afraid that bringing up Mom would pitch his daughter back into the deep sadness he'd seen in the past. This is a common reaction from the surviving parent, be it blissful optimism, denial, or a protective mechanism.

My response to this stepmom was, "How could everything be fine when this girl has lost her mom?" Think about it. The bottom line is everything will be fine until it's not. Why not deal with the task of taking time to grieve now, while the kids are still relatively young? Why wait until later when the life stakes are higher?

I have been through, with my own stepkids, the phases of thinking, "They seem happy. Everything must be fine." It's so much easier and harmonious to do nothing, I know. But what experts recommend, and I can second from personal experience, is that it's healthier to help your grieving child chip away at the underlying hurt, which was no doubt bottled up inside this stepdaughter, not to mention her younger brothers who seemed even more "fine" than she did. This stepmom took some action in the form of seeking counseling for herself. I hoped she could take the time to gather some informed perspectives on stepfamily development and then find the courage to encourage some conversations about Mom and about the grief being experienced within her family.

What is a stepparent to do in a situation where no one wants to rock the boat? Open the door to talk. If your family members walk through the door toward you, continue. If they don't reach out to you, don't force it. Work behind the scenes to make sure they can reach out to someone: a relative, pastor, friend, teacher, mentor, etc. The kids can grow up better than "fine" if they have the support and encouragement of loving adults.

REFLECTION PROMPTS

1. Recall a time when you were supported through your grief. What helped you the most?
2. How can you adapt your knowledge and experiences to help your stepfamily members grieve?
3. Which memory-keeping ideas to honor the deceased are you most likely to try first?

POINTS TO REMEMBER

◆ Grief support techniques vary due to the age of the person grieving.
◆ Don't let death-date and birth-date anniversaries go by without some kind of recognition. Use the ideas provided to stimulate your own celebration ideas.
◆ Memory-keeping holds the highest healing value when activities are meaningful and sincere to those re-grieving their losses. Thus, invite your grieving family members to be involved with the creation of your family's memory-keeping activities.
◆ Make the implicit—what's on everyone's mind but is not said or seen—explicit in your home.
◆ Don't assume everyone is "fine."

EIGHT

A Heart for Differences

"The heart has its reasons which reason does not understand."
–JACQUES-BENIGNE BOSSUET

Brittany: Ten years old
Ian: Nine years old
Years since their mom died: Four-and-a-half
Years since our remarriage: Almost three
Season: Spring

AS SNOW PILES LIQUEFIED AND TREE BRANCHES *sprouted green fuzz, I felt a new surge of career-based motivation. I learned to facilitate several workforce courses from Wilson Learning, one being a fun, understandable behavioral and personality-style model. It occurred to me that our family might like to sample the program as well—it could be a great opportunity to reveal more about each other.*

I talked it up to the kids, who were actually curious about my new work. I suggested that we all do personality profiles, and to make it more fun I also offered that we should include our pets. The kids loved the idea that the animals would be part of the experience.

During the session, we sat around the kitchen table just like we did for our family meetings. I set up my flip-chart on the easel, and drew a four-quadrant matrix. I walked my family members through the profile process, asking everyone but the spotlighted character to answer the same set of pre-designed questions about that person or pet. At the end we'd decide on a behavior style for each and talk about the different needs of each style.

Our Australian Cattledog, Shayla, served as the perfect icebreaker. An unknowing participant, Shayla lay on the rug gnawing her Nylabone.

"What do we know about the way Shayla expresses her needs?" I asked. "Is she more assertive or more shy?"

We were referring to the dog that Brian and I had years ago nicknamed "Incorrigible."

"More assertive," the kids said.

Brian and I nodded in agreement.

"Oh yeah," said Ian, high fiving Brittany.

"Although there isn't a right answer, the fact that we all agree puts her clearly on the right side of this picture." I pointed to the matrix. "We call that behavior 'tell-assertive.'"

"Now, is Shayla more comfortable interacting with people, or do you think she's more comfortable executing her daily tasks by herself?" I asked.

"People," Brittany said. "She's always with us."

I gestured to the bottom right of the model. "That puts her down here. The intersection of tell-assertive and people-oriented is called an Expressive."

"But she can also go off for an hour and gnaw on a bone," Ian said.

"Right," I said. "Any style can and will exhibit traits of the other three styles at various times. The question is, which style is most common and most comfortable for Shayla?"

I felt that Ian was on-the-mark about Shayla; she was a people-oriented dog, but first and foremost, she found things to do to keep busy. Upon further discussion, we changed her profile to task-oriented and tell-assertive, the combination that defines a Driver.

That evening, the four different styles emerged, differentiated by each person's or pet's most comfortable way of navigating life. I made it clear that no style ranked any better than the others. I also challenged everyone to share something he or she liked about every style.

The results? The Drivers (Ian and Shayla) take charge, the Analyticals (Diane and Brittany) collect and act upon information and observations, the Expressives (White Sox the cat) thrive on attention and people energy, and the Amiables (Brian) try to keep harmony and peace among them all.

I felt so good that night after our family session. I taught the kids something new, they were interested, and they even aligned on most of their viewpoints despite their differences. We laughed at ourselves when being profiled and also listened to the highlights of each other's strengths. We learned about each other in a way that made each person think twice about relating to other people. Our session was a rare and delicious interlude, so different from some of the stresses we'd had in past years.

Following the predictions of the Stepfamily Cycle, daily life was becoming more about communication and relating, characteristic of the Middle Stages, and less about power struggles and surviving—throwbacks to the Early Stages. Day-to-day life yielded a more predictable rhythm than it did in the Early Stages.

Embarking on the personality exercises together reminded our stepfamily members that we approach life each in our own way. Stepmom Marin offered some examples of differences she noticed right away in her stepfamily. "Some lifestyle preferences came along with Grace and Kiefer. One simple example was food choices. I am more natural and whole wheat, and they were raised with convenience foods. Changing that is tricky—you can't come into a household and change everything. Even traditions like Christmas … it's hard to establish your own traditions without considering theirs," she said. "I also noticed that senses of humor were different; I'd think something was so funny, and they wouldn't get it."

I believe it's important to remember that *any* type of family (not just stepfamilies) will be challenged by the many levels of variety amongst its members: gender, personality, generational differences, chemical make-up and possible imbalances, preferences, views of the world, etc. The list goes on.

Stepfamilies have the additional layers of the Stepfamily Cycle to consider as the family members learn to live with each other. Re-grief will still surface from time to time, challenging the progress we're making through the various stages. I find it useful to view these phases as exceptions to the progress, rather than setbacks.

Identifying differences is one step toward developing an open heart. Other steps include demonstrating tolerance for those differences and developing compassion for every individual in the family. We can only embrace and control these additional outcomes for ourselves—we cannot force anyone in the family to be more compassionate, for example. Developing empathy, finding common ground, and calling out the good in your stepfamily provide a running start toward this healthy family goal of developing a heart for differences.

Developing empathy

Merriam-Webster defines empathy as "the feeling that you understand and share another person's experiences and emotions; the ability to share someone else's feelings." In order to acquire empathy, we have to be aware of and sensitive to our family members' feelings, thoughts, and experiences. Then we learn how to demonstrate empathy with our words and actions.

Sometimes empathy has to be taught to us by our family members. Marin said, "I was really mad at Rod and the kids one time and I remember saying, 'I'm stuck with you guys.' And I remember Rod saying, 'Well, we're stuck with you too!' And then I realized, *Ahh, it goes both ways.* I always thought it was all me—I'm the only one whose feelings are hurt here. And actually it does really hurt for them too." Marin explained what a shift in her stepfamily outlook she experienced that day.

Empathy requires removing the lenses through which you look at the world in order to try on someone else's view of life. You may have heard the phrase of Native American origin, "Don't judge a man until you have walked a mile in his shoes." That is one of the earliest descriptions of empathy. A more modern definition of empathy comes from a blog I subscribe to, *Meaningful Mama*:

EMPATHY is
Seeing with the Eyes of Another
Listening with the Ears of Another
And Feeling with the Heart of Another.

You can see why knowing a bit about "another's" personality style could help cross the bridge from intolerance to empathy. Because we can observe what others say and do, and how they speak and act, we can approximate their personality style. That style tells us something about how they see life, albeit just as a starting point.

Using the language from my Wilson Learning example, I'm more task-oriented and my husband is more people-oriented. I need to consider his style preference when working with him, or to help him when he's down. If I want him to discuss curfew guidelines with the kids, the last thing I should do is direct him or leave him a dry, written list of topics. I need to connect with him personally and explain my feelings about the curfews. I need to hear him out and sense his level of buy-in in order to see how on-board he is with my ideas, and which ideas he wants to contribute.

If Brian feels down, and I schedule "Help Brian" as a task on my list, he'll feel overlooked when all he wanted to do was turn to me when he's struggling. When I open my ears to listen first, and then communicate with him about the balance of what he needs and what's on my plate for the day, he feels like I care. I know I care either way, but staying rigid in my task-oriented style doesn't "get through" to him as an extension of my love.

Thinking ahead accompanies empathy. We plan or imagine the views of the other person before we act. This extra step of forethought and attempt to understand another person paves the way for compassion, which is a heartfelt awakening to the deep feelings another person may have. When you feel nervous during your child's performance, or you're moved to action by a cause, that's compassion. Compassion goes beyond a cognitive connection with another's situation; it's a natural "opening" of your heart toward feeling another person's joy or pain.

Compassion may or may not stir amongst your stepfamily members, so it's best to start by practicing empathy. I've used any and all of the following short scripts to help me empathize at-the-ready:

+ This person is different than I am.
+ There's not a "best way" to navigate the world; everyone finds their way.
+ This person is entitled to their views ... ask them what they're thinking and feeling.
+ If I impose my way or the highway, it represents intolerance.
+ Intolerance implies that I think I'm better than the other person.
+ If I want to achieve relationship with this person, I need to be versatile.

The word "versatile" in this case means flexible. In order to build relationships with people I need to work with, I flex my own style toward that person's style in order to make them more comfortable to relate to me, to contribute, or to help me.

Here is a personal example of applying versatility among all my family members by taking the four styles into account. To get projects accomplished in a household, a family sometimes acts like a little work unit. If I want to launch a spring cleaning project, I can't get this project done very effectively if I don't involve the whole family team.

+ With the Amiable style (people-oriented and questioning approach): I take time to relate and discuss my feelings about the state of the house. I ask for a team approach. I secure a commitment on the calendar so the project doesn't linger, or provide a countdown to action.
+ With the Analytical style (task-oriented and questioning approach): I approach the situation intellectually, using knowledge

and reason to describe consequences of clutter. I also make myself available to provide resources and/or work side-by-side with the individual.

◆ With the Expressive style (people-oriented and telling approach): I use humor, perhaps painting an absurd verbal picture of what our family room would look like if we never put things away. I appeal to the fun in working together. I also provide a countdown to action.

◆ With the Driver style (task-oriented and telling approach): I focus on the result of the project, such as "Clean in Five Simple Steps." I offer options of how to get the work done, so this person retains some say in the project progression. I allow this person to work independently.

Of course, versatility has to go both ways in a stepfamily. As kids mature, they can see their parents as multi-dimensional people with personal styles, not just as the flat roles of "mom" and "dad." Also, stepmothers in particular have a huge stereotype to overcome: the "wicked stepmother" we discussed earlier, who emanated from the stuff of fairy tales. This stereotype may have further developed from the tough character of stepmoms living through the war generations, when people suffered more losses and rough times, and probably had to toughen themselves up just to cope.

McBride shared her theory about the wicked stepmother. "Being domineering and aggressive may have been a way to overcome insecurity, and that style gave stepmothers a bad rap. Then, the stereotype was reinforced in movies where stepmothers boss their stepchildren and even plot to harm them." Your demonstrations of empathy can refute stereotypes like these.

Finding Common Ground Among Differences

In the early years of developing a relationship with Brittany, Shayla played an important role. Shayla was the intelligent, curious, and determined canine I brought into our stepfamily. She enjoyed playing games and going for walks, not to mention chewing on bones.

Until meeting me, Brittany had only owned cats and one dog when she was a toddler. That dog went to another good family when Ian was born. By eight years old, Brittany was fascinated by my stocky, black-and-tan pup who provided many hours of entertainment both inside and outside the house.

I can see why they enjoyed each other—both were as sharp as the Vermont white cheddar they munched for snacks or reward treats. I found it such a gift that Brittany and I both enjoyed animals, because that gave us something in common to break the relationship ice.

In a stepfamily, finding common ground can be trial and error. First of all, the ages of your children—if too young or too teen—can affect productive communication. Also, if the kids are traveling between two homes, you miss the time and exposure advantage that occurs when they live with you fulltime. More likely, the kids do live with you fulltime and you just haven't been a stepfamily long enough to feel comfortable trying a one-on-one relationship.

The bottom line is that finding common ground with your stepchildren is a logical step to having some kind of one-on-one relationship; one that stands without a third party or spouse as an intermediary. And whatever time it takes to build that relationship is really okay, as long as you're consciously putting in the effort.

Start with the status quo. Let your stepchildren become

accustomed to the rhythms and routines of their new lives. Look to them for cues about when and how to contribute what you know, as opposed to forcing your hand.

For example, what if you would like to take your relationship with your stepdaughter to a deeper level? Start with assessing where the relationship stands now. Is your stepdaughter coming to you with questions? What are the questions about? Or are you starting at square one, just hoping to jumpstart a relationship? What can you offer to the relationship that's helpful yet not intrusive?

In order to find common ground with your stepdaughter, possible areas to explore include:

School: How would she feel if you volunteer? If it's not cool or even possible to be in the classroom, you can still help with general school needs, such as newsletter mailings or media center/library volunteering.

Sports or hobbies: Do you have a specialty, especially one neither of her parents could claim; one that lines up with her interests? For example, a sport, a fine art, a craft, a foreign language, a scientific curiosity, or a domestic interest like cooking?

Spiritual beliefs: Do you share the same faith? If you don't, can you attend a variety of faith-based programs and learn together?

Recreation: Notice what she does when she hangs out. Does she read? Play games? Listen to music? Spend time on the computer? Do you have anything in common?

Pets: Would the whole family agree to choose and care for a pet together?

Looking back, canine care and obedience training was a topic with which I felt completely secure; something I knew well and could contribute to the new family. Luckily, Brittany was interested in these activities with Shayla and me.

Ian and I had less in common but occasionally stumbled upon some wacky thing we were both willing to do together, like indoor beach-ball volleyball during the winter. As long as I kept my sense of humor about side-outs we could play an entire tournament on a weekend.

Ian and I also shared a love of Chinese food, and we'd seek out Chinese restaurants in the various cities we visited. We'd compare hot-and-sour soups and lo mein dishes in the early days, until his palate graduated to even more sophisticated dishes. As a family, we even took a Chinese cooking lesson we bought from a silent auction, and for many years enjoyed making and consuming fried dumplings in the comfort of our own kitchen.

If you don't have anything in common with your new family members, let life run along. Eventually you'll dig up something to share.

Find the good

As we face the multitude of differences among the people we love and live with, developing a heart for differences helps us carve out relationships. Even knowing that, I needed some resources to help me when, despite my best intentions, my compassion allowance ran low. When I became too tired or too wrapped up in my own work and life issues to empathize with my kids, I lost sight of what I call "the good."

Before my stepchildren became young adults, we lived together full-time. The relationship tension was more frequently "edgy," as opposed to now that we don't live together under one roof. During times when my rope came undone, I think my stepkids often shouldered the impact. When I unraveled, I became humorless and controlling. Never insulting, I hope, but certainly autocratic.

In hindsight, I'm guessing that I wasn't employing enough self-care to rejuvenate the energy I needed to cope and respond with a lighter mood. Another strategy I could have used then was a model to help me reconnect with the good in the kids' behavior. A model, for example, like one I found later in the book, *Raising a Daughter*, by Jeanne and Don Elium. I feel this strategy applies to raising a son as well. The authors recommend we "name

the positive intent" in our children's behavior. What is the positive possibility that lies within the immature behavior you find so irritating? If you could jump ahead twenty-five years, what life skill would have grown out of your child's current actions?

The Eliums put together a chart of some immature behaviors and their possible mature form. Think of this as a puzzle to solve. One way to start the puzzle is to name the behavior (for example, talking back) and then think about what could blossom when the child is older (boldness, willingness to speak up).

Here are a handful of their examples:

Immature Form	Possible Mature Form (Positive Intent)
Temper Tantrums	Self-Assertion
Whining	Compassion
Pouting	Thoughtfulness
Laziness	Rich Inner Life
Stinginess	Conservation
Aloofness	Independence
Bossiness	Leadership Abilities
Pickiness	Discernment
Giddiness	Zest for Life
Moodiness	Inner Searching
Secretive Ways	Healthy Privacy and Boundaries
Conforming	Team Player

Because I had a tendency to get autocratic, I looked for ways to change my autocratic responses to responses that assumed the child's positive intent. Here are a few to consider:

Child: I don't want to clean up my room.

Autocratic response: You march in there right now, young lady, and don't come out until it's finished.

Positive intent response: You don't like it when I tell you what to do. You'd rather organize your own time.

Does the positive intent mean the child gets away without cleaning the room? No. But it gives you a more communicative entry point by recognizing that the kid is not a problem with legs—the kid is a person.

Child: I'm never sitting by Lila at lunch again!

Autocratic response: It's not nice to say things like that about your friends.

Positive intent response: It sounds like Lila might have annoyed or hurt you. Let's talk about it.

By naming some possible young feelings, this positive intent response engages the young person and hopefully gets them talking to you.

This next example pertains to teens.

Child: I'm going to hang out with my friends on New Year's Eve.

Autocratic response: What! There you go trying to break up an important family holiday again.

Positive intent response: You have a group of friends you really enjoy, and you'd like to spend time with them. We want to spend this holiday time with you too. Let's figure out how we might be able to do both.

Our abilities to recognize positive intent won't happen overnight, but positive intent certainly is a step toward helping us refocus on the person instead of the problem behavior. Maybe a little positive intent from you will help your stepchildren see you as a person too.

While Brittany attended college, we were fortunate enough to have her close to home. One evening she dropped by for a visit, quite animated and wanting to share something she'd learned.

"I took the True Colors quiz and, oh my gosh, it's so accurate!" she said. One of her classes included a personality quiz, and a discussion of the results as well as the True Colors four personality types.

"Dad is so blue, I knew it! And he's just like Chris." Brittany referred to a former boyfriend.

"You're gold," she said to me. "Like Kayla." Kayla was Brittany's current roommate. I enjoyed this news; Brittany liked Kayla a lot.

"What color are you?" I asked.

"Green—that fits," she said. She handed off the descriptions of all four styles. The only one she hadn't yet mentioned was orange, as no one in our immediate circle matched that profile.

I felt excited about how much this newfound knowledge meant to Brittany, driving her to share the results with us. The seeds planted in our Middle Stages discussions of behavioral style had taken root and sprouted a connection to something she could apply toward developing a heart for differences in her young adult life.

REFLECTION PROMPTS

1. In the resource section, you'll find several suggested personality quizzes you can access online. If you haven't done this type of exercise with your stepfamily members, which of these would you be most likely to try? Are there any that your stepchildren have already been exposed to at school?

2. In the big scheme of your stepfamily development, how much of the conflict comes down to differences among family member styles, make-up, and preferences?

3. Which strategies will you try first to develop a heart for differences in your family?

POINTS TO REMEMBER

- All families can learn to identify and cope with differences among family member styles and preferences.
- Families that understand and practice a versatile approach to family projects may gain more family cooperation.
- Practice with tolerance-building statements like empathy and positive intent can mature into real compassion among family members.
- Strive to find the good and find common ground in your stepfamily.
- We can't force our family members to have open hearts, but we'll enjoy our relationships more when we engage our own hearts.

NINE

Straight Talk
and Honest Communication

"Honesty is the first chapter in the book of wisdom."
–THOMAS JEFFERSON

Brittany: Twelve years old
Ian: Almost eleven years old
Years since their mom died: Six
Years since our remarriage: Four-and-a-half
Season: Winter

IT COULDN'T HAVE BEEN A MORE PERFECT day at the beach. Our family took a late-winter vacation, basking in the sun in bathing suits while friends home in Colorado waddled around in heavy coats. Globelike clouds floated across a startling blue sky. Seagulls glided and cawed overhead while Brittany and Ian strolled ankle-deep in the water, looking for shells.

I focused on Brittany as the breeze pushed back her dark blonde hair and the bright sun glowed off her skin. I plunged my hand into the beach bag for my camera. At twelve, she was fast developing the curves typical of a young woman, and I felt that if I didn't capture this blossoming moment I would lose it forever.

The vacation was as idyllic as it sounds. To top it off, by the fifth day I harbored a delicious bit of knowledge. I was late menstruating ... just barely, but most definitely late. In whispered tones, I shared daily updates with Brian at our hotel.

I remember how, several times over the years, we'd talked with the kids about the possibility of a new baby in the family. We'd asked them how they felt about it, and different conversations brought up a variety of thoughts and reactions. The words ranged from, "It'd better be a boy," (Ian) to "Will I have to share my room with the baby?" (Brittany). My desire to have a baby had never been a secret, and we had given them plenty of opportunities to ask questions.

But nearly five years had gone by and no baby had been conceived. As I approached thirty-six, Brian reminded me that my mother didn't birth me until she was thirty-six.

The blissful vacation came to an end. As soon as we set down our bags at home, I jumped back in the car to raid the early-pregnancy-test section of my local pharmacy. I surveyed the selection of boxes and descriptions. One line, two lines, pink lines, blue lines ... how does a woman choose a test stick?

Meanwhile, Brian felt nervous. It's one thing to agree to start over and entirely another to do it. When we'd started trying to conceive, Brittany and Ian were in early elementary school; now they were almost in junior high and relatively independent. Brian wondered, "Am I stepping backwards?"

Nerves notwithstanding, the pregnancy test was positive. Despite his contemplations about timing, Brian scooped me up in a huge hug. We wanted to proclaim baby construction a go in the Fromme household. The decision at hand was when and how to spill the news to Brittany and Ian. I didn't see any point to waiting until I was farther along to tell the kids. I wanted to share interesting baby developments with them along the way. For example, what if I had morning sickness and couldn't come down to help with breakfast? What would I say about the increased number of doctor's appointments? We decided to tell the kids at our next regular family meeting.

In preparation for serving ice cream at the meeting, I set a fifth bowl and spoon at the table to see if either of them noticed. Not one to miss much, Brittany guessed the surprise right away, and Ian acted as if he knew. Had they overheard our conversations at the hotel?

Regardless, the family meeting gave us time and structure to talk about the new addition. Pregnant for the first time, I had no idea of the emotions a new baby would stir in all of us down the road. Thus the discussions at this family meeting focused on logistics. Where would the nursery go? (Brittany was excited to switch bedrooms and occupy the front office with the bay window.) What would we name the little one? (We threw out lots of options, but Brian and I were not ready to decide.)

The meeting ended in laughter when Brittany asked, "Who'll watch the baby when you guys go out?" We sat in total silence for many seconds until Ian suddenly backed away from the table chanting, "Not me, not me!"

By handling the larger-than-life topic of a new baby straight from the beginning, the *idea* of a new baby in our family was not a surprise or inconvenience. Family meetings remained a good forum to talk about baby realities as they developed, and of course there were many. I think we devoted one whole meeting to how a crying baby affected each member of the household.

By making a time and a place for this kind of straight talk, every stepfamily can benefit. Communication shapes our ability to sustain our stepparenting skills by deepening our relationships with clarity and honesty about important family topics.

Willing Attitude
Acceptance
Stepfamily Education
Sustainable Stepparenting
Communication
Support
Grief Education

Effective communication is a way to reach out and show you care. Remind family members that although straight-talk conversations can be difficult, they are a sign of a family who cares for one another. Expressing our feelings is essential to loving relationships.

Another aspect of maintaining healthy communication involves humor. A good sense of humor can go a long way to break the ice in challenging conversations. However, humor should be used as a strategy, not a substitute, for getting to the heart of issues.

For example, how would you react to a five-year-old who calls you a "poopyhead" for telling him to eat his vegetables? Would you:

a. Demand an immediate apology

b. Put the child in time-out

c. Give him a spanking

d. Say "Shhh! You can't tell anyone my secret name!"

Gina Shaw, who wrote the article "The Lighter Side of Parenting" for WebMD, said that answer "d." breaks the tension with silliness and helps you form a bond with the child.

With older children, you can try other forms of humor including:

- Exaggerate the situation using well-known literary or movie situations. For example: "At least you don't top Adam Trask in *East of Eden* regarding your ex's behavior after a breakup!" (His ex attacked him and tore his shoulder.)

- Accomplish a task with reverse psychology: "Whatever you do, don't let me catch you smiling today."

- Create a game to get what you want accomplished, such as, "Anyone who finds the most undone chores and completes them gets to choose where we eat dinner tonight."

- Suddenly use another voice or accent, or declare that the next few hours are "English accent only" or "Pig Latin only."

- Make requests via social media, using funny memes or emojis.

When it's difficult to make honest communication fun, you can at least recognize your family's efforts. One family plunked "communication coins" into a jar every time someone used candid statements to navigate through a fog of bad feelings. The fund became available for family or one-on-one outings.

The challenge of honest communication

Honest communication in your stepfamily can be difficult, but it is possible. Without it, good intentions wither into dried-up habits rather than ripen into fruition. When you build straight talk into your family repertoire, no subject should be taboo: whose turn it is to clean toilets, why Mom or Dad is so annoyed by crumbs on the counter, celebrations of what's going well in the new family, what family members miss most about the parent who died, and everything in between.

Honesty around such bigger issues as fallout from the parent's death can surface when you least expect it. I noticed that many candid statements burst forth from the mouths of my stepchildren while we drove from place to place—home to school, school to football, home to ice skating. Perhaps the vehicular motion and occasional potholes rattled loose the truth.

For example, one day on the way home from the ice rink, Brittany wondered, "What will a new baby call you? We call you Diane." I explained why our child would naturally call me Mom. She replied succinctly, "I'll probably never call you Mom."

Ian's concerns on these rides were different. "If you and Dad split up because he's unhappy, I'll go live with Dad," he said once, seemingly out of the blue.

Belying the feeling of someone churning my insides into butter, my immediate response to their statements was always something like, "It's more complicated than that," or "That's certainly your choice." What I really wanted to say was, "That hurts my feelings," or "You have no idea what you're saying!" But how can you ding a kid for being honest? How can you think fast and reply with the appropriate amount of truthfulness?

Talk about what you see

What doesn't get said or expressed in your stepfamily relationships will linger. Christy Borgeld, founder of National Stepfamily Day and Week, said in an article on this organization's website,* "Holding everything inside will only result in your stomach keeping score." While you don't have to point and counterpoint everything anyone in your stepfamily says to you at the exact moment they say it, it is important to find a time to explain how certain behaviors or actions made you feel.

Re-grief can trigger raw honesty. Sometimes this honesty wears a mask of criticism. For example, on the drive home from high school on one of Cathy's death-date anniversaries, the time when Ian said, "You just married my dad to have a baby," I used straight talk to jump to the root issue. I was somewhat prepared for anything that day, having experienced ten of these anniversaries so far.

"I know you may not believe me, but I'm truly sorry your mom is gone," I said softly. "I know life would have been easier for you if she hadn't died."

"Fair enough," he replied.

I also told Ian that I knew his statement simply wasn't true in my world. I encouraged him to talk to his dad about why Brian thought we got married. Later, I went to Brian, told him what had transpired, and nudged him to seek out his son. Brian later reported that they did talk, with no major change in Ian's attitude. We didn't think to create the opportunity for the three of us to discuss explicitly why anniversaries trigger re-grief. In hindsight, that would have been an outstanding example of straight talk.

As you experience communication challenges like these, you might keep a journal. Ask yourself, "What behaviors or statements can I let go? Which are really worth discussing with family members?" Observe your family's behaviors and take notes on what you see and what you hear. To balance your perspective, ask your spouse to give you the same type of feedback about your own behavior.

In the highest functioning stepfamilies, members talk about what is

---

* http://www.nationalstepfamilydayandweek.com/

seen but not heard. What is not being spoken that needs to be? According to psychologist Benn, "When the issue is on the table, then maybe we can do something about it." Benn acknowledged that most emotions start in cognition. "We have a notion in our culture that just because we are aware of something, it will change the way we feel. But it doesn't ... we still feel the same. So talk about what you see."

One common communication challenge in grieving stepfamilies is that the kids may not let themselves get too close to the stepparent. The conflicts that spring from loyalty to the deceased parent feel too risky, or the children may be slow to develop trust in the stepparent. Thus, communication may feel stilted or unfinished due to what remains unspoken.

How do I put my thoughts about puzzling or hurtful distancing behavior "on the table"? I verbalize them. For example, I tell young adult Brittany, "It seems that every time I feel I get close to you, you suddenly start communicating only with Dad." Now I've spoken. I'm not stewing over this alone in my bedroom.

"You may get no response right now," Benn said, "but then the next time she pulls back, maybe since it's been put on the table, she might say to herself, 'Oh, I'm doing this again. Maybe I don't really want to do this. Maybe this is impacting my relationship.'" Possibly her realization will progress to an interactive conversation with me, or maybe that particular behavior will stop.

Adam used straight talk to diffuse the entire loyalty conflict for his stepdaughters. He said, "When the girls' father died, I had a talk with them. I said, 'I can't fill the shoes of your father, and I'm not going to try to be your father, but I'm here to support you.'"

Adam put himself in a position to have the girls seek him out when they needed him. I, on the other hand, spent a lot of time and energy attempting to engage Brittany and Ian in family togetherness. Now that Brittany and Ian have left the house and live on their own, I feel more freedom to let them call the shots with me. I've relaxed the "lead" part of the dance among us. By the same token, I don't want them to think or feel that I don't care. I do care about them very much; however, all the wisdom I've gathered from counselors, authors, and experienced stepparents advises letting relationships with the adult children be more of a two-way street. Putting thoughts on the table about my new way of relating with the kids might look like this: "How do you feel when I call you? Do you feel like it's enough? Too much?" or "When I contact you, do you feel like you have to respond, or do you feel like you have to take care of me? How often would you like to see each other? Help me know what's best for you."

Benn said, "We teach people how to treat us. If I'm doing something to you in the relationship that you don't like, and you let me keep doing it, then I'm flunking a test I didn't even know I was taking. So I'd rather you tell me you don't like that behavior, to honor our relationship. I believe in honesty and genuine relating over faux harmony any day."

I've always been a very honest person, and yet I just cannot bring myself to have this "to the mat" conversation with either Brittany or Ian. I prefer to extend myself when my heart moves to do so, and I accept the situation if they don't reply. The good news is, usually they do reply, and we do see each other on a semi-regular basis.

Benn advises that we stepparents act in ways that are the most honest for us. Maybe someday I'll feel moved to ask some of the harder relationship questions that will take our family to a new level. Those questions might include:

- What was your best memory of having me as your stepmom?
- What was the most challenging part of having me as your stepmom?
- Do I need to know anything that's still bothering you … that maybe is still feeling unresolved?
- If not, do you have someone you can talk to about our history?
- Where do you think our family goes from here?
- What role would you like your father to play?
- What role would you like me to play?

How to talk

The hardest part of changing or building a straight-talk communication habit is getting started. It's a bit like learning to ski beyond the bunny hill. You may feel terrified to make that first turn on a run that seems too steep. But if you put 110% attention and effort into making the first turn, the next turn seems less scary. And, of course, the more turns you practice, the easier skiing becomes.

The most important guiding principles for sharing stepfamily issues are sincerity and clarity. But what do these terms really mean? One of author Sue Thoele's twenty guidelines for stepmothers is "communicate clearly and truthfully from the heart." Sincere communication does not come from a place of wanting to control but rather from a place of seeking and expressing your truth. Keep in mind that the process of expressing your truth may not feel very good in the moment. It's the end result—after baring your souls and wrestling through the process of understanding each other—that helps family members break through to deeper relationships. Remember, too, that task-oriented personality styles might not relate to this baring of the heart as well as people-oriented styles. Task-oriented styles may seek and express truth first by stating the facts and sharing thoughts about that information, then warming up to processing feelings.

Clarity, or communicating clearly and thoroughly, is a catalyst for positive behavior in the family. Without clarity, messages can be mixed or vague. Communicating clearly involves saying what you mean and checking for understanding. For example, if you've just explained a new weekend curfew to your teenage stepdaughter, you could say, "Tell me what you heard so that I know I communicated clearly." Or you might say, "I want to make sure we're on the same page, so would you please explain the new curfew back to me?" Share all the details necessary to assist the other person's understanding of the topic.

Circumstances in a grieving stepfamily can provide ample opportunity to engage in these honest communication techniques. When Brittany was fifteen, we got into a difficult verbal exchange about a boyfriend. This conversation occurred on the anniversary of her mother's birthday, which falls just two weeks before Mother's Day. As a high school sophomore, she dated a high school graduate. I surprised myself by boldly telling her why I thought he wasn't right for her. That initial interaction served as a kindling pile.

As recently as weeks before this interaction, I had asked Brian what Cathy would have thought of the age difference. He felt that she wouldn't have approved. Motivated by the anniversary date, I told Brittany that in the spirit of her mother, who would want what was best for her, Cathy wouldn't approve of her dating this boy. This was the first time I'd been able to bring myself to say something this direct about her mother. I took a risk, knowing that honest communication isn't always easy. My words fanned the kindling into a full-blown fire, a blow-up that was necessary for Brittany to get to the heart of what she wanted to say. Brittany informed me quite clearly that she couldn't have this conversation with me. I called her out of her bedroom to the kitchen table and listened.

"Why can't we talk about this?"

"I just don't feel that you're a mother to me, in my heart," she said.

Rather than letting those wounding words shut me down, I recognized that Brittany was taking a communication risk as well, and encouraged her to speak what she'd never spoken before.

"This is really important," I said. "Tell me more."

Perhaps these feelings had been cooking from the very beginning, for seven or eight years. I told her that it was really crucial to her health that she express how she felt, so we could both move on and develop a better relationship without feeling hurt or guilt. I was able to share with her how having a baby had given me insight around how she must feel without her mom to guide her.

After that conversation, I felt that my relationship with Brittany improved for a while, until the next set of developmental bumps brought up new issues to work through. Though the stepparent does not always have to dive into every deep conversation, this particular one was critical to developing a relationship with Brittany.

What to do when it's too difficult to talk

Given that clear and sincere communication isn't always easy, do you ever feel it takes too much effort to say what you mean? Can you imagine that sometimes your stepfamily members feel the same way? Saying what *needs* to be said may not feel natural or sincere. One self-help strategy is to identify non-verbal ways to show what does feel sincere. Then our actions serve as our straight-talk.

For example, while I didn't always have the emotional energy to seek out deep conversations with Brittany and Ian, I loved to keep up with their activities. I was excited to see many of Brittany's ice skating and horse competitions, junior high band concerts, and high school swim meets. I made almost every one and felt nervous and excited for her when she competed. I felt the same positive anticipation about attending Ian's football games or watching him study the instrument-panel controls prior to his aviation club's rocket missions. To see them growing up and participating in these activities made me proud. I was not their birth mother, but I hoped that my willingness to be so actively involved in their lives communicated to Brittany and Ian that I cared.

When stepfather Adam is not comfortable going head-to-head on stepfamily issues, he acts as what he calls "a bridge for communication" between the surviving parent and child. "When Lily and one of her girls are having difficulties communicating, I need to jump in and get things going again," he said.

He shared an example of what happened after Lily and her young adult daughter Rachel, who had come to visit for a few hours, had an argument. Lily had gone outside to their garden to work out her frustrations by hand-cultivating a flower bed. Rachel stayed inside. Adam knew that Lily wouldn't want to leave that conversation unfinished, but Rachel wasn't going outside. As stepparent, Adam didn't want to confront Rachel directly and tell her what to do. But he could talk with Lily. "After a while, I went out to Lily and told her to quit doing yardwork and get in there and talk to her daughter," Adam said. When Lily protested that Rachel hadn't come to seek her out, Adam strongly encouraged her to be the one to take the first step. By doing so, Adam gave Lily the strength to follow through, yet he didn't have to face Rachel himself.

Another self-help strategy is for the stepparent to enlist help from the surviving parent. In our family, I asked for Brian's help as family conversations continued about having a younger sister in the house. I had begun to realize how my bond with Amy was different than the one I had with the other kids—more instinctive and natural. I didn't care any less for Brittany and Ian, but the bond with Amy felt deeper. I then had an epiphany: Of course Brittany and Ian also couldn't feel the same way about me as they felt about their mom. Yet, despite my awakening, I couldn't bring myself to share these realizations fully with them. I asked for Brian's help, and we decided it was more important for Brian to tell his children that having a new family member did not mean *he* loved them any less. That way he could validate his love with positive straight talk, while I could validate mine with physical presence. I made a point to continue watching them at their activities. Until they were older teens and out of the house more often, I maintained the same quality and quantity of stable presence in our home.

What to do when your kids won't talk

All parents, not just stepparents, have stories to tell about that one child who just won't talk to them. Some personality styles prefer to navigate through many of their thoughts and feelings privately. Or parents may just be encountering a non-communicative phase. In these situations you have to strike a delicate balance. Letting children handle everything solo leaves them drowning in their thoughts and feelings, and can be viewed by children as lack of caring. Meanwhile, too much pressure from you to reveal what is going on can be perceived as nagging, then backfire to the point where you'll get less communication than you did before.

You can sample and rotate through the following five straight-talk strategies to draw out your stepchild and hopefully discover a few connections that seem the most comfortable. Share these techniques with your spouse to reinforce that he or she will often be the main communicator with his or her children.

◆ **Create chat havens.** Notice where your stepchild seems to be comfortable hanging out and become part of that environment. A younger child might like to build forts, for example. Figure out a way to play with the child in the fort. Once relaxed and engaged with you, your stepchild may answer your questions more readily and even bring up some of his or her own. An older child might really love to sketch and draw. Go to a coffee shop or gallery that has some fascinating artwork and chat while you're strolling.

◆ **Direct conversations by naming feelings.** Sometimes you can release tension by offering another person a description of how you perceive their emotional state at that moment. You might say, "You seem a little angry today. Is there anything I can do to help?" Be aware that this communication technique makes some people even more upset. But then you may get the *real* feeling stated in their blowback: "Oh, you think I'm angry? You don't know anything! Try violated! That's what I'm feeling right now ... completely violated."

◆ **Observe behaviors.** State factually and unemotionally something you saw or heard. Separating the facts from the feelings can de-electrify the conversation. Here's an example: "Honey, I saw you pull a bench across the hall just as Katie was coming around the corner toward it, which caused her to ram into it with her shin. What was going on?" In response to your observation, most children will immediately elaborate on why they acted that way. "Katie took my favorite book and stashed it in her room earlier today. I was just trying to ambush her to get it back." Then you can ask more questions about how the child handled this situation and suggest other ways to get the book back.

◆ **Ask open-ended questions.** It's very easy to get caught up in a circle of yes or no questions and then feel like you barely had a conversation at all. Open-ended questions can't be answered logically with a simple "yes" or "no." As kids get into their teen years, it's important that these questions don't feel like an interrogation. Weave questions into the rhythms of daily life—while cooking dinner, during a shopping trip, while walking the dog, etc.

- **Express their value.** Since kids and adults fundamentally want to be appreciated, give the person a quick reminder that their thoughts and feelings are important to you. You might say, "Hey, I just want you to know that I wouldn't ask if I didn't care about you."

One goal of straightforward communication is to reach out and show caring. Another is to plant seeds of wisdom for the children's consideration. You may not get a response every time, or even half the time. But if your mission becomes strictly to force family members to talk, the push may be just enough to seal their silence for a longer period of time. One place to avoid the invitation to straight talk is during family meals. The risk of saving up a bucket-load of questions for mealtimes is that kids might then make a negative association with eating meals together. In general, mealtime should be a time of light conversation—reinforcing that meals together are intended to be enjoyed with one another.

If your stepchildren just won't talk to you or the natural parent, you both can reassure them that you're there if they need you. Tell them you really mean that, and hopefully whatever is blocking them from communicating will dissolve over time.

Marin, who has been involved with her now adult stepchildren since they were very young, offers some hope: "Things have really evolved. It took time and patience. I remember when Grace had a dog show in Austin and I went with her. After many years of spotty interaction, it was really neat to just have time alone with her and be friends."

How to listen

Listening skills can be your life vest in the stepfamily ocean. Learn to be patient and listen with your ears, not your mouth. That means you listen for understanding rather than interrupting or listening for the points upon which you will build your next comeback.

When it's your turn to speak, you might even take an additional minute to validate what you heard before you share your views or perspective: "What I heard you say was (fill in the speaker's words and not your own paraphrase). Is that accurate?" For example, "What I heard you say was that you would get ready for the dance at Melissa's and then come back to our house at 3:30 p.m. Is that right?" This approach provides family members the opportunity to say "yes" or "no," and elaborate further if the answer is "no." Perhaps they didn't even realize that wasn't what they meant to say, until you pointed out what you heard.

With children, be prepared for them to say, "That's not what I said!" Don't get dragged down into the argument. Just move them right on to, "What did you say, then?" which gives them another chance to express their ideas. When I miss or misinterpret what my kids have said, I sometimes use humor with a joke about my age or my memory.

Thoele calls these skills "heart listening." Kit confirms that heart listening was a key stepparent-stepdaughter strategy. When Lana got frustrated or angry, Kit would hear out her opinion. Kit wouldn't always agree with Lana's opinion, but she would listen and repeat back what she thought she had heard from Lana. That type of exchange helped both stepmother and stepdaughter communicate clearly.

Empathy also plays a part in listening skills. Kit said, "I would let Lana voice her opinion on everything. I would listen and say things like, 'Yes, I know having an 11:00 curfew really stinks. But let's just do it this way right now, and as things change and you get older we can talk again.' Lana told me later that it really helped her when I would say 'that stinks.' I would say it a lot about her mom: 'That really stinks that your mom died. That was just a rotten deal.'"

A brief empathetic statement like Kit's can encourage kids to keep listening or keep talking.

The Power of Family Meetings

Zero communication is the worst trap of all in a stepfamily. Assumptions fill the gaps and family members behave based on the assumptions. One way a stepfamily can ensure some sort of regular communication is family meetings. Many professionals advocate regular family meetings as the forum to discuss problems, make suggestions, ease conflicts among family members, air general complaints, or celebrate successes.

Before our stepfamily launched family meetings, I wondered:

How can I help the rest of the family look forward to these meetings?

What will make each person feel like an important contributor?

What meeting formats work well?

We started family meetings when Brittany and Ian were about ten and nine. They surprised Brian and me with their openness to family meetings. We applied the following practical guidelines to make our family meetings work.

Commit to a regular frequency for family meetings, i.e., we will meet once per month, or once per week, etc. In a highly-scheduled family, pick dates so that everyone can get them on their calendars, and provide the busiest kids frequent reminders.

Pick a meeting time of day that is not over a main meal. Make the meeting special and separate, with its own character. Keep mealtimes free from discussions that can get too heavy.

Decide who will facilitate each meeting. In a stepfamily with kids from both parents, each parent should trade off facilitating the meeting. If the kids are only from one parent, let that parent facilitate for many months until the family is comfortable with the meeting format. Then the stepparent can trade off running the meeting.

Prepare for the meeting in the form of a meeting agenda. Ask family members to contribute agenda items ahead of time or build the agenda together on a white board.

Provide a speaker's prompt—an object (preferably one that makes noise) that can be passed to the person who is speaking. If someone interrupts, the speaker can simply set off the noise as a reminder that he or she is still speaking (as opposed to getting into a squabble). Our family used a small soda can filled with about ten pennies. We duct-taped over the opening and it lasted years.

Set several meeting rules. This activity can be part of the first family-meeting agenda. Rules might include: Speakers must ask for speaker's prompt. No interrupting the speaker. Someone will take notes at each meeting. Meeting will not exceed one hour's duration. Decisions will be made by family vote (consider other methods if you think this will cause problems).

Use the straight-talk strategies to encourage honest communication. This effort will take multiple meetings and practice.

Make the meeting fun. Our very first stepfamily meeting was an ice cream sundae bar, and it was a big hit. Not all the meetings have to incorporate a big event or theme, but consider what you might do for each meeting so that your kids look forward to them.

Brainstorm ways to reward or recognize great communication during the meetings.

Follow up on action items. There is nothing more discouraging than baring your soul at a family meeting only to see that no one is behaving any differently.

Be clever about ways to make family meetings "required" in order to maintain other privileges. For example, you can say, "I'll move your monthly allowance into your bank account as soon as we hold the family meeting and make sure there's nothing else you need or owe." Or try, "My car (or the gaming system, or the Internet) will be available as soon as our family meeting is done."

Stand together to resolve family conflicts

Entire books have been written about conflict-resolution theories and techniques. With regard to resolving stepfamily conflicts, the most important principle is to apply a united parenting approach. When you and your spouse line up on your problem-solving strategies, you reduce the number of possible options you and your stepchildren need to sort through to get to "yes."

Adam said, "One of our biggest successes is that Lily has always backed me up, even if I'm wrong. Whether subconscious or not, the kids have tried to divide us, and yet we have stuck together. Actually, she sticks by me more than I stick by her. When she's making mistakes, I'll sometimes say to Lily about one of the girls, 'She has a point here.' That helps me bond with the kids too."

Adam and Lily choose to face conflict in their stepfamily and to support each other. Other types of reactions to parent-child conflict may be driven by fear responses. According to Thoele, the parent who is too harsh is driven by the fear of failure, and the parent who is too giving is driven by the fear of rejection. Neither of these extreme conflict resolution techniques helps our stepchildren in the ways we intend.

Psychologist and author Mary Pipher confirmed a child's need for consistent middle ground during tumultuous times. In her book, *Reviving Ophelia*, Pipher noted through her extensive research with adolescent girls that a balance at home between love and structure helps increase a teen girl's self-esteem. Too much structure with low expressions of love alienated the parent-child relationship. Too much love with little structure left the children boundary-less and insecure.

I believe that the following tips are among the most useful to consider when family conflicts erupt. Of course, the list doesn't end here. Grab your spouse and decide which conflict management resources you'll commit to and pursue.

- ◆ Separate the facts of a conflict from the emotions. Tell what you see and hear. Another way to say this is to separate the problem from the person.

- Make a goal of being loving but firm.
- Respond from a place of sadness or disappointment, rather than from anger.
- View conflict as an opportunity for growth, rather than as something bad.
- Be grateful for the wisdom conflict brings.
- Meet in a neutral place to discuss conflict. If in the home, meet in the kitchen or family room. Even better, leave the house and go to a completely neutral zone like a coffee shop.
- Meet one-on-one with all parties involved in the conflict. Hear each person out in order to better understand each point of view.
- Listen with your ears, not with your mouth.
- Agree to disagree.
- Put solutions in writing, if verbal agreements aren't being followed.

REFLECTION PROMPTS

1. What makes communication go well in your family? What factors challenge communication in your family?
2. How much do you, the stepparent, get involved in communication with your stepkids? How do you split parent/child communication with your spouse?
3. How can you engage your stepkids in conversation in ways that they accept?
4. Do you hold family meetings? If so, what do you think makes those successful? If not, is there a reason you have not implemented them thus far? What might need to happen for you and your spouse to begin to hold regular family meetings?

POINTS TO REMEMBER

- Honest communication is not easy, but it's possible.
- An emotional blowup may happen before family members can

bare their souls.

- A state of brokenness almost always yields wisdom.
- If something is truly bothering you, put it on the table, even if you won't get an immediate response.
- Listening from the heart can provide relationship breakthroughs.
- Communicate to understand and be understood.
- Step back sometimes, but don't give up.

PART III

Equilibrium: Finding Balance Day by Day

Maintaining emotional balance across many months and years of daily stepfamily living requires a wide variety of strategies. We can't substitute for the time and experience spent stepparenting. During every phase of the Stepfamily Cycle we gain more perspective. Read this section of the book in the order that works for you. Scan the headings and subheadings. Find the topics that appeal to your curiosity, and study the strategies that might help equalize your particular stepfamily rhythm.

TEN

Zigzag Evolution

"Challenges make you discover things about yourself that you never really knew. They're what make the instrument stretch—what make you go beyond the norm."
—CICELY TISON

Brittany: Fifteen years old
Ian: Thirteen years old
Years since their mom died: Nine
Years since our remarriage: Seven
Season: Late fall

THE CALENDAR THAT MORNING REVEALED THAT IT *was once again November 16. Although in most people's lives, this is just another day, for Ian and Brittany, that date was and will always be the anniversary of their mother's premature death from cancer. During the morning scurry to get out the door to school, neither Brian nor I asked the kids about ideas for anniversary date plans.*

At the end of the school day, Ian didn't arrive home from junior high at the usual time. Parents usually accept a grace period after the end of school during which all is still considered well, so we didn't worry at first. Brian and I both worked from home so I continued my project on the computer.

When Ian didn't show up by 3:15 p.m., the grace period ended. The next hour shattered into fragments of slow-motion minutes.

3:16 p.m. I made a number of phone calls to Ian's friends' houses while Brian drove around our suburban neighborhood to see if Ian was walking around or hanging out anywhere. Neither effort turned up any results. I thought, Has he at least ridden the bus all the way to our home bus stop? I grabbed the phone book to look up the district phone number, hoping to reach Ian's bus driver. In the middle of my research, Brittany got dropped off by her high school friend. Ian hadn't contacted her on her mobile phone, so she knew nothing.

3:30 p.m. One of Ian's friends called back on my mobile. He remembered that Ian had been on the bus home. This encouraging news meant Ian couldn't have gone too far. I gave Ian's friend a huge verbal thanks, then Brian and I drove to the bus stop in one car. I got out, Brian drove one way, and I walked the other way. I relied on sheer intuition to choose my path, taking a left out of our immediate neighborhood onto the sidewalk bordering the main road.

About 150 yards down the sidewalk, a black-and-white object took shape as I drew closer. I could see that it was a tennis shoe, but wouldn't realize that it was Ian's tennis shoe until I got right up on it. No other clues—not even a sock—lay nearby. I didn't see any signs of a struggle or of another person's presence or belongings. I navigated through a jumble of feelings: relief to find a clue so soon, perplexity, and an undercurrent of fear for the unthinkable possibility of kidnapping. Ian was stocky and strong. My gut told me he was probably fine. I couldn't resist a nervous chuckle knowing how he could hardly wait to kick off his shoes at the end of a day. I called Brian.

3:45 p.m. Brian met me at the shoe and started drawing emotional connections about Ian's MIA status. The shoe sat on a sidewalk that led to a nearby open space area. The recreational trail lay like a concrete ribbon across a wide expanse of prairie grassland. Ian's mother had been vital in convincing our city that this tawny terrain should be preserved. She fought for the open space rights until she passed on. The city purchased the land and posthumously dedicated the prairie in her name.

3:50 p.m. Brian and I agreed on a plan. He would continue on foot to-wards the trail and I would drive the car back to the house and check for mes-sages. Brian started down the hill that plunges through accompanying groves of honey locust and pine trees to the trail connector below.

3:56 p.m. I entered the house and gave Brittany, who was parked on the couch watching Cartoon Network, the updates. In between mouthfuls of popcorn, she asked for the details. She didn't seem too worried—the blessing of daylight was still with us, and Ian was known for being impulsive. Driven by adrenalin, I attacked some kitchen cleanup and kept my phone nearby.

4:02 p.m. Brian called, his voice uplifted with the good words, "I've got Ian." I threw down my dishrag, fist-pumped the air, and told Brittany the news. Brian found Ian on the trail connector walking back toward the neigh-borhood. He was walking in his socks and holding one shoe.

Brian got the lowdown from Ian later that day and reported to me that Ian was very matter-of-fact about his actions. Ian said he didn't connect the anniversary date but rather that he'd had a "bad day." When I asked him later what "a bad day" meant, he said he'd had a headache all day and he felt sad. When he got off the bus he decided to go for a walk on the prairie. It didn't occur to him that this was unusual, or that people would be worried, or that there was a specific trigger for his sudden impulse. Ian knew what he was moved to do, even if he didn't know why.

We know that this anniversary date fostered Ian's re-grief. He felt the symptoms in his body and searched for relief in just the right place—a place where he could connect with his mom. While re-grief is defined as re-grieving a loss, the rollercoaster of recurring re-grief behaviors contributes to a phenomenon that Stepfamily Cycle originator Patricia Papernow calls "zigzag evolution."

The essence of the zigzag concept is that stepfamilies do not evolve in a straight, predictable line. Rather, they grow more along the lines of a one-step-forward, two-steps-back analogy. While it's true that all families zigzag to some extent, stepfamilies typically have more obstacles to their evolution: a shorter history together, less "instant" (unconditional) love, and the challenge of merging cultures and traditions.

Here are some examples of zigzagging:

- A fourth-grade stepdaughter holds her stepmom's hand (a first) several times during summer vacation but then doesn't show any physical contact that fall when her stepmom volunteers in her classroom at school.

- A teenage boy who called his stepmom "Mom" for seven years wakes up one morning and starts calling her by her first name from that point forward.

- A natural parent grows weary of being caught in the middle between spouse and kids and becomes irritated with the spouse for demanding too much time.

- A seventeen-year-old stepson moves away from his family and lives with friends during senior year of high school. The same young man moves back in at twenty-one.

- A stepdaughter who now has her own baby asks her stepmom for lots of advice.

- A stepdaughter who has moved away goes through waves of constant communication or no communication at all.

We stepparents can also zigzag:

- A stepdad who has been patient with his stepdaughter's dramatic outbursts of re-grief suddenly feels like he can't tolerate that behavior anymore.

- A stepmom who has craved the love and attention of her stepchildren for more than fifteen years finds herself retreating from them when they, in their twenties, start to show her that attention.

- A stepmom feels uncomfortable the first times her adult stepchildren do call her Mom.

- A stepdad struggles with hurt feelings as he watches his oldest stepdaughter's grandfather walk her down the aisle at her wedding.

- ◆ A stepmom and her husband notice how parenting their birth child helps her find more compassion for her stepkids.

Zigzag is a real, heartfelt dynamic in stepfamily life.

Stepparent zigzags help you gain perspective

An oversized light bulb clicked on when I realized that what I used to call a "funky phase" actually represented my own zigzag in our stepfamily. Stepparent zigzags can take as many different emotional and behavioral forms as those from other stepfamily members: sadness, desperation, frustration, anger, disconnection, and bossiness, for example. Our zigzags may be triggered by stepfamily member re-grief or may occur on our own cycles.

Back in the Early Phases of the Stepfamily Cycle, when I waged my battle with Ian's plastic bat against the old chaise lounge in my backyard— that was a zigzag. A buildup of angst brought me to the point at which my thoughts and feelings crossed to the dark side until I let them out.

Another zigzag pattern I see in my behavior comes when I've been upbeat and accepting of any behavior that comes my way, and then suddenly I start obsessing over something a stepchild or a relative is doing, such as misunderstanding my intentions without taking the time to get to know me. Or I might be stressing over something they are "not doing," such as not returning my calls or emails.

I believe that underlying any of these fixations is my heartbreak over not having a better relationship with my young-adult stepchildren than I do. But the key word there is "better." At least I have some relationship. And, our relationships have grown to the point where we can discuss our feelings and opinions about other family members or about factual happenings in our lives and in the world. Someday, I hope I can also discuss my feelings about our relationships and have a productive dialogue. For that conversation to happen, I still need to get over some fear—fear of that old cycle of trying too hard without much relationship improvement, and fear of possible buried, unspoken grudges that the kids will either hold forever or dump out all at one time.

I know I'm supposed to get all the cards out on the table. I know I'm supposed to be the big girl and make the first move. Sometimes I get blocked up because our relationships are not always what I would call a two-way street. When I keep in mind the kids' ages and busy lifestyles—working and thirty something—along with the fact that neither of them chose me as their role model growing up, the lack of initiation is not surprising. However, for me that means that each new engagement with the kids, during which I try something new or try again, takes more emotional effort than with people in my life who are reciprocal with their time and emotional investment. For now, my relationships with my stepkids are approachable, and sometimes we have fun as well. I'm grateful for this state of our relationships. I understand that the dynamics of all my feelings are examples of zigzag. I do my best to honor the status quo, I do relax and go with the flow of what's present in the moment, and I do coach myself to reach out and dig deeper when I'm ready.

In my conversations with Marin, she recognized one of her own zigzag dynamics. "Grace and Kiefer are both adults, and they do call me Mom now. Now it feels good, but at first it felt funny," she said. "I had feelings of not deserving it. They would address cards to Mom, and I would sign my cards 'M,' which can cover both names! They had moved on, and this was my hang-up."

Adam felt he sometimes fell short being the father figure his stepdaughters needed. "All girls want to be their dad's princesses, and I haven't treated my stepdaughters as princesses … I treat my own daughter that way," he said. "I need to push more; I need to be more active with them. They want to be cherished."

Adam expressed some regret, an emotion that borders on guilt. Neither regret nor guilt feels good, and both emotions point to a dilemma. I believe that we stepparents engage in a balancing act between sincere actions—which we sometimes think are "not enough"—and acting the way we think we should, which our stepkids may think is "too much." We have to allow ourselves the grace to try both strategies, see how they work, and forgive ourselves for the ones that aren't well-received. Armed with the courage to try the straight-talk method of putting things on the table, we may be able to clarify which strategies our stepchildren prefer. We also benefit from learning strategies to weather every family member's zigzag phases.

Asking others for a new perspective can also help stepparents rise above stresses. I often find I am sorely in need of a new view, sometimes when I least expect it. Once, when young adult Ian moved back into our basement, we all believed the stay would be super short. A night turned into weeks, and I hadn't yet been down to the room that my husband set up for him. When I walked in there to offer to change the sheets, I saw something that I firmly support, yet it still made my stomach do a flip-flop. Ian had two pictures of his mother up in the room. My head knew this was good—good for him and healthy to keep connected. That didn't, however, change how my insides deflated.

I mentioned my experience to my cousin, who has always been very honest and truthful with me, and is a psychologist to boot. She said, "I'm guessing that having you in his life in such a supportive way has allowed him to also cherish his mom and his memories of her." This was a V-8 bonk-on-the-head moment. Why didn't I think of that?

When I was younger and felt down when reflecting about the kids calling me Diane, another mom told me that her son (not her stepson) calls her by her first name. When she asked him to call her Mommy, he said, "But you're my DeeDee!" It triggered a memory of Brittany telling her friends that I was "her Diane." I guess that wasn't so bad! I was "hers," no matter what.

When I talk to other stepparents and parents, and hear stories about their kids, I help normalize a zig or a zag. Every time I've reached out, I've learned that many issues with children are universal and not just limited to a stepfamily setting.

Try it. If you're struggling with something in the stepfamily arena, cast out for a fresh view. That which you reel in may be just what you needed to hear.

How Do You Deal with Zigzag?

Where do you turn when stepfamily dynamics have you in a mood? The stepparents I chatted with offer a variety of strategies based on the common theme of taking care of yourself.

Marin read a lot of novels. "I loved to get lost inside a good book," she said. She also talked with friends, either in person drinking coffee or on the old-style corded phone. She chuckled at these memories. "I'd be chatting and moving around while the kids would be playing games with the phone cord and getting tangled in it." If everything seemed just too overwhelming, Marin's other "go-to" was to sleep.

The always active Ella kept busy. "I immersed myself in my activities—church, choir, bird-watching, and exercise. I kept going with the things that interested me," she said.

Adam and Lily turned to their faith, as did Kit. "What do you do if you are in uncontrollable situations and you don't have a higher power?" asked Kit. "Prayer has really gotten me through and this hardship has brought me closer to God."

My go-to coping strategies were and still are physical and spiritual. I am blessed to still be strong and healthy, and I'll push my body to feel the endorphins that come with vigorous physical exercise. I can only recall a few times when a good workout did not help lift my mood and change my perspective somehow. I also enjoy reading motivational quotes and reflections. Some are secular and some are spiritual. Since I like to read, I'll often search a topic such as "disappointment" or "frustration" at a website called Goodreads. By reading other authors' viewpoints, I get a quick new perspective on my feelings. Sometimes, I also pick up a tip about a book I'd like to read or a reading suggestion for my kids.

I especially love this quote about disappointment, found on Goodreads. It seems like the perfect quote for zigzag, because it questions whether the thing you're feeling down about was even real to begin with:

"It was one of those times you feel a sense of loss, even though you didn't have something in the first place. I guess that's what disappointment is—a sense of loss for something you never had." —Deb Caletti, *The Nature of Jade*

A quote collection called *Starting Your Day Right* by Joyce Meyer has helped me see light during a dark zigzag time. Sometimes her commentary on a biblical verse seems to be speaking right to me.

"Love bears up under anything and everything that comes, is ever ready to believe the best of every person, its hopes are fadeless under all circumstances, and it endures everything." —1 Corinthians 13:7

Joyce's commentary: "If your feelings get hurt because someone looked at you crossways or because friends or family forgot your birthday, you need to spend more time with God. He will fill you with so much love and such a sense of self-worth that you won't feel ill-tempered or touchy toward anyone ..."

In the end, I know that relationships go through phases. A zigzag is not the happiest phase, but it's also not the worst. Time will rush forward, something will evolve or change, and new phases will be born. Though I look forward to the relationship upswings, I'll work on being content with where things are right now.

What to do when you feel angry

"Speak when you are angry and you will make
the best speech you will ever regret."
                              —Ambrose Bierce, author and journalist

I have blown communication with my family members on more than one occasion due to anger. No good ever comes out of a screaming match with your stepchildren. They just see you as scary and out of control. A yell-fest with your spouse isn't much fun either. I follow three cardinal rules now when I feel angry at a member of my family. They are:

Rule #1: Spill my anger first outside of my family, or at least with my spouse. If I'm angry at my spouse, I'd better hole up and get on the phone with a good friend who will listen to my rants without judging. Or sometimes I exercise or dance away the physical feelings of anger.

Rule #2: Don't burn any bridges. If, even after talking to someone about my feelings, I'm still angry enough to make grandiose statements that start with "You always …," or "You never …," or "I hate when you …," then I am probably not yet ready to talk it out. I could definitely say things that I will later regret. I'll never forget when I was sixteen and my mom told me that she hated me. I forgave her, of course, but I'll never forget how lost I felt after those words. I would have been even more put off if she were my stepmom.

This leads to Rule #3: Be willing to step away. If I start a discussion and my anger is taking over, I'm learning to tell the other person that I need a timeout. I walk away until I'm ready to try again. I've found that a good test for readiness is when I can calmly describe why I felt angry without experiencing the anger-driven flush of my cheeks and tensing of my body. I've been focusing on ways I can "come down" from feeling angry so that I don't affect my health or leave my family with the impression that I'm a lunatic.

I think that we stepparents have an opportunity for ongoing education when we tell our families that we were angry and why. Our sharing might spur another stepfamily member to speak up about his or her anger. This process might move zigzags forward at a faster rate.

Sometimes I get angry because someone in the family has, unknowingly or not, pushed one of my hot buttons. For example, I've learned that when no one in the family seems to understand me or what I'm feeling, I become angry. Feeling misunderstood is a hot button for me, and I illogically think my family members should be able to read my mind. Nevertheless, getting to know my hot buttons helps me process my anger, so that I don't overreact when those buttons are pushed. Other hot-button examples for me include:

- feeling underappreciated
- feeling like someone I trusted has crossed me
- perceiving a lack of respect (from any family member toward any other member)

When these topics come up for me, I know I have to take extra time to evaluate what's really going on, and then I can react in an appropriate and constructive way that doesn't do harm to my stepfamily members.

Here's an example. After multiple years of awkward Mother's Days, I came to know that on Mother's Day I might feel underappreciated. Before I believed in my heart that Mother's Day wasn't my holiday to celebrate with my stepkids, I would feel angry that no one in the house took the initiative to celebrate Mother's Day with me or even say why they couldn't or didn't want to. So I made a point of planning something special for myself on Mother's Day weekend; something I gave as a gift to myself, even if just time to be outdoors (a likely choice for me). Then, no matter how I felt about Mother's Day, I became part of the solution to help myself enjoy it, and I didn't transfer any anger to my husband or stepkids.

Measuring stepfamily progress

The cliché epithet, "a watched pot never boils," couldn't be truer in the case of stepfamily zigzag. Zigzag evolution explains why it's so important not to judge the success of your stepfamily on a short-term basis. What looks like progress one season might reverse itself during another season.

Rating your stepfamily growth along a spectrum of weeks, months, or years creates a false context for measurement. If you feel you need to catalog success, look instead at growth in the context of the Stepfamily Cycle. Over the years, is your stepfamily moving from the Early Stages to the Middle Stages by shedding stepfamily myths and trying out more realistic roles and more productive communication? In moving from the Middle Stages to the Later Stages, does your family engage in less power struggles and experience less stress around "step" issues? Are all family members getting comfortable hanging out in one-on-one pairs, such as stepparent with one child at a time or parent with one child at a time? These Stepfamily Cycle benchmarks give you more useful feedback about your stepfamily progression than any time-based measurements.

Another perspective may emerge from practicing a "from the blimp" view of your family. If you were flying in a blimp over hundreds of houses that had viewports through their roofs, do you believe that your household would stand out as the dysfunctional, "in trouble" household? Or would it mostly look like the other households? I learned that our stepfamily interactions were not that different than other family interactions, based on the number of times I heard friends respond, "It's like that in my house too!"

Stepparent Adam offers this view: "Over the years, we probably are getting to be a closer stepfamily. Sometimes we go different ways, some phases are better than others, but overall it is progressing."

One final perspective on stepfamily growth comes from the analogy of earnings on an investment account. A balanced, diversified financial account in standard economic times suffers some losses, boasts some gains, yet overall measures up and to the right. A stepfamily is an emotional investment. Even a zigzag is contributing to the overall gains in your stepfamily.

REFLECTION PROMPTS

1. Identify two recent examples of zigzag in your stepfamily. How did you react in each circumstance?
2. What coping strategies will you use to work through family zigzags?
3. How have you tried to measure your stepfamily growth? Which approaches have worked for you and which approaches have not?

POINTS TO REMEMBER

- Key milestones and anniversaries can subconsciously trigger changes in behavior.
- All family members zigzag, not just the kids.
- Not all stepfamily members move forward at the same rate.
- Keeping a steady vigil over your stepfamily success works against you. Relax and trust the Stepfamily Cycle.
- Talking to other parents about the issues they face with their kids can help normalize a zig or a zag.

ELEVEN

Acceptance, Not Attachments

"My happiness grows in direct proportion to my acceptance, and
in inverse proportion to my expectations."
–MICHAEL J. FOX

Brittany: Seventeen years old
Ian: Sixteen years old
Years since their mom died: Almost eleven
Years since our remarriage: Nine
Season: Late summer

THAT SATURDAY MORNING SEEMED LIKE ANY OTHER weekend morning until Ian walked into the kitchen and said, "Good morning, Diane." After so many years of calling me "Mom," I thought his renaming was a joke or a posture he was putting on for the day. Maybe it was a dare. I thought it would go away, but at the day's end, the weekend's end, and the following week's end, he was still calling me Diane. All I could get out of him the following Saturday was that he'd decided I had forced him to call me "Mom" all those years ago. Now he wanted the choice to be his.

A cry of injustice welled up inside. I didn't force any name; in fact, I gave both kids choices instead of mandating a name like many families do. I moved out to our front porch for some air and brought with me all the clementine oranges I planned to prepare for a fruit salad. While peeling, I recalled every detail of that chain of events. When Ian was eight and Brittany nine, I asked them to decide if they could call me a pet name. I hoped that they would go for Snoopy, who was their dad's favorite Peanuts comic strip character. However, Ian started calling me mom, and Brittany said she really couldn't call me anything but Diane. Now, at sixteen, Ian felt empowered to make a different choice, and he did.

I threw the bright-orange curls of rind into the green Tupperware bowl. You could cut Ian's transition with the peeling knife. And he wouldn't elaborate on his reasons, which left me unsteady and squirmy in my stomach. As the weeks neared a month, a relationship that had once been playful turned almost utilitarian. Rather than acting wacky and goofing around, Ian's demeanor with me about-faced to matter-of-fact and undemonstrative. I masked my hurt by distancing myself for protection.

Loss usually involves a bargaining phase, during which you'd give almost anything to return to the way things were. I skipped over bartering; I didn't believe I could ask Ian to re-choose any other name when the un-choice represented something more significant. Brian agreed. He had gone for a few walks with Ian and asked him what was going on. Ian was re-processing his sixteen-year-old understanding of the time when Brian and I became a couple, and had developed negative ideas about my motives and intentions in the relationship.

I looked straight into the eyes of an important but difficult phase of the grief cycle: choosing acceptance of the way things are in the moment.

This is the chapter I had to write to myself and then read over and over. I crave intimacy and harmony in relationships, so much so that I have a hard time accepting those relationships on any other terms. I know I can't expect all results to land my way, nor will family times always be peaceful, so I need to constantly work on accepting things the way they are.

My gut reaction to Ian's rite of passage stands in direct contrast to Brittany's similar expression of independence about two years earlier, when she told me I'd gone too far in judging her nineteen-year-old boyfriend and that I had no right to do so, since she didn't feel like I was her mom. Somehow I was prepared for that, and I kept control of my emotions, all the while encouraging her honesty. I remember what joy and pride I felt at being objective and making progress in what could have been a highly-charged emotional mess. In comparison, I remember how miserable and rejected I felt about Ian's crossroads. Why?

A good look at our family dynamics at the time when Ian changed his mind suggests one possible answer. That summer represented the last few months before Brittany's freshman year of college. Change was in the wind for our family. With our oldest ready to fly free, the rest of the family became more vulnerable. Ian was about to take on the role of the oldest child at home, Amy was "losing" her big sister, and I imagine we all harbored some separation anxiety. Plus, Brian and I were managing the transition involved with Brittany's "summer-before-college" curfews and guidelines regarding the wheres, whats, and whoms of what seemed like nonstop outings. This continual vigilance required extra emotional outlay and consistency on our part, even though we knew she would soon be leaving us. It's fair to say that my confidence and emotional peace were not at their peak.

Stepmom Kit also went round and round about accepting her naming and identity with Lana and Brad. "I wanted so much to be a mom. I craved being a mom. I craved for the word 'mom.' That didn't last too long. I didn't dwell on it because I think I knew with them that it wasn't a possibility, that I was their aunt and I would always be their aunt."

Faced with many family situations and choices that are out of our control, our sustainable stepparenting formula would not be complete without the addition of acceptance.

You won't run out of opportunities to practice acceptance in your step-family. For example, you may already have accepted that blood is thicker than anything or that your stepchild has not chosen you as a confidante. Acceptance comes into play as well when you honor the place of the deceased parent in the family, or when you punt on the way you want to discipline because it's not your place to deliver the rules. Thinking back to the gardening model of our stepfamily that I once drew, we can let in the light, clear the weeds, plant the seeds, and watch what grows. But we can't attach ourselves to the way the garden will shape up. The final result is out of our control.

What do you do when your heart yearns for a different outcome than you're experiencing? Will you let disappointment or attachments to expectations hold you back, or will you find ways to regroup and forge ahead? Consider these forward-looking strategies:

- Flip your perspective by choosing a new attitude
- Practice daily gratitude for what's amazing about your life
- Confront the reality of inevitable dissonance
- Strive for authenticity—you're a person too
- Assess your ego

Through techniques such as these, I've discovered how to look at my world in new, positive ways, recognizing and shaking off my attachments in order to focus on my own growth.

Choose your attitude, choose your gratitude

In doing research for one of my writing projects, I became inspired by this quote:

"The last of one's freedoms is to choose one's attitude
in any given circumstance."

–Viktor Frankl, Austrian psychotherapist,
author, and Holocaust survivor

These powerful words remind us that every day we are in charge of our attitudes and behaviors. I believe that repeated buildup of unwelcome stress during vulnerable times yielded a message for me: worry and negativity just bring me and everyone around me down. Choosing love and gratitude will always work for the greater good of my stepfamily; however, that choice is not always easy.

I wasn't in control of my emotions one Super Bowl Sunday when I let a lively conversation between Brittany and one of my good friends upset me to the point of stealing away to have a good cry in my bedroom. Fourteen-year-old Brittany shared with my friend the answers to almost every question about school, life, and boys that I had asked Brittany the day before. I received controlled, one-word answers when I hoped Brittany would confide in me. Before I started that conversation, I became attached to my desire that our relationship had progressed to that point of sharing. I ignored bigger-picture thinking that at Brittany's age, natural separations from parents are the norm. Because of my attachment to an imaginary result, Brittany and my friend's free-flowing, fun conversation tipped me over an emotional edge.

What I didn't do, in my attachment blindness, was choose my attitude in this situation. The fact that Brittany was capable of being happy and upbeat with someone meant that she was feeling self-confident and having a good day, for which I should have been thrilled. And I learned everything I wanted to know from my original questions—just not directly.

What choices, then, don't work in stepfamilies?

- Choosing to ignore the good in a situation
- Choosing power
- Choosing control
- Choosing the family role we're convinced that "the kids need"
- Choosing to find fault
- Choosing isolation from the family
- Choosing to dwell on immediate gratification

How do we learn to receive what's good in stepfamily relationships and to remain positive? How do we let go of our attachment to expectations?

I remember a college class I took covering several Eastern philosophies that offer helpful insight about the link between expectations and suffering. According to Ven. S. Dhammika, "When we want something but are unable to get it, we feel frustrated. When we expect someone to live up to our expectation and they do not, we feel let down and disappointed. When we want others to like us and they don't, we feel hurt."* All of these outcomes derived from attachments represent types of personal suffering I've put myself through in reaction to interpersonal stepfamily dynamics.

Also insightful, but surprising to me, are the synonyms I found for expectation: belief, assumption, presumption, hope, wish, desire. I didn't see the connection, at first, between belief and expectation. Now I do. For example, when I believe something—such as, "kids want boundaries"—it's easy for me to subconsciously expect my spouse to share that belief. If my spouse doesn't line up on my page, I've set myself up to feel disappointed. But I never stopped to confirm my spouse's belief, so I'm losing something I never had to begin with.

I definitely thought hope, wish, and desire were significantly different than expectation, because they are "wants," not "musts." But now I believe that all of those postures trigger attachment too. I recall sitting in our counselor Dr. G's office, recounting my hope that "in time" Brittany and Ian would seek out a deeper relationship with me.

"I've heard that when kids go to college, they often appreciate their parents more," I said.

---

* www.buddhanet.net

Dr. G. shook his head. "Not necessarily."

"Well, a lot of moms have told me that when Brittany has children, she'll probably turn to me," I said.

Dr. G. raised an eyebrow.

"I can hope for that, can't I?" I said.

"Not necessarily."

I've also looked up the word acceptance in the dictionary. Definitions include: a willingness to receive, the treating of something as welcome, a favorable regard for something, the recognition of truth. These phrases sounded so uplifting, they made me want to be accepting! In other words, acceptance involves seeing things as they are and welcoming that very state instead of wishing and hoping for more.

Rather than constantly struggling to get what we want, we can modify our wanting. As Viktor Frankl said, choose your attitude in any situation. Stepdad Adam was floored when his stepdaughter Laurel chose to go to a father-daughter dance with a friend's father instead of with him. "Sure, it hurts when they don't include you," Adam said. "But what was I to do? If she didn't feel comfortable going with me, it's something she had to resolve in her mind and heart. I had to let it wash over me and remind myself that I'm still a father figure. If I made a big deal of it, it would be worse."

One small step that can influence an attitude shift is a daily practice of gratitude. While "an attitude of gratitude" might be vague and cliché, exploration of the specific things you're thankful for can help recast the spirit of any day in a more peaceful light.

Author Laura Ingalls Wilder said, "As the years pass, I am coming more and more to understand that it is the common, everyday blessings of our common everyday lives for which we

I've also looked up the word acceptance in the dictionary. Definitions include: a willingness to receive, the treating of something as welcome, a favorable regard for something, the recognition of truth. These phrases sounded so uplifting, they made me want to be accepting!

should be particularly grateful. They are the things that fill our lives with comfort and our hearts with gladness—just the pure air to breathe and the strength to breathe it; just warmth and shelter and home folks; just plain food that gives us strength; the bright sunshine on a cold day; and a cool breeze when the day is warm.""

If you need a push toward gratitude, perhaps you'll find motivation in the words of keynote speaker and author Steve Maraboli who said, "Be wise enough to be grateful. Be courageous enough to be happy.""" Many gratitude experts suggest writing down five things every day for which you're grateful. If you practice this in the evening, the act can bring positive closure to your day. By practicing in the morning, you feel more alive as you launch your day. By focusing on what we appreciate, we choose to shift our focus away from things we can't control.

Inevitable dissonance

Our attempts to grow relationships crash into a lot of human nature. Creatures have strong wills of their own, wills that cannot be controlled or fixed. T.S. Eliot, in his *Old Possum's Book of Practical Cats*, illustrates this concept.

> "The Rum Tum Tugger is a Curious Cat:
> If you offer him pheasant he would rather have grouse.
> If you put him in a house he would much prefer a flat,
> If you put him in a flat then he'd rather have a house...
> Yes the Rum Tum Tugger is a Curious Cat –
> And there isn't any call for me to shout it:
> For he will do
> As he do do
> And there's no doing anything about it!"

Eliot uses cats as an analogy for human behavior. Family members are

---

** https://www.goodreads.com/work/quotes/11151
*** https://www.goodreads.com/work/quotes/25086973?page=3

going to do what they're going to do, unless, thanks to their higher intelligence, they see a reason to change their behavior. That reason is often extreme pleasure (positive motivation) or extreme pain (sinking to their lowest point).

The ultimate nature of your step-relationships is also out of your control and may not meet your expectations. The inevitable state of emotions is dissonance— a disharmonious state of being that may seem frustrating at first, but which ironically may release us to get past our attachments to having results the way we want them. Instead of continuing to look ahead at a goal of stepfamily peace and harmony, what if we accept a state of dissonance as the way things are? What if peaceful co-existence is an unrealistic expectation?

Psychologist McBride said, "Stepparents, particularly stepmothers, think that they have to be in charge of everything. Everything has to be choreographed perfectly, and that's how it's got to work, but it just doesn't work that way. Life doesn't work that way."

Could we liberate ourselves by accepting that the default mode of family dynamics is chaos? Then, harmonious moments would stand out as interludes for which we're so grateful. Stepfamily ministry expert Ron Deal, in his "Enduring Disharmony" article at smartstepfamilies.com,**** takes this dissonance concept a step further: "Rubbing your rough edges against someone else's rough edges smooths both and eventually ... are you ready for this? ... gives way to connection. The struggle produces trust, respect, and appreciation for one another ... the working through of disharmony actually moves you forward as a family."

It's okay to imagine the possibilities in your stepfamily, but when you become attached to any particular possibility, you may struggle. Aspire to let people be who they are with all their idiosyncrasies. This unconditional acceptance requires you to discipline the many emotions that make you want to either get back at others or avoid them. Why not, instead, focus your energy on allowing yourself to be who *you* are in the stepfamily mix?

**** http://smartstepfamilies.com/view/enduring-disharmony

You're not just a role, you're a person

Stepmom Ella didn't have any illusions about her role with her stepdaughters. She said, "Joanie and Merle never saw me as a second parent—just as Walter's second wife. They learned to like me, and that's all. And I learned to accept it. My biggest challenge was to earn their respect, not as their father's second wife, but as a person."

In the quest to "do good" for our stepfamilies, or even just to manage ourselves within our stepfamilies, we can forget who we are. Each of us is a real person, valuable inside and outside of our families, no matter our current phase of relationship building or stepfamily development. Take it from me, who learned the importance of authenticity as fast as wood petrifies: it's much better to show your stepfamily members who you really are than to flood them with who you think you're supposed to be.

In her work with stepfamilies, McBride observed what works to help kids feel comfortable with a new parent. She nodded her head as if to accentuate the suggestions. "Time, familiarity, and accepting, not forcing," she said. "When things aren't shoved down their throats, the kids can let the routines and rhythms of life take them into familiarity." Once again, we hear the message that we must allow time and the natural evolution of relationships to carry us through the phases of the Stepfamily Cycle. From this perspective, letting the real you shine through can warm the whole stepfamily over time.

Being authentic with your stepchildren may be easier when you join your stepfamily while the children are still young and still developing their familiar routines. Children in their teens may already be set in their ways, and they're also already engaging in the developmental work of separating from their parents. With teens, your actions of authenticity may look different. Being authentic may mean being as civil and polite as you would be with your co-workers, with flashes of explaining to the teens what you believe in and why. This strategy of civil co-existence mixed with revealing who you are could get you to a Middle Stage phase where you can then practice the straight-talk technique of asking them for input on how you and they build relationships. If these approaches are not working, you still bring the family a valuable gift: the role of supporting your spouse during the kids' teen years.

With the paucity of resources formerly available for stepparents of grieving children, I did latch on to a television series called *Everwood*, about a New York City neurosurgeon who loses his wife and then moves with his teen son and young daughter to small Everwood, Colorado. Although this was only a fictional getaway into the life of a grieving family, I could relate to the natural dad slogging away at communication with his fifteen-year-old son, while his nine-year-old daughter still adored him. Dad didn't feel like he had a lot of openings to be authentic with his son or talk about deeper issues. The dad felt like anything he tried yielded the same net result: "My son hates me."

I felt a similar despair with Ian after my fateful transition from Mom to Diane. Distancing myself didn't restore our relationship and took a tremendous amount of energy on my part. The only sane solution was to put myself back into the relationship and accept whatever was going to happen. In the years between high school graduation and young adulthood, I welcomed him back into our home for several stays when he needed assistance. Although Ian and I don't share a lot of the same interests, we were able to converse over cooking. He often grated cheese or chopped vegetables to help prep for dinner, or occasionally cooked the whole dinner himself. Our daughter Amy really enjoyed when Ian stayed over. Ian's playful side came out again with Amy as he wrestled her or shot rubber bands at her, and instead of being jealous, I found myself glad for both of them.

Sharing our hearts explains who we are and can advance even a difficult relationship ... even if the other person doesn't react right away. Author and speaker Stephen Covey calls this "making deposits in the emotional bank account." Over time, the deposits will grow into something significant.

These examples remind me that every little step toward authenticity counts. We may take a risk and reveal our hearts but get no apparent yield from our young people. Yet the alternative, the strain of being someone we're not, can tax us. By doing the work of letting go of attachments and accepting without conditions, we'll begin to understand some of our step-family's dynamics deep in our hearts. We can use our straight-talk skills to explain to our stepchildren when our feelings are hurt, or to ask them how they want the stepparent-stepchild relationships to unfold. Given time, your family members can choose to see that "you that shines through."

There's No E-G-O in A-C-C-E-P-T-A-N-C-E

When I was six or seven, I had two pet names for my father—Naa and Ego. Although I don't remember their origin, I suppose I was following suit from seeing the diminutives my parents used for each other on Christmas gift tags and Valentine's Day cards. (P.B. and E.S., which stood for something sweet and romantic.)

Naa died out quickly but Ego remained. I'm not sure why my father let me call him Ego—he didn't have a large one and I didn't know the word's true meaning. Now, ego has become a caution sign on my road through stepparenting life. By becoming aware of my ego, I have been able to move into a phase of life where I mostly accept my evolving relationship with Brittany and Ian.

"But you are their mom," insist many who learn of our story. It's not that simple. As we've learned, their mom is still their mom, living or deceased.

A Thai exchange student whom I supervised on her exchange program in the USA stated it well. "You have to respect your mom. She is the one who gave birth to you." Thank goodness for the Asian culture of honoring their elders.

The acceptance dance can be boiled down to a pretty straightforward dynamic. When I release my ego's need to be loved in specific ways by Brittany and Ian, then I accept whatever behavior comes my way from them. But when I become upset when they, for example, choose to call only their dad for support and reinforcement, then I know my ego has flared.

> The ego wants recognition and justice. For any of us who have kids, including biological children, since when does being a mom or dad net you these rewards? I can at least protect my ego by reminding myself that my service heart makes me a good mom. Like the stepparent version of Eliot Ness, I continue headlong into the world of "doing good."

REFLECTION PROMPTS

1. Write down three to five things you're grateful for today. Do you notice a shift in your feelings or awareness as a result?
2. Which of your expectations make you feel the most trapped? What do you need to do to let go of those expectations?
3. How much of the real you are you showing your stepchildren?

POINTS TO REMEMBER

- When it comes to attitude and gratitude, you own the choice.
- Family life may contain more dissonance than harmony. What if you accepted the dissonance as the new normal?
- It's healthier to show your stepfamily members the "you that shines through" rather than the person you think you're supposed to be.
- There is no E-G-O in A-C-C-E-P-T-A-N-C-E.

TWELVE

Milestones and Miracles

"Life appears to be too short to be spent in nursing
animosity or registering wrongs."
– CHARLOTTE BRONTE

Brittany: Twenty-four years old
Ian: Almost twenty-three years old
Years since mom died: Eighteen-and-a-half
Years since our remarriage: Sixteen-and-a-half
Season: Winter

I WAS SO GLAD I PICKED UP the phone on Valentine's Day afternoon.

"Hiiiiiiii!" Brittany's voice filled the receiver. It was unusually high-pitched and sing-songy.

"Are you sitting down?" she asked.

"You mean like sitting down good, or sitting down bad?" I wasn't sure where she was heading.

"We're getting MARRRRRRRRR-IED!" she crooned.

That wise fiancé of hers, knowing how hard it is to surprise Brittany, hadn't told a soul he planned to propose to her on Valentine's Day. Brittany sounded so happy.

As the story of the proposal unfolded and Brittany retold it over the weeks to follow, I figured out that I was one of the first people Brittany had called. Maybe even the very first. I thought of all the times I had either missed her calls or queued up her messages for later in the day due to work obligations. I felt so fortunate to have had the presence of mind to pick up the phone and be the recipient of this milestone.

Melting away were memories of less happy times, such as when Brittany shooed me out of her hospital exam room when she was fifteen, or when she gave her dad and me the silent treatment for the entire week of family vacation in Arizona.

Those recollections were drowned out by her swell of enthusiasm now. Strong and passionate voices of encouragement from well-meaning stepmoms and moms also rang in my ears: "Just wait until she finds the love of her life. Just wait until she starts having children. You'll be the first to know."

Whether or not they were right, I could treasure this moment. I hung up with Brittany, called Brian, and opened with, "Are you sitting down?"

When I looked deep into Brittany's blue eyes that day long ago at the softball field, about half a year after her mom died, I couldn't predict that I'd ever be receiving this special phone call. The thought of her wedding ceremony brought up a combination of joy and panic. I recalled a scene from Chris Columbus's movie *Stepmom*, in which a terminally ill mother and her children's stepmother-to-be discuss their feelings about the young teen daughter's far-off wedding day. The mom tells the stepmom she's afraid her daughter won't remember her on her wedding day. And the stepmom tells the mom how terrified she is that her stepdaughter will be consumed with thinking of her mother. This scene, while fictional, is on-target as a heart-wrenching example of real-life milestones families and stepfamilies live through.

Adolescence alone buzzes with a swarm of coming-of-age milestones and ceremonies. Teens celebrate with bat mitzvahs and bar mitzvahs, confirmations, quinceañeras, formal dances, sweet sixteens, driving privileges, and graduations, to name a few. Young adults are often sorting through the pressures of college, or entering the workforce and taking on many new responsibilities. Dating relationships may become more serious and lead to commitment. Teens and young adults grapple with the incongruities in life that they notice every day, such as a parent drinking at a party and then driving the family home.

Milestone occasions in stepfamilies are characterized by some of the most joyous times and yet some of the trickiest emotional times: holidays, graduations, weddings, births, funerals, and other losses. Family members' feelings often peak and valley during ceremonial times.

It helps to think ahead to upcoming known milestones so that you don't let them become millstones. For example, you might anticipate that extended family you barely know may visit or become otherwise involved during special occasions. Plan how to relate to them before the big event, always keeping the spotlight on relatives' relationships with the kids.

Take all big occasions a step at a time. You'll have time to forecast graduations, and hopefully weddings and births as well. Your stepchildren will be old enough at the times of these milestones to think about what atmosphere they want at their ceremonies, so ask questions to determine what's important to them. How do they want extended family to be involved during high school graduation? How will we recognize the deceased parent at a wedding? How do they hope or imagine the stepparent will be involved at that wedding? Is it important to your stepchildren to name one of their babies after their deceased mom or dad?

Funerals and other losses will likely present the biggest opportunities for growth through a milestone. All the rules and lessons of re-grief apply here. You may experience unprecedented withdrawal, anger, or catharsis from your stepchildren, depending on their ages and stages of life. Or, they may be joyous to reunite with immediate through extended family during these times. The best gift you can give is to tap into your wisdom about re-grief and make yourself available to your spouse and family members.

Continue to ask questions and be an active listener— the family will help you discover which next steps to take, even if that means backing off for a while.

Even during milestone-related zigzags, remember to celebrate the miracles. For example, when Brian's mom was in her final hours at the hospital after an unexpected build-up of fluid in her lungs, our immediate family and Brian's dad, Paul, gathered to support each other. Several of us actually shared the moment of being in the hospital room when Phyllis passed. While that was, on one hand, a painful moment, it was also a miracle of togetherness and the opportunity to hold each other up. Even our ability to make it to the hospital in time was a miracle. In the weeks to follow, our family time zoomed through the roof as we worked to assist Paul and honor Phyllis.

Wedding ceremony balances honor and acceptance

I knew Brittany's wedding would merge three families' wants and ideas: her mom's family, her husband to be's family, and our family. Cathy's family always lived in the eastern United States, while Zach's and our families lived in the middle of the country. Who from Brittany's mom's family would attend? How would the wedding ceremony provide integration between past and present? What would be my role in the wedding? Would Brittany demonstrate sadness that her mom wasn't there? What support, and from whom, might she need?

One miracle during the wedding planning was that the answers to all of these questions worked out quite naturally. Brittany's vision drove the anticipated feel of the ceremony, and a small "village" of her close friends banded together to provide support. I had the good fortune of living just up the road from Brittany, and she turned to me as her main wedding planner. I treasured this opportunity to help organize her wedding and reception. The project tapped into my natural planning and organization skills, which made it easy for me to play a sincere and significant role in this milestone event.

Brittany and Zach wanted an outdoor fall wedding. Picture a green pasture lined with rows of white chairs, each tied with a purple or silver ribbon. The pasture lay just east of a long windbreak lined with magnificent Cottonwood trees, behind which peeked the Colorado Rockies' mountaintops.

At the ceremony itself, Brittany's Aunt Anne on her mom's side and the wedding officiant, who was a friend of our family, made sure to honor Brittany's mom in two ways: visually with a picture and in the context of the story of Brittany's life, told prior to the exchange of Brittany's and Zach's wedding vows. Anne was the only member of Cathy's family physically well enough to fly out from the east, and we were all grateful that she did. The ceremony would not have been complete without someone who had been close to Brittany's mom. Anne and Brittany positioned Cathy's picture on a high, small table nestled to the right of the flower-laden wedding arch. Next to the picture Brittany placed a candle in a hurricane lamp. After Ian escorted Anne down the aisle, Brittany and Ian lit the candle together before they sat down. It remained lit for the duration of the ceremony.

The chaplain told the story of the influences of love in Brittany's life. The love story began with Brittany's mom and dad, and it continued with my arrival on the scene as a new parent. The groom grew up in a more traditional family, and the chaplain commented on his story as well.

The bride and groom designed their wedding's overall theme around how their love together was a reflection of the love they had each experienced in their families of origin. We were all included as part of that history. Brittany remained in high spirits, and no family member felt left out of the wedding ceremony.

For the reception we moved indoors, complete with dancing and an outstanding buffet dinner donated as a wedding gift by one of the groom's culinary friends. At the reception, I enjoyed witnessing Brittany and Zach's community of friends amongst all the pockets of family. So many walks of life gathered together in one room to celebrate.

As I consider the emotional complexity of this event, it seems that the outcomes of the wedding—fun, honor, sentiment, love, and inclusiveness—were all miracles. An event like this could have gone very differently and been much more tense and stressful. I attribute the smooth outcomes of Brittany and Zach's wedding to several dynamics:

- The bride and groom are outstanding young people who worked hard at holding on to the wedding and reception they wanted, in the midst of many other influences
- Brittany handled everything about her wedding with maturity and without any bitterness
- Brittany and I had been developing a better relationship during the pre-wedding years and each made more effort to respect the other

A nice coincidence about the date of Brittany's wedding is that it was held over the annual National Stepfamily Day weekend. National Stepfamily Day (September 16) was put in place to recognize the beauty and unity of stepfamilies. All in all, this wedding was symbolic of Brittany's natural family and her stepfamily coming together to make up the story that is hers alone—her own miracle.

What I've Discovered I Like about Being a Stepparent

In the spirit of being grateful, I've reflected upon what aspects I enjoy about being a stepparent. I see these revelations as mini-miracles as well. I've presented these thoughts, which range from tactical to abstract, in the old "David Letterman" style. I came up with nine instead of ten things, because I want you to fill in the tenth spot—what do you like about being a stepparent?

10. *Your revelation goes here!*

9. My good friend of twenty-plus years thinks I'm a "saint up for a promotion." I laugh at this one, because I did not take on stepparenting to be recognized for it ... but it's nice to know that someone sees that the job requires rising above some adversity.

8. With regard to adversity, stepparenting has taught me how to give and persevere, even through the hard times. For someone like me, who prefers harmony over arguments and peace over discord, this is a huge growth experience for which I could not be more thankful.

7. As a child, I was extremely sensitive to criticism, and all through young adulthood I used to take a lot of things personally. I started my stepparenting journey in the same vein, but being a stepparent has thickened my skin, which is handy for life in general. In fact, some might say I could use a little more sensitivity back in the mix again ... and I'm working on that. The bottom line is that I don't waste a lot of time or energy anymore feeling wounded or slighted. If I do feel these emotions, I process through them a lot more quickly than in the past.

6. I have three children but only had to experience labor and delivery of one. If you've carried and birthed multiple babies, you know what I'm talking about. After going through the birth process, I might have wanted two children max, but instead, as a stepparent I received the gift of parenting three.

5. I think it's cool that my stepkids have three sets of grandparents and that I had the pleasure to know all of them as part of the kids' and my history. I appreciate the ability to see how each of them has fit into my kids' personal stories.

4. I'm part of a family group that gets its own U.S. holiday—National Stepfamily Day is September 16 and can be celebrated anytime in the week surrounding the date. Founded in 1997 by Christy Borgeld, the mission of National Stepfamily Day is to recognize the beauty and unity of stepfamilies everywhere.

3. Professional counselors advise that I turn over the most difficult parent-child negotiations to my husband—their father (whew!). I don't feel guilty during times when I choose to be a pal or even an observer instead of a parent to my stepkids.

2. My parenting run with Brittany and Ian prepared me to be a more relaxed, mature parent with my daughter Amy. I'm finding this especially helpful through the teen years. I notice that some of Amy's friends' parents are still sorting out which battles to choose with their teens. Thankfully, I have a jumpstart on that wisdom.

1. As an educated stepparent, I have a deep well of knowledge about parenting and family dynamics that I could not have otherwise obtained or understood. Through time, experience with successes and failures, and my self-study, I've become an expert in this area.

I offer my sincere thank you to Brian, Brittany, and Ian for my growth as a person.

Celebrate the miracles

Humankind has a tendency to take the positive things in life for granted but make mountains out of the challenges. With this frame of mind, it's easy to miss the stepfamily miracles that happen along the way. When I look back on our stepfamily formation, I make time to remember how many little joys have sprung forth—from the time when I first helped the kids make cool Halloween costumes, to playing indoor volleyball with ten-year-old Ian, to sharing the wine country with twenty-one-year-old Brittany, to hosting a "family-favorite" Chinese dumpling party where adult Brittany, Zach, and Ian enjoyed doing the production line work together.

I view the mistakes I've made in the context of how much I've learned and grown, not only as a stepparent and parent, but as a person. Most importantly, I understand in my heart how much the kids must miss their mom and how much I need to honor that relationship.

As you forge forward with your stepfamily, continue to be courageous. Be aware and be kind. Show compassion or admit when you can't. Honor the parent who died. And, last but not least, notice and celebrate those miracles.

REFLECTION PROMPTS

1. What family milestones do you have coming up? During these milestone events, how will you shine the spotlight on the needs of your stepchildren?
2. What do *you* celebrate about being a stepparent to a grieving child?

POINTS TO REMEMBER

- Milestones may trigger family member re-grief.
- Planning for stepfamily milestones can prevent them from feeling like millstones.
- Taking time to celebrate your stepfamily miracles, large or small, is as important to your stepfamily health as taking time to grieve.

Supplemental Material

Each of us has our own specific questions or challenges within the topic of stepparenting a grieving child. While it's not possible to anticipate every query you might have and provide an exhaustive list of answers, I've assembled supplemental material to address frequently-voiced ponderings written by readers of my blog and website, as well as from my conversations with other stepparents. Additionally, I have included a list of resource material such as books and websites that can further assist you as you give your time and love to your stepfamilies.

Common Stepparent Ponderings

"Insanity is doing the same thing over and over again
and expecting different results."
– ALBERT EINSTEIN

How to handle Mother's Day and Father's Day

No matter whether you are a biological parent, stepparent, or both, Mother's Day and Father's Day can be emotionally-loaded holidays. If your stepchildren are in elementary school, they may feel especially emotional simply because everyone in the classroom is making something for Mom for Mother's Day, and they dutifully follow along. Father's Day gifts might be created at summer day camps or church camps. Although more teachers are now taking the variety of family structures into account on these holidays, the traditional approach is a one-size-fits-all gift.

Over the years I found that my expectations for Mother's Day became my biggest enemies. Here's the bottom line—I've learned that if I have expectations for Mother's Day I need to fulfill them myself! For example, I often want to get our yard trimmed up and blooming on Mother's Day, so I carve out part of the afternoon to work in the yard. I ask my family to join me too, which can provide some additional help achieving a nice outcome for our home.

The following wisdom has worked for me to make these parent holidays so much more pleasant over the years.

- Take Mother's Day or Father's Day into your own hands. Plan something that makes it your day, as opposed to waiting for someone else to do something for you. What did songwriter Tom Petty say? "The waiting is the hardest part." Don't wait. Take action!

- Be bold enough to celebrate an entirely different day with your stepchildren. I really believe (but only after years of experience!) that these holidays are not ours to celebrate with our stepkids, unless the kids are moved from the heart to execute their own ideas to celebrate with us. Your stepkids have a mom or dad, whether dead or living, and this is the day to honor those relationships. We can even help with activities or tributes to Mom or Dad in the same ways that we help memorialize those loved ones with and for the kids.

- There is such a day as Stepmother's Day, which is, according to several Internet sources, the Sunday after Mother's Day. According to the National Stepmother's Day Facebook page, the holiday originated from one daughter's wish to celebrate a day for her mom and a day for her stepmom. National Stepfather's Day also appeared briefly on the radar, according to a 2013 article in the *San Francisco Examiner*. Unofficially, that falls on the Sunday after Father's Day. You could ask your stepfamily if they would be open to starting one of these new celebration traditions with you.

- When you're in a blended family with kids of your own, I suggest using your family meeting time to decide together how best to recognize these commemorative days. One option is certainly to divide along biological lines; however, that approach may feel too awkward. Before the day arrives (*before* is the key word here), go around the table at a family meeting and see if every family member can voice an opinion about how to celebrate that day. You can explain that whatever the family chooses does not have to extend to the following year. Your family can try this approach and then discuss how it went for everyone.

♦ If your parents or in-laws live close by, or if your family has "adopted" some local parent or grandparent figures, do something special for them and with them. If the activity is something you enjoy too, all the better! If weather permits, do something outdoors. Or catch a special movie together. Giving can feel as good as receiving—maybe even better.

No matter what you choose to do on Mother's Day or Father's Day, remember that it will feel best if all parties are sincere in what they can give. If the sincerest gift is to offer nothing, I believe that is better than something that feels forced or contrived.

How to process your feelings about your stepchildren and your own children

In the early phases of stepparenting, before I bore a child, I observed through my stepchildren's actions and reactions that blood relationships are thicker than anything. While I was raising my birth child, I deepened this realization through a simple interaction with other moms.

I had dropped off my daughter, Amy, then eight years old, at a Saturday sleepover party. The moms chatted on the front stoop before taking off to enjoy their evenings. One of them mentioned a phrase that caught my attention: "… after I check on my kids at night to make sure they're still breathing."

"Oh my gosh!" I exclaimed. "I thought I was the only one who went in and checked if my kid was breathing!" I also joked about thinking I was a bit of a freak for doing so. Around the circle, all the moms acknowledged that they checked every night.

On the way home, I felt solidarity around my parenting instincts. But at the same time, a sadness flooded me. I couldn't remember ever once checking to make sure Brittany or Ian was breathing after I tucked them in at night. Maybe it was because their father played that role. Maybe it was because I hadn't taken care of them since birth. But no matter the reason, it never even occurred to me to check their breathing.

I wondered if this made me a selfish or bad stepmom. I thought back. I did some pretty nice tuck-ins, with stories and backrub games, like "guess what letter I'm drawing on your back." I concluded that my lack of mama-bear intuition simply underscores a difference between my parenting and my stepparenting. As a stepparent getting to know the kids mid-development cycle, I learned to take care of them as opposed to acting from protective urges. As stepparents, I think we need to become okay with the differences between our feelings while parenting a stepchild and a birth child. Neither approach and neither set of feelings are right or wrong—they're just different.

Just as important, let's realize that our stepkids also see their relationships with stepparents and with natural parents in different lights. Yes, we're turning the tables on this question. We've learned that when Mom or Dad is deceased, the natural connection still lies with the birth parents. We may witness different expressions of how stepchildren accept our love and parenting as compared to how they might accept the same from their mom, dad, or even from a treasured aunt or grandmother. All those years, I took the variations in their expressions of love personally … while at the same time I was doing my own unconscious form of loving differently.

When we're feeling down or frustrated, we can hold on to the fact that a distinct set of dynamics defines stepfamily relationships. These relationships are a two-way street. I'm learning more and more about empathy by flipping my perspective and considering the views of the kids I'm raising. If you, like me, started stepparenting before you had children of your own, the process of bringing a new baby into the family may open the door for you to see your stepchildren with new eyes and hearts.

For stepfamilies who are struggling with whether or not to have a baby, only you and your spouse can make that decision. Whether you pendulum, pray, or run pros and cons, peace will fill you as you gain guidance toward a decision. Sometimes one of you wants to move ahead and the other doesn't. My husband and I got through that phase by exploring what was behind his fears and then realizing that none of his concerns were life-threatening. Then he gave me the gift of fulfilling my wishes. Other than the temporary frustration that came with some sleepless nights, he has never regretted the decision that grew into our daughter.

Another important question is whether your children and stepchildren will be on board for this family expansion. A new baby is certain to cause some kind of a shift in stepfamily dynamics. How can you make this a positive shift?

The most authentic response is to be realistic by acknowledging that a baby signifies extra work, yet also promotes the benefits of widening your circle of love. Yes, there will be changes in the family. And yes, you'll experience some hard moments with a new baby in the home. But you'll also see a new side of life and experience a lot of joy. The baby can be a family project for everyone.

My stepchildren jumped in and out with the baby project. Their choices of when or when not to participate were fun to observe. Ian could sit on the floor and play the Elmo toy with eight-month-old Amy for an hour, or watch Baby Einstein videos with her. But once she started to say "no" and talk back, he was "outta' there" for a year or so. Brittany didn't much like the infant phase but interacted more and more during the toddler and preschool years. While Brittany was getting dolled up for prom, she let three-year-old Amy wear her old ninth-grade formal dress around the house and she curled Amy's hair.

It's especially important for the surviving parent to reassure his or her children that there's plenty of love to go around in the family, even with one additional member. The parent backs up his or her promise by still spending time with each and every child.

The new addition will deepen the parenting skills and perspectives you and your spouse bring to your entire stepfamily. In fact, a new baby will challenge a stepparent to think, again or for the first time, about the different kinds of love that are possible in a family. Having a baby may help stepparents clarify how to play more realistic roles with their stepchildren.

How to manage school breaks and time off

"The days are long
But the time is short."
                    –UNKNOWN

Consider bitter-cold winter break days. Think about long, hot, unstructured summer days. Either or both of these types of days may be hallmarks of school breaks in your region. If your children and stepchildren spend three-quarters of the year in a school building, be honest: Does the thought of school breaks excite you or do you dread them?

Some of us see the opportunity that "time off" presents to build relationships with our stepkids. However, many of us have a hard time getting past the fact that there are more people in the house, more messes to clean up, and in general more demand on the parents. Stepparents may have to field questions and situations that the parent normally handles, which requires the natural parent to set boundaries with his or her kids about who is in charge.

No matter how you feel, school breaks present opportunities for your kids to relax and get back in touch with their authentic selves. School breaks mean you'll have more face time with your children. With those goals in mind, stepparents and parents don't need to fill up every moment with activity. But when activity is needed to break the boredom syndrome, sometimes we need creative input.

To help make school breaks mostly relaxing and enjoyable, consider these strategies and ideas.

- Take time to ponder what each child in your family likes and needs … who will bounce off the walls if they don't stay scheduled and busy? Who prefers the downtime of free play or free choice of things to do? Can you help match each child's needs to a fitting situation? What would all family members like to do for fun?
- Hold a family meeting (fondue party? barbeque? ice-cream-sundae bar?) to discuss fun and also to set break-time expectations

and boundaries. The household will generate more dishes to do, more family-room cleanup, more sibling arguments, more phone calls, more nonstop television or social media ... how will you handle this as a stepfamily?

- Discuss whose discipline prevails—parent's, stepparent's, or both? How will the natural parent get their children's buy-in if the stepparent is in charge? What activities or forms of expression are simply not allowed—such as having a party while both parents are gone at work? How will you administer consequences?

- Balance doing things with your kids and stepkids alongside continuing your own groove. Break time doesn't mean giving all your free time to others.

- Got teens? Help them get into at least one volunteer opportunity or paid position. For younger teens, use your network of contacts in the community to find unadvertised possibilities such as dog walkers, house sitters, weeders, mowers ...even readers to young children or to the elderly.

- In the summertime, if you have the funds available, join a community pool. Another option is to schedule a weekly excursion to the public pool ... start some traditions with water toys and crazy, fun snacks. Or set up a slip-and-slide in your yard or nearby common area. Water can be a great common denominator for a wide range of ages. When Brittany and Ian were still in elementary school, we decided to add an above-ground pool to our backyard. The biggest challenge was to keep the pool warm enough in which to swim—for the first few years the kids braved 68- or 70-degree water temperatures. The addition of a solar panel finally brought some 78- to 80-degree swimming days, on the very hottest weeks of the summer. But the kids and their friends were resilient, and we witnessed many days of vortex-making, noodle fights, sunbathing, and general water mayhem to make that backyard pool memorable and worth it. Amy and her friends still enjoyed that pool until the beginning of their teens.

- A great way to start or end the summer is a water fight. You can buy 100 water balloons for a few dollars. Get creative and play a game of Capture the Flag using water bombs for being caught in enemy territory.
- Explore classes offered by your community's recreation department. Most offer an overwhelming number of options from art classes to sports camps to writing clinics, at a reasonable cost.
- Schedule family reading time. Pick one book appropriate for all family members and take turns reading it out loud to each other. Have post-reading discussion but keep it light—don't make it feel like school and you'll keep your audience engaged.

All of these ideas and strategies can be scaled for long weekends too. Beyond the traditional Fourth of July and Labor Day weekends, holiday weekends for stepfamilies can include National Stepfamily Day on September 16 and whatever Saturday is closest to it. National Stepfamily Day recognizes a strong commitment to support stepfamilies in their mission to raise their children.

Here are some additional ideas to add spice to a long weekend:

- Rent or borrow a pop-up camper (or your trusty tent) and take a camping night away from home. Gather around the campfire and stargaze. Or, just camp in the backyard.
- Ride your bikes together. Take whomever is home and head out on a route that you've been wanting to try. Maybe the path ends up at an ice cream shop or a movie theatre. If weather and time permit, pack a picnic to take along.
- Pick someone in need to visit over the weekend. Perhaps you know someone in the hospital or in a nursing home. You can always call nursing homes or assisted living facilities and ask if they have anyone in special need of a cheerful visitor.
- Pick out a theater movie your whole family can get excited about. Discuss the movie afterwards over dinner or coffee-shop drinks.
- Plan and make a meal at home together. For fun, pick an international theme; perhaps something that relates to the kids' heritage.

- Make a hike a scavenger hunt. (This takes the focus off the effort of hiking.) Parents, make up your lists ahead of time. Split your family into teams (suggestion: mix siblings and stepsiblings on a team so it doesn't become "Family Feud.") Treat everyone to a snack after the hike/hunt. Or, just make a home-based or neighborhood-based scavenger hunt.
- Learn and play some new games. You can start with some basic card games like Poker and Rummy. Board games range from quiet word games to crazy, loud performance games.
- Set up a jigsaw puzzle in your home, in a place where it can stay until it's completed. Observe the family dynamics that occur while building the puzzle. This exercise could be not only fun but also insightful.

No matter how you handle school breaks and long weekends, you may have fabulous days and you may have more challenging days. I've learned that despite the harder days, each new day presents a fresh opportunity to do things a little differently to make things better. If you model this behavior, your stepchildren and children can pick up on it for their own self-management.

How to ride seasonal energy to make your own changes

Sometimes families get stuck in their routines, habits, and ruts. We can look to small miracles in nature to jumpstart our motivation to make changes, either in ourselves or with our families.

In many regions of the world, the turnover of the seasons is a natural reset point. Take fall as an example. If fall is your region's back-to-school time, neighborhoods buzz with the back-to-school sounds of rumbling buses and kids chatting in packs as they walk to or from the bus stop. With its changing landscapes and temperatures, fall inspires.

The first few weeks of a new year, coming off winter break, represent another natural milestone. Regardless of your location, the New Year offers a slower pace and time to reflect upon where we've been and which goals lure us to forge ahead.

If your climate gets cold and snowy, that type of weather drives us indoors where it's warm and cozy. This indoor time together can spawn family activities, such as cooking, breaking out the movies and the board games, or completing indoor projects together.

Spring presents natural signs of re-awakening and re-birth. As temperatures warm, neighbors emerge from their houses and sounds of children playing outdoors drift in through open windows. Little splotches of bulb color brighten our gardens.

Warmer weather beckons us to return to the outdoors. Summer across most of the world represents some time off for students. This season gives kids and families chances to plan vacations together or try new skills like fishing, camping, paddleboarding, and in some regions skiing.

With natural change momentum in place, maybe it's a good time to try something new in your stepfamily. I remember the spring when my husband dumped his young adult lectures and switched to more of a question-based approach with Ian, then twenty-one. I caught the change and felt that I could also model this questioning: "How did that work out for you? What's your next step?" Ian made the change that spring to move back out, reclaiming his independence after six months of living at home.

I can ride the seasonal energy to be bolder and braver in my attitude and actions. The change that occurs when the kids go back to school allows me to recharge and refresh during the day. My newfound energy leads to more stimulating and "hip" conversations with my stepkids as we talk about school or life happenings, activities, and friends.

Maybe these change points are great times to have the straight-talk conversations you've been delaying, for example, the "I know I'm not your birth parent and yet I'm here to help you" conversation. Or perhaps you'll find the words to communicate something else important to your relationships with your stepkids, something that you've not yet been able to utter.

If the emotional conversations are too heady, seasonal changes are perfect times to try new logistics or organizational systems. The kids can catch your fever to clean out the garage, get a new closet system going, rearrange the family room, plant a garden, or build a deck. Let seasonal changes act as your tailwind to get things done.

How to help people of varying ages with their grief

Here's a re-cap of strategies to help family members with their grief, no matter their age or stage of life.

Ages four or younger

- ♦ Repeat your short, honest answers
- ♦ Provide lots of reassurance and nurturing
- ♦ Help kids maintain a consistent routine
- ♦ Create opportunities to play as an outlet for grief

Ages five through eight

- ♦ Talk with the kids while they are engaged in quiet play
- ♦ Initiate symbolic play using drawings and stories
- ♦ Continue the child's regular physical outlets
- ♦ Encourage expression of a range of feelings
- ♦ Answer questions factually with an added level of detail for these ages
- ♦ Explain options for expressing grief, and allow for choices

Ages nine through thirteen

- ♦ Reinforce that death is a natural part of life and give examples of various life cycles in our eco-systems
- ♦ Have patience
- ♦ Be available to listen, to talk, to nurture
- ♦ Encourage verbalization and self-expression
- ♦ Help children separate the facts from their feelings about the death
- ♦ Plan family activities as requested by the kids, within reason

Teens

- ♦ Apply the pre-teen interventions
- ♦ Ask what kind of support they would like from you
- ♦ Encourage teens to talk to each other within pairs or groups
- ♦ Provide reminders that denying death through risk-taking

behaviors won't make grief go away

- Help teens find a creative outlet for grief and self-expression, such as painting, music, journaling, etc.

Adults

- Just be there for them—your loving presence may be in silence or through verbal or physical exchange of love
- Let your spouse talk about their loved one
- Ask about the fears you perceive they're displaying
- Let your spouse be angry or sad
- Provide the type of pampering your spouse desires
- Engage professional help if severe grieving persists or if your spouse doesn't respond well to your assistance
- Don't give up on your spouse
- Don't criticize the person who died
- Don't offer platitudes such as "She is in a better place"

How to recognize when a child isn't coping well

When your stepchildren tell you they're fine, you know now that you can't take that statement at face value. They may be fine in the moment of speaking those words, but they can always benefit from ongoing age-appropriate grieving work.

How do you know, then, if a child is having trouble coping to the point that periodic grief-management work is not enough help? These symptoms are a good starter list of indicators that could be cause for concern:

- Ongoing trouble sleeping, eating, or concentrating
- Lack of belief that things will get better
- No recognizable moments of pleasure or happiness during the roller coaster of grief
- Any indication of feelings of despair, helplessness, hopelessness, emptiness, loneliness
- Any talk about plans or desires for suicide
- Any self-harm, such as cutting or burning

- Inability to function at school
- Signs of the condition called "complicated grief," such as persistent thoughts and images of the loved one, yearning for the loved one and imagining life still with that person, as well as extreme anger or bitterness over the loss

As a member of a grieving stepfamily, I think it's always a good idea to have a counselor or therapist in mind—someone you keep in your back pocket. If you witness any of these symptoms in your stepchildren, please contact that counseling resource to ask for more help. If you feel the need is more urgent, such as a stepchild who is talking about suicide, please call the National Suicide Prevention Lifeline at 1-800-273-8255.

How to keep connected with adult stepchildren

When you and your stepkids live together full time, you may have those long days where you wish for some separation. When your kids move out, however, you lose that valuable face time and you may have to keep in touch on social media. Don't get me wrong—Facebook and other social media have their place. Without Facebook I wouldn't have seen this post that I loved:

Seen on a blackboard outside a coffee shop:

No Wi-Fi!

Talk to each other!

Call your mom.

Pretend it's 1993!

Live!

Ironic, isn't it … that this post encouraging face time appeared on social media? I couldn't have laughed over this post and its humor if I hadn't seen it on Facebook.

But I'd feel empty if all I had were Facebook relationships. Real face time (and I don't mean the Facetime app) trumps Facebook.

One strategy to remain connected with your adult stepchildren is to say yes when they ask for a temporary move back into your home. This agreement requires a lot of boundary setting, of course, about how long an adult child can stay, and which house rules apply to the adult child. I do remember, however, that our stepfamily reconnected with a lot of face time when each of my young adult stepkids stayed with us during the year, living in our basement one right after the other. Instead of just marking "Like" on a Facebook comment, it was nice to be able to hear the expanded version of the latest. We even managed to eat some meals together without much pre-planning.

Do I wish that they lived in the house permanently? Well, no, and at their ages I know they are also eager to be independent. But living under one roof, and acting (mostly) like adults with each other, was a relaxed way to catch up and stay in touch. The time together deepened our relationships.

Brittany, then twenty-four, and her then fiancé managed to live in what was basically our basement storage area for four months. My stepdaughter got to know our then eleven-year-old, her little sister, much better. What a boost for my young one to have her older sibling around and to play Wii together! We had one dog and they brought two more, so I was often greeted by the mythological three-headed Cerberus when I came in the door. A little chaotic? Yes. Was it worth it? Absolutely, extra dog hair and all!

Planning my stepdaughter's wedding was certainly not something that could have been done on Facebook. Facebook definitely augments our knowledge of what's happening in each other's lives, but, like texting, I consider it a supplement and not a replacement for relationship.

Brittany was talking about their new house before they moved out and joked, "I'll bet you can't wait to get rid of us!" I replied, "No, actually, it's been nice to have you here." She just smiled. As recently as four years prior, I wouldn't have honestly meant that. Kids do grow up, and we all can change the way we relate to one another.

Ian's stay piggybacked on Brittany's and he was twenty-three at the time. Ian has a keen interest in politics and loves to talk about what's going on the world, country, and city. I don't run at the mouth regarding these topics. This mismatch makes a typical conversation between us go a bit flat.

When he lived here during that year, we had more opportunities to chat about everyday things. For example, a ready subject was the canine miracle of nature who lived with us (a very sweet and very needy dog). Or we could comment on various aspects of education when Amy brought home school assignments and projects.

When Ian moved out again, I missed the low-key discussions in the kitchen. I missed him offering a hand by sautéing the ground beef and chatting while I was making the rest of the evening's casserole.

As quickly as we were able to reconnect when he lived here, now we hardly connect at all. We see each other at planned family events or when he drops in (which is still better than Facebook). But everyone else also attends those family events, so he and I find little time for one-on-one. His rigorous food-industry work schedule overlaid upon my life and schedule doesn't leave a lot of room for get-togethers. And Ian isn't even on Facebook! So in conclusion, I would have to admit that while face time trumps Facebook, Facebook trumps no time.

Another strategy to keep handy is planning special events—be they for holidays, special occasions, or just for fun. Our family seems to trend toward traditional holiday and birthday celebrations; however, we've also worked in some game nights or dinner-and-drinks meet-ups as well. Perhaps you'll be even more creative.

If your stepchildren don't live close to you, I believe your relationships will blossom from an occasional visit to their parts of the world, or from times you help fly them in to stay with you. What doesn't work with adult stepchildren is to wait until you're reacting to a crisis phone call—a request for money, an illness, or other chaos. These types of higher-stress interactions do not provide the best foundation for relationship-building. Your guideline for reaching out to your stepchildren should still be to remain sincere and extend the part of yourself you feel you can give without giving yourself away.

How Can I Best Help
My Stepfamily Overall?

"How would your life be different if..you stopped worrying about things you can't
control and started focusing on the things you can? Let today be the day..
You free yourself from fruitless worry, seize the day and take effective action
on things you can change."
– STEVE MARABOLI

SOME NEW STEPPARENTS ARE STARING AT THE big job ahead of
them and feeling overwhelmed. Most of you want to know how you can
help, and if you can help your grieving family. Becoming a contributing
stepparent—one your stepchildren will respond to—takes time. My advice
is to pursue the goals that will help you strive for long-term, sustainable
stepparenting. Our sustainable stepparenting formula best sums up those
goals:

Derived from our formula, here are some of the best ways you can help your grieving stepfamily:

- Support your spouse or partner, first and foremost
- Assess your willingness to stepparent, and gather support to increase that willingness
- Learn the stepfamily myths to make sure you're not trapped by any of them
- Learn the Stepfamily Cycle to understand how stepfamilies grow and evolve
- Learn ideas to help your stepchildren process their grief
- Include the deceased parent(s) as part of your family
- Participate in honoring important family anniversaries
- When your stepfamily is in the Middle Stages of the cycle, suggest that more family activities occur in one-on-one pairs
- Also in the Middle Stages, make sure your stepfamily holds family meetings where all members have a chance to speak their minds
- Make sure that you have your own support system to relieve stress, share ideas, and get feedback when you are stuck or need help
- Shed your expectations of what your stepfamily is supposed to be and accept its organic growth through the Stepfamily Cycle
- Reclaim the authentic you and reveal your gifts to your stepfamily
- Celebrate stepfamily miracles large and small

We can and will learn and grow from stepparenting a grieving child.

Resource Guide

PLEASE EXPLORE OR USE THESE RESOURCES AND references for further reading, research, and contemplation.

Grief and how to help grieving children

WEBSITES, WHICH INCLUDE LINKS TO BOOKS
Center for Loss & Life Transitions
    http://www.centerforloss.com/
The Dougy Center: The National Center for Grieving Children & Families
    http://www.dougy.org/
National Alliance for Grieving Children
    https://childrengrieve.org/

BOOKS
Corr, Charles A., Clyde M. Nabe, and Donna M. Corr. 2009. *Death & Dying, Life & Living*, Belmont, CA: Wadsworth Cengage Learning.
Emswiler, Jim and Mary Ann Emswiler. 2000. *Guiding Your Child Through Grief*. New York: Bantam Books.
Hipp, Earl. 1995. *Help for the Hard Times: Getting Through Loss*. Center City, MN: Hazelden.
Krementz, Jill. 1981. *How It Feels When a Parent Dies*. New York: Alfred A. Knopf.
Worden, J. William. 2001. *Children and Grief: When a Parent Dies*. New York: Guilford Press.

Crisis hotline

National Suicide Prevention Lifeline
  http://www.suicidepreventionlifeline.org/
  1-800-273-TALK (8255), 24/7 hotline

Mother loss and father loss

WEBSITES, WHICH INCLUDE LINKS TO BOOKS
Hope Edelman, Motherless Daughters
  http://hopeedelman.com/
Fatherless Daughter Project
  http://fatherlessdaughterproject.com/

BOOKS
Diamond, Jonathan. 2006. *Fatherless Sons, Healing the Legacy of Loss.* Hoboken, NJ: John Wiley & Sons, Inc.
Edelman, Hope. 2006. *Motherless Daughters: The Legacy of Loss.* Cambridge: Da Capo Press.
Schuurman, Donna. 2003. *Never the Same: Coming to Terms with the Death of a Parent.* New York: St. Martin's Press.

Stepparenting and building healthy stepfamilies

WEBSITES, WHICH INCLUDE LINKS TO BOOKS
Ron Deal
  http://familylifeblended.com/
  http://smartstepfamilies.com/index.php
National Stepfamily Resource Center
  http://www.stepfamilies.info/
Dr. Patricia Papernow
  http://www.stepfamilyrelationships.com/
Carri and Gordon Taylor. Opportunities Unlimited
  www.cgtaylor.com

BOOKS

McBride, Jean. 2001. *Encouraging Words for New Stepmothers*. Fort Collins, CO: CDR Press.

Norwood, Perdita Kirkness with Teri Wingender. 1999. *The Enlightened Stepmother: Revolutionizing the Role*. New York: Avon Books, Inc.

Papernow, Patricia L. 1993. *Becoming a Stepfamily: Patterns of Development in Remarried Families*. Cambridge: GestaltPress.

———. 2013. *Surviving and Thriving in Stepfamily Relationships: What Works and What Doesn't*. New York: Routledge.

Thoele, Sue Patton. 2013. *The Courage to be a Stepmom: Finding Your Place Without Losing Yourself*. CreateSpace Independent Publishing Platform.

ARTICLES

Deal, Ron, "Enduring Disharmony." *Smartstepfamilies.com*. Published electronically July 2008. http://smartstepfamilies.com/view/enduring disharmony.

Special resources for grandparents raising grandchildren

http://grg.colostate.edu/parenting.php

International stepparenting resources

Australia
www.stepfamily.org.au

Great Britain
http://www.happysteps.co.uk/Pages/default.aspx,
http://www.beingastepparent.co.uk/

Japan
http://web.saj-stepfamily.org/

Personality sorters

Enneagram
> http://www.9types.com/rheti/index.php (free sample test sponsored by founders)
> https://www.enneagraminstitute.com/ (official site by founders)
> http://www.enneagramtest.net/ (free sample test not linked to founders)

Keirsey Temperament Sorter
> http://www.keirsey.com/

Myers-Briggs
> http://www.myersbriggs.org/my-mbti-personality-type/mbti-basics/

Social Styles
> http://www.wilsonlearning.com/wlw/articles/w/hidden-cost-comm (official site by founders)
> http://www.smallworldalliance.com/documents/SocialStyles-Assessment.pdf (free self-assessment not linked to founders)

True Colors
> https://truecolorsintl.com/about-us/what-is-true-colors/ (official site by founder)
> https://lonerwolf.com/true-colors-personality-test/ (free self-assessment not linked to founder)

Acknowledgments

ALTHOUGH I EXPRESS GRATITUDE EASILY, MY BIGGEST fear is to forget someone who has been a huge support along the journey of creating this work to help stepparents of grieving children. Nevertheless, I plunge into this gratitude to the many parties who have supported me along the way.

I can't express enough thanks to my stepchildren for being brave enough to let me share our family stories in order to help explain my insights to readers. In the same light, I thank my husband, my daughter, and all of our extended family—mine and Brittany's and Ian's—whose stories helped shape this book. These examples will serve to teach others for years to come.

I found the encouragement to keep moving forward with this project from a number of helpful souls and sources. My current writing critique group, Broad Horizons Writers Group of Fort Collins, Colorado, has supported me from the very inception of this work, literally from the seeds planted to form this book. Thank you from the depth of my heart for all the years of reviews and discussions. Another former critique group at the First Presbyterian Church in Fort Collins also contributed many hours of thoughtful insight.

Deep gratitude goes to the families who allowed me to interview them, for their further anecdotes brought this material to life. I also want to thank the readers who joined my mailing list and emailed me their suggestions for what they wanted to see in this book. You have no idea how your contact with me kept me going, convincing me that people needed this book, even when I had shelved it in order to refresh and re-evaluate my perspective.

A notable group of psychologists, therapists, and stepfamily and grief experts gave me the courage to pursue this work as well, either through deep involvement over time or positive validation in conversation. A shout out to all of you, including Ron Deal, Jean McBride, Mark Benn, Patricia Papernow, Mary Ann Emswiler, Carri Taylor, Jen Krafchick, Stephanie Crandell Seng, Donna Schuurman, Jen Aberle, Jeffrey Glasser, Pat Tahan, Christy Borgeld, and Tina Blount.

Thank you as well to my dear friends—you know who you are—who listened to me process my feelings during the days of daily stepparenting, and again when I gave updates about this book over the years. You've stuck by my side through my angst and my determination alike, and you always asked how this project was going. I couldn't have kept on without your support.

The physical form of this book would not have come to fruition so beautifully without the editing, production, marketing, and publishing help of Donna Mazzitelli of Merry Dissonance Press, Polly Letofsky of My Word Publishing, and the cover and interior layout design of Victoria Wolf and Andrea Costantine.

Last, but certainly not least, I want to thank my mom, who also stepparented grieving children, and my dad, who adopted a son that pulled away from him but ultimately reunited. Although my parents cannot read these words here on earth, their examples always give me the courage to carry on.

With gratitude to all,

Diane Ingram Fromme

About the Author

DIANE INGRAM FROMME BIRTHED *Stepparenting the Grieving Child* when she craved but couldn't find the stepparenting information she needed to help raise two children who lost their mom to cancer. She latched on to the idea of a stepparenting-through-grief resource while sitting on the floor of a beloved indie bookstore, surrounded by self-help books that addressed either stepparenting or understanding grief, but not the layering of both topics. Diane decided to summon her powers of observation, journaling and writing expertise, and interviewing skills to produce a guidebook for stepparents of grieving children.

A writer at heart from the tender age of eight, Diane's writing and communication experience ranges from her Stanford University B.A. degree in communication, to training and facilitation work, to freelance writing of personal essays and articles. Diane relies on writing to help her process beautiful as well as difficult phenomena, much of which emanates from her life experiences. In all of her writing, she expresses how education, social interactions, and family dynamics improve, challenge, or change our lives. Diane Ingram Fromme has published her personal essays in literary collections and online, while her educational articles have appeared in local, regional, and international magazines.

Diane is a native New Yorker who now writes from her cozy home in Fort Collins, Colorado. She lives with her husband Brian, her teen daughter Amy, and a spunky canine. She is fortunate to see and keep in touch with her adult stepchildren, Brittany and Ian, who also reside in Northern Colorado. Diane wears many hats as a mom, stepmom, writer, speaker, training expert, and international student-exchange coordinator, and she enjoys each and every role.

To learn more about Diane, including how to book her for speaking engagements or your next group event, be sure to visit her website at www.DianeIngramFromme.com. There you will also find samples from her other published works to date.

You are invited to join the conversation about the joys and challenges of stepparenting grieving children by filling out the contact form at www.dianeingramfromme.com. Be sure to include your Facebook name in the comments box, and you will be invited to a private Facebook group monitored by the author.

About the Press

MERRY DISSONANCE PRESS IS A BOOK PRODUCER/INDIE publisher of works of transformation, inspiration, exploration, and illumination. MDP takes a holistic approach to bringing books into the world that make a little noise and create dissonance within the whole in order that ALL can be resolved to produce beautiful harmonies.

Merry Dissonance Press works with its authors every step of the way to craft the finest books and help promote them. Dedicated to publishing award-winning books, we strive to support talented writers and assist them to discover, claim, and refine their own distinct voice. **Merry Dissonance Press** is the place where collaboration and facilitation of our shared human experiences join together to make a difference in our world.

For more information, visit http://merrydissonancepress.com/.

More Praise for
Stepparenting the Grieving Child ...

Clarion Rating: ★★★★★
Reviewed by: Olivia Boler
February 1, 2017

Drawing from the author's personal experiences, this is an excellent, essential guide for stepparents of grieving children.

Diane Ingram Fromme's *Stepparenting the Grieving Child* offers helpful guidance to stepparents, guardians, and professionals who work with children who are mourning the loss of a parent.

Fairy tales like Cinderella and Snow White paint stepparents—especially stepmothers—as harridans out to get rid of their stepchildren. Perhaps, Fromme muses, some of this is based on old-fashioned, rigid behaviors. Stepparents, not having parenting books to inform them that building trust and forming attachments could take years, turned to harsh disciplinary tactics.

Fromme did not have a guide, either, when she became the stepmother to two young children whose mother had died of cancer. She found books for new stepparents and books for people grieving the loss of a loved one, but not one self-help book focused on being the stepparent of children whose parent had died.

With some engaging moments that read like a memoir, this book is primarily an accessible parenting guide for navigating a new, special family dynamic. Using interviews with other stepfamilies in which a natural parent had died as well as documented research, the book offers advice on everything from deciding when it's the right time to remarry to understanding the cycles of grief.

Fromme views her own story as a cautionary tale: were she to do it again, she might have waited a while longer to marry her widower husband, in consideration of his and his children's grieving. Instead, she "bought into a common myth—one of the many that new stepparents encounter," that given time, the family would "start to feel loving and cohesive."

Instead of bonding instantly, though, or viewing her as a mother figure, Fromme's stepchildren sometimes seemed emotionally removed from her, and looked to their father as their main caregiver. Their relationship, now more than twenty years in, is still a work in progress with emotional ups and downs.

Fromme uses fieldwork to support her declaration that stepparent-stepchild relationship fluctuations are perfectly normal and acceptable. She uses examples that will bring comfort to stepparents who might be at a loss for the "right" way to treat their grieving stepchildren.

Chapters begin with pivotal moments from Fromme's stepparenting journey that serve as introductions to specific topics—from stepparenting mindsets, to dealing with feelings of jealousy or rejection, to honoring deceased parents and acknowledging them as part of the family. Each chapter ends with questions to consider and listings of the main topics covered. At the end of the book is a resource guide that includes books, websites, and organizations for grief, suicide prevention, and the National Stepfamily Resource Center.

Written with clarity and in an agreeable voice, *Stepparenting the Grieving Child* is an essential guide full of excellent parenting strategies for stepparents, parents, and caregivers.

—*Foreword* Clarion Reviews

BlueInk Review
Reviewed: January 2017

Among the many challenges stepparents face, one of the most difficult involves caring for stepchildren after the death of a birth parent. As a new stepmother to two children who lost their mother to cancer, the author was dismayed that even with her best efforts, her new stepfamily "didn't gel like magic." Now, using her decades of stepparenting experience plus anecdotes from other stepfamilies, including readers of her blog (www.dianeingramfromme.com), Fromme provides wide ranging insights and strategies for those faced with the challenges of blended—and grieving—families like her own.

Fromme recommends stepparents first explore their own feelings before focusing on grieving stepchildren. As stepparents come to understand their own beliefs, expectations and needs, they're better able to free themselves from emotional burdens and move towards empathy for the child, she says. For example, when her stepdaughter said "you're not a mom in my heart," Fromme focused on a positive outcome from the conversation—a teen finally opening up to suppressed feelings—rather than the pain the statement caused her.

The author moves on to debunk stepfamily myths, such as the idea that adjustments occur quickly to young children or that the original family is the only valid one. She includes valuable strategies, including how to build a support network, understanding the age-appropriate stages of grief, working on honest communication and moving toward empathy. A resource guide follows.

Fromme prefaces many chapters by relating a challenging personal family situation. Here, she includes the interesting technique of stating each child's age, time since their mother died, and how long she had been stepparenting at this point. This moves readers from early childhood through teen years, demonstrating relationship changes and insights.

Fromme isn't a mental health professional, but she has endured in the school of hard knocks. Her wealth of practical suggestions can provide

support and comfort to stepparents, surviving parents, other family members, and teachers coping with a child's grief when a parent has died.

—BlueInk Review